THE PRACTICE
OF GOVERNMENT
PUBLIC RELATIONS

American Society for Public Administration

Book Series on Public Administration & Public Policy

Editor-in-Chief
Evan M. Berman, Ph.D.
National Chengchi University, Taiwan
evanmberman@gmail.com

Mission: Throughout its history, ASPA has sought to be true to its founding principles of promoting scholarship and professionalism within the public service. The ASPA Book Series on Public Administration and Public Policy publishes books that increase national and international interest for public administration and which discuss practical or cutting edge topics in engaging ways of interest to practitioners, policy-makers, and those concerned with bringing scholarship to the practice of public administration.

The Practice of Government Public Relations, Mordecai Lee, Grant Neeley, and Kendra Stewart

Promoting Sustainable Local and Community Economic Development, Roland V. Anglin

Government Contracting: Promises and Perils, William Sims Curry

Strategic Collaboration in Public and Nonprofit Administration: A Practice-Based Approach to Solving Shared Problems, Dorothy Norris-Tirrell, and Joy A. Clay

Managing Public Sector Projects: A Strategic Framework for Success in an Era of Downsized Government, David S. Kassel

Organizational Assessment and Improvement in the Public Sector, Kathleen M. Immordino

Ethics Moments in Government: Cases and Controversies, Donald C. Menzel

Major League Winners: Using Sports and Cultural Centers as Tools for Economic Development, Mark S. Rosentraub

The Formula for Economic Growth on Main Street America, Gerald L. Gordon

The New Face of Government: How Public Managers Are Forging a New Approach to Governance, David E. McNabb

The Facilitative Leader in City Hall: Reexamining the Scope and Contributions, James H. Svara

American Society for Public Administration
Series in Public Administration and Public Policy

THE PRACTICE
OF GOVERNMENT
PUBLIC RELATIONS

EDITED BY
MORDECAI LEE
GRANT NEELEY
KENDRA STEWART

CRC Press
Taylor & Francis Group
Boca Raton   London   New York

CRC Press is an imprint of the
Taylor & Francis Group, an **informa** business

CRC Press
Taylor & Francis Group
6000 Broken Sound Parkway NW, Suite 300
Boca Raton, FL 33487-2742

© 2012 by Taylor & Francis Group, LLC
CRC Press is an imprint of Taylor & Francis Group, an Informa business

No claim to original U.S. Government works

Printed in the United States of America on acid-free paper
Version Date: 20110603

International Standard Book Number: 978-1-4398-3465-7 (Hardback)

Visit the Taylor & Francis Web site at
http://www.taylorandfrancis.com

and the CRC Press Web site at
http://www.crcpress.com

For Brad Brin, Ernie Franzen, and Charlie Wright—good
friends who were there when I needed them.

Mordecai Lee

For Sabrina and Jordan, the loves of my life.

Grant Neeley

For Fred Carter and Louise Majors—the first to teach me about
the importance of government public relations; and for Jimmy,
Paxton, and Paisley, who never let me forget what's important.

Kendra Stewart

Contents

CD-ROM Contents

Preface

An understanding of the practice of government public relations helps contemporary public-sector managers *do their jobs*. Along with such traditional management tools as budgeting, human resources (HR), planning, and leadership, this volume is intended to make the case that the twenty-first-century government administrator needs new tools to address the changing context of government communication.

First, civic life in modern times is now much more dominated by the news media and by related public communications technologies. Public administration practitioners, as well as students studying to become public administrators, need to understand the importance of media relations as part of their profession. Second, public administration itself is increasingly an act of communication. Government public relations is a vital tool that can help all public sector agencies implement their missions and increase accountability. For example, public relations can be used to *educate* the citizenry ("only you can prevent forest fires") and is cheaper than regulation; *inform* the public of new programs and services they may be eligible for; and *persuade* the public to serve as the eyes and ears of the agency (such as elder-abuse hotlines). External communications is especially important during times of crisis and emergencies.

Third, the public context of public administration is what differentiates it from business administration (and nonprofit management). External communications techniques can be used to help fulfill the obligation of government managers to the public: to *report* to the citizenry on the accomplishments and stewardship of the agency; to be held *accountable*; and to contribute to an *informed public*, the basis of democracy. Fourth, mass communications technologies continue to evolve and change. Social media—a form of communication that didn't even exist at the turn of the century—are now powerful, even dominant methods of interaction. Managers who want to succeed need to understand the potential of these new venues for communicating in *both* directions with the citizenry.

These are some of the reasons that public relations has recently been coming out of public administration's closet. More and more training programs are recognizing the importance of external communications and are adding the subject to their curricula. It has been that rise in interest that contributed to the preparation of this volume. The book presents an up-to-date examination of the specifics of government public relations and how it can help practitioners. It seeks to provide an understanding of the uses of public relations as tools to advance the goals of public agencies, including media relations, contributing to an informed public, listening to the citizenry, and crisis management. While no manager can be an expert in all aspects of public administration, this book will help managers know what external communications tools are available to them for advancing the mission and results of their agencies.

Who Is This Book For?

The book is intended to be helpful to both public administration practitioners as well as students who are practitioners in training. We want to demonstrate in tangible ways how public relations can help government managers at various levels of administration do their work. This includes practitioners seeking to specialize by developing skills in public relations, those assigned to communications offices wanting to explore new ways to fulfill their responsibilities, and program managers who are seeking innovative and inexpensive ways to implement their programmatic missions. Also, this book is intended to help general managers who are at the middle and senior ranks. The latter work at a level where they could enhance organizational performance by understanding how public relations can help do that. For example, when civil servants who have policy area expertise (aging, health care, public works, etc.) move up the hierarchy, they find themselves overseeing public information offices, but are not quite sure how those offices can help them accomplish their programmatic goals or democratic responsibilities.

The book focuses on practitioners throughout the public sector, including the U.S. federal government, state and local governments, and public administrators outside of the United States. Given the size and scope of the American federal government, some illustrative descriptions and cases frequently come from it. However, they are presented here in a way that would be useful to public administrators at other levels of government or in other countries. The main focus is on government managers who are *implementing* policies already adopted by elected officials, politicians, and political appointees. Certainly, in the real world, all public administrators are involved to some degree in policy making. Still, this book is less for political appointees (serving at the pleasure of an elected chief executive) and more for the daily work of permanent career civil servants, whether senior or junior.

We have included several features intended to maximize the usefulness of the volume to practitioners and students. Similarly, the accompanying CD includes case studies, PowerPoint slides, checklists, and other resources intended to enhance the benefit to practitioners.

Acknowledgments

Our heartfelt appreciation to Professor Evan Berman, the editor of the ASPA Series in Public Administration and Public Policy, and to all the professionals at Taylor & Francis who brought this book to fruition. Evan played several very important roles in conceiving and developing this volume. He first raised the possibility of a book on government public relations for practitioners with Mordecai, who welcomed the opportunity and began working on it. A few months later, Grant and Kendra contacted Evan expressing a similar interest in working on a book on public relations. With Evan acting as matchmaker, the three of us enthusiastically joined efforts. It turned out to be a fortuitous match, as each of us had strengths (and weaknesses) that jibed well with the skills and interests of the other two. Truly, if two are better than one, then three are even better. We enjoyed working with one another and are grateful to have had an opportunity to collaborate on a subject that we feel is of importance to public administration practitioners.

Our thanks to all the authors who agreed to submit chapters reflecting their areas of specialization. They cheerfully dealt with our seemingly endless questions and requests for minor revisions. Our appreciation goes as well to those who authored case studies and other supplemental materials. In our opinion, they definitely strengthened the usefulness of the book. Mordecai also wishes to thank Andrea Zweifel, the program associate at his school, who carefully proofed his contributions. Grant thanks his colleague Don Vermillion, guest speakers and, most importantly, his students, for their enthusiasm and questions about the need for and the importance and practice of government public relations. Kendra thanks the Research Committee and the Graduate School at the College of Charleston for providing funding to support the writing of this book.

We hope readers will find the book helpful and we welcome feedback and suggestions from practitioners and instructors. Please address comments through the corresponding coeditor, Kendra Stewart (stewartk@cofc.edu).

Mordecai Lee
Grant Neeley
Kendra Stewart

Editors

Mordecai Lee is a professor of governmental affairs at the University of Wisconsin-Milwaukee. In the field of government public relations, he authored *Congress vs. the Bureaucracy: Muzzling Agency Public Relations* (Norman: University of Oklahoma Press, 2011) and *The First Presidential Communications Agency: FDR's Office of Government Reports* (Albany: State University of New York Press, 2005). He also was the editor of *Government Public Relations: A Reader* (Boca Raton, FL: Taylor & Francis, 2008). Before joining the academy, Dr. Lee served as legislative assistant to a congressman; was elected to three terms in the Wisconsin Legislature's State Assembly and two terms in the State Senate; and was executive director of a faith-based nonprofit involved in public policy advocacy.

Grant Neeley received his B.A. and M.P.A. from Texas A&M and his Ph.D. in political science from the University of Tennessee in 1996. He has served on the faculties of Texas Tech and Ball State and joined the University of Dayton as an associate professor in 2005. He is the director of the MPA program and teaches courses in political science and public administration. His primary research interest is public policy and administration, but he has conducted research in the areas of urban politics, political behavior, and interest groups. His work has appeared in the *American Journal of Public Health, Political Research Quarterly, Social Science Quarterly, Public Performance & Management Review, Policy Studies Journal, State and Local Government Review*, and *Evaluation Review*. Dr. Neeley currently serves on the executive council of the National Association of Schools of Public Affairs and Administration. During 2010–2011 he was mobilized as Press Desk Officer, J9–Strategic Communications, US Forces Iraq, and serves as a Reserve Public Affairs Officer in the United States Navy attached to the Commander, 5th Fleet in Bahrain.

Kendra Stewart is an associate professor and director of the Master of Public Administration Program at the College of Charleston in Charleston, South Carolina. Her research interests include state government reorganization, government and press relations, nonprofit networks, and homeland security. The articles she has authored have appeared in *The Practice of Strategic Collaboration: From Silos to Actions, Urban Affairs Review, Public Finance and Management, Frontiers, Perspective in Politics,* and various scholarly books. Prior to her current position, Professor Stewart was a faculty member at Eastern Kentucky University and worked for the state of South Carolina in public information and other capacities.

Contributors

Shannon A. Bowen is associate professor in the S. I. Newhouse School of Public Communications, Syracuse University. Dr. Bowen specializes in public affairs, issues management, and organizational policy. Her Ph.D. (2000) in mass communication and business management (marketing) is from the University of Maryland and her dissertation won the International Communication Association's Public Relations Division Outstanding Dissertation Award for 2000–2002. Prior to the three years she spent as a research analyst, she worked on Capitol Hill as a public relations specialist for Congressman Floyd D. Spence (R-SC), Chairman of the U.S. House Committee on National Security.

Napoleon Byars teaches in the School of Journalism & Mass Communication at the University of North Carolina at Chapel Hill. Before joining the school, he was the director of policy and communications for the Air Force Association. A former public affairs officer in the Air Force, Byars has a broad background in government communications including serving as public affairs officer to the Chairman of the Joint Chiefs of Staff, and deputy publisher for *Pacific Stars and Stripes* newspaper in Tokyo. He has lectured at national conferences and symposia and conducted media relations and crisis communication workshops in China and Russia. He is an award-winning teacher and has written broadly on public information and national security affairs and the evolving phenomenon of digital governance.

Jenifer E. Kopfman is assistant professor in the Department of Communication at the College of Charleston. Dr. Kopfman earned her Ph.D. in 1995 from Michigan State University. Her research in social influence and health campaigns has focused on topics including organ donation, cancer screenings, blood donations, and women's health issues. Prior to her return to academia, Dr. Kopfman worked as a researcher for the Centers for Disease Control and Prevention, conducting audience analysis research for campaigns designed to promote folic acid consumption by women of child-bearing age to help prevent birth defects, and conducting evaluation research for an autism awareness campaign. Her research has been published in journals such as *Health Communication*, the *Journal of Applied Communication Research*, *Transplantation Proceedings*, and the *Journal of Health Communication*.

Kevin R. Kosar is a researcher at the Congressional Research Service, a nonpartisan government agency in the Library of Congress. He is a contributing editor to *Public Administration Review*, the author of two books, and the editor of another. His writings have appeared in scholarly journals, such as *Presidential Studies Quarterly*, and in popular media, including *The Weekly Standard* magazine, and the *Chicago Sun-Times* and *Philadelphia Inquirer* newspapers.

Abbey Blake Levenshus is a Ph.D. student in the University of Maryland's Department of Communication. Her research centers on government public relations, including crisis communication and social media. Her professional experience includes serving as communication director for a U.S. representative, a political technology company, and a government consulting firm in Washington, DC. Levenshus teaches courses in public relations theory, principles, and writing. She received her M.A. in Public Communication from American University in 2007.

Brooke Fisher Liu is an assistant professor in the University of Maryland's Department of Communication. She received her Ph.D. in mass communication from the University of North Carolina at Chapel Hill in 2006. Her research primarily examines how government organizations manage communication during crisis and noncrisis situations. She is particularly interested in developing new models and theory that accurately reflect government public relations practitioners' unique experiences. Dr. Liu's research has been published in the *Handbook of Crisis Communication*, *Journal of Applied Communication Research*, *Journal of Communication Management*, *Journal of Public Relations Research*, *Public Relations Review*, and *Natural Hazards Review*. Her research has been funded by the National Consortium for the Study of Terrorism and Responses to Terrorism (START), the Plank Center for Leadership in Public Relations, and the Arthur W. Page Center for Integrity in Public Communication.

Diana Knott Martinelli is the Widmeyer Professor in Public Relations at the West Virginia University P. I. Reed School of Journalism. She worked for nearly 15 years in various public relations positions, including those in federal programs, health care, and broadcasting, before earning her Ph.D. as a Park Fellow at the University of North Carolina at Chapel Hill. Her research has been presented and published nationally and internationally. She also has served as a communications consultant for various state and federal agencies and programs, and has conducted workshops in strategic communications, media relations, and crisis communications at regional and national conferences for government officials.

Amanda Ruth-McSwain is an assistant professor in the Department of Communication at the College of Charleston. She earned her doctorate in agricultural communication from the University of Florida. In addition to her teaching background in corporate communication, Dr. Ruth-McSwain has professional experience in public relations in the nonprofit sector. Her journal publications include articles in *Science Communication, Communication Quarterly, Journal of Extension,* and the *Journal of Applied Communication.* Dr. Ruth-McSwain has served on the board of the Charleston chapter of the American Marketing Association and the Lowcountry chapter of the Public Relations Society of America and is currently the advisor for the College of Charleston Public Relations Student Society of America.

Leila Sadeghi is an assistant professor with the department of educational leadership in the Nathan Weiss Graduate College, Kean University. Dr. Sadeghi's research interests include the use of social media in the public sector, and how new media technologies are being used in the classroom to enhance student learning. Dr. Sadeghi has published numerous chapters, articles and reports on these topics and regularly trains public officials on the use of new media. She can be reached at sadeghi.phd@gmail.com.

Jerome Sadow headed public affairs for a national research center of the U.S. Department of Transportation (DOT) and for a regional office of the U.S. Department of Housing and Urban Development (HUD). He served as press secretary to a U.S. senator in Washington, DC, and also to a Massachusetts attorney general. Sadow was a news editor at a Boston TV station and a reporter for the *Boston Globe.* He currently teaches in the College of Communication at Boston University.

Maureen Taylor is professor and Gaylord Family Chair of Strategic Communication at the University of Oklahoma. Dr. Taylor received her Ph.D. from Purdue University. She has significant experience in monitoring and evaluation (M&E) of political transition grants to nongovernment organizations (NGOs) and independent media in Armenia, Bosnia-Herzegovina, Croatia, Indonesia, Jordan, Kosovo, Liberia, Serbia, and Sudan. Dr. Taylor specializes in adapting traditional social science methodologies for use in fast-paced, conflict-prone environments.

Anne Zahradnik is assistant professor of health care management in the School of Management, Marist College in Poughkeepsie, New York. She has a B.A. in English from the University of Pittsburgh and an M.A. in communication and a Ph.D. in public administration from Western Michigan University. She comes to academia from a successful career in business-to-business and health care marketing and public relations. Her research focuses on health care access issues and on communication surrounding health care policy issues.

Chapter 1

Introduction

Grant Neeley and Kendra Stewart

Contents

Although the news media and technological advances play significant roles in the lives of most Americans today, the field of public administration has virtually ignored the topic of public affairs in government. However, effective communications strategies not only advance the mission of a public agency, but also provide an important and required public service. Public information is one of the key aspects to government accountability. Today's practitioners (and students training to be practitioners) greatly benefit by understanding the crucial role that the news media plays in public life, how to deal with the media and, more generally, how external communications efforts can be used to advance the work of public agencies. Public relations is an important tool of governance just like other tools we teach in public administration programs or offer training for in government agencies.

Some of the uses of public relations in government are pragmatic, intended to advance the mission of the agency, but in unorthodox ways that reduce costs. For example, public service campaigns are ways to influence public behavior in a way that is less expensive than policing. Similarly, advertising the availability of new programs and services is a way to reach potential clients and customers through a wholesale approach, rather than the more expensive retail one-by-one outreach effort. Besides these pragmatic uses of public relations, external communications can also be used to advance the goals of a democratic society. These would be situations of "information for information sake" rather than to accomplish a more tangible management goal. Examples of this aspect of government public relations include reporting to the public on agency activities as a way of contributing to an informed public, disseminating information as a prelude to citizen participation in agency decision making, and listening to public opinion.

Purpose of This Book

With the recent change of administration in the U.S. executive branch, we have seen increased attention to issues of public information, transparency in government, and government and press relations in the United States and abroad. In addition, rapidly evolving technology and its influence on public communication have left many in government struggling to remain current in this area. Citizens and constituents learn to use interactive tools when searching for information, utilize technology for communications, and now expect government information and services to exist in the same information space as private entities. This book is an effort of leading experts in the field to assist public managers in understanding the nuances of the rules and regulations governing public information, innovative ways to use new technology, how to respond in a crisis, and how to think strategically in crafting a public image. The very practical and applied treatment of these topics should generate the interest of practitioners and policy makers due to the lack of available information on issues of public relations in the public sector. Several chapters contain a "Best Practice Checklist" as well as other supplemental material (all provided on the CD-ROM that came with this book) that can be used to implement the strategies outlined in the book.

This book is intended to serve as a single source of information for all aspects of governmental public relations. As the U.S. government transitions into a period of more relaxed restriction of public information, public administrators need a book with practical guidelines and applicable tools to assist in this new era of government public communication. In addition, the decline of traditional journalism and the rise of social media are moving targets that are continuing to evolve and require renewed and sustained attention for public administrators to the public relations function. This book addresses some of the common issues and approaches to consider when dealing with this rapidly changing environment.

This book is aimed at providing a very practical, hands-on approach for the planning, implementation, and evaluation of various aspects of government public relations. The conception of the book is to serve as a practitioner counterpart to the academically oriented *Government Public Relations: A Reader*, which was published by Taylor & Francis in 2008 to serve as a textbook in university-level courses. The majority of the chapter authors are current or past practitioners of government public relations crossing all the levels of government, extending outside the United States and in other areas of public service as well (such as nonprofit and nongovernmental organizations [NGOs]). While their writings are informed by the latest research, their interests and orientation are to improving practice. Each chapter is intended to be useful to someone practicing in the field and looking for guidance, resources, practical advice, and best practices.

Overview of This Book

Beginning with Chapter 3, the book is divided into two sections: "Reaching the Citizenry: The Tools of Public Relations," and "Managing Government Public Relations." Chapter 2 provides an introduction to the scope, purpose, and practices in the field of government public relations by Mordecai Lee, one of the foremost leaders in the field. Lee focuses on how public relations can help public administrators do a better job at implementing policy, accomplish an agency's mission, and promote democratic accountability.

Section I: Reaching the Citizenry

The first section, "Reaching the Citizenry," begins with Jerome Sadow's chapter on media relations focusing on the role of government communication directors as they work within their organization and most importantly with the media. Particular attention is paid to communication methods, especially writing for press releases, speeches, executive point outlines, issue backgrounders, op-ed columns, letters to the editor, and TV and radio interviews. Sadow presents a straightforward discussion of public relations (PR) strategies and tactics, how to handle media criticism, crises and issues management, and the use of leaks, and identifies the important personal relationship of the media relations expert with senior agency officials.

In Chapter 4, Napoleon Byars analyzes the growing use of the web by government to disseminate information and achieve greater transparency. The chapter examines the web operations of a number of agencies including the White House, the U.S. State Department, Department of Defense, and Treasury Department. In particular, the Defense Department maintains the most extensive and perhaps effective online presence on the web. A thorough examination of how that came to be, along with where things may be headed will provide a practical and helpful perspective to practitioners at all levels of government. This chapter discusses the purpose of each website as it relates to public information as a management function and how websites have become central in helping maintain relationships with key stakeholders. In addition, the chapter presents agency tactics for directing citizens to its website and encourages them to return time and time again as part of an ongoing dialog among all levels of government and citizens.

Jenifer E. Kopfman and Amanda Ruth-McSwain cover the use of public information campaigns in Chapter 5. Saying no to drugs, buckling up, donating blood, and preventing forest fires: public information messages are prevalent in our daily consumption of information and in governmental public relations. Although public information campaigns are used by nongovernment entities, they are classically government-sponsored campaigns developed to address various social problems and communicate information to a large number of citizens to achieve positive societal results. A well-crafted public information campaign can raise awareness, change attitudes, motivate behaviors, and even impact public policy by providing crucial information to a defined target audience. This chapter presents multidisciplinary insights and theoretical perspectives as well as the experiences of the authors to provide a practitioner guide for planning, implementing, and evaluating public information campaigns. Historical and contemporary public information campaigns provide a background for reviewing campaign development stages and analyzing successful communication strategies of public-centered messages across local, state, and federal government agencies. A practical checklist facilitates the development, implementation, and evaluation of a public information effort.

Crisis, emergency and disaster public relations, the subject of Chapter 6, is a major focus of many government agencies and one that has increased in importance in the shortened news cycle and increased use of mobile technology. Brooke Fisher Liu and Abbey Blake Levenshus focus on this important crucial function for government public relations practitioners. In addition to providing a valuable overview of how to prepare and manage a crisis communication plan, the authors include recent research by effectively framing disaster messages, exploring types of frames that resonate with the media, and explaining what obstacles and opportunities practitioners face when managing crises and disasters that are unique to the public sector.

Social networks are changing the communications landscape in public administration. More recently, government agencies and elected officials are using social media channels to engage citizens and arouse support on social issues. As demonstrated by the political campaign of President Obama, social networking encouraged millions to participate in the political process. Until recently, citizens had very little interaction with government, and therefore fewer mechanisms of information sharing. In Chapter 7, "Web 2.0," Leila Sadeghi looks at how government is utilizing social media channels to engage the public and adapting to these changes in communication. This chapter also explores issues that are important in the current environment such as how government can effectively respond to tweeted service requests and complaints, practical strategies for government and universities to inform citizens of their actions, and how government and universities can monitor and measure the effectiveness of their social media strategies. Saghedi also highlights some of the best practices currently adopted by state and local governments. The emphasis is on the use of social media to enhance communication, improve service delivery, and foster greater civic engagement.

Section II: Managing Government Public Relations

In Chapter 8, "Strategic Communication Planning," by Diana Knott Martinelli, the focus is on an oft-neglected area of government public relations. Many government organizations are so busy with the things they *must* do, that they don't take the time to strategically think through and plan their public relations activities, except perhaps in the case of special campaigns, where outside counsel is often secured. Martinelli argues for the need of every organization to develop an annual strategic communications plan that will identify priorities and allow for efficient use of valuable resources. This chapter presents the process of developing an annual communications plan for government entities that supports the overall vision, mission, and goals of the larger institution. This activity not only helps move the larger organization forward, but also helps the smaller unit become more visible and valuable to management. Examples taken from government and government-funded entities show how to apply these principles along with a step-by-step process that functions as a template for any organization wishing to better organize and strategically deliver its communication messages.

Chapter 9, by Shannon A. Bowen, explores the ethical challenges facing professional communicators in government public relations. Topics explored include media relations, stakeholder relations, providing public service information versus concealment for community or national security purposes, public accountability, relations with the myriad publics of the government, grassroots communication and use of the mass media, ethical use of research and data in lobbying, the ethics of constituent relations, and relationships with NGOs and advocacy groups. Using a public policy issue case study provides a real-world lens to examine how different ethical frameworks underlie governmental public relations.

As first mentioned in Lee's chapter, government public relations is fraught with the potential for misuse, abuse, and misunderstanding by lawmakers. In Chapter 10, Kevin R. Kosar focuses on practical guidance for government professionals "Doing Right and Avoiding Wrong with the Law and Politicians." Many modern democratic governments have laws or political norms that differentiate between appropriate and inappropriate public relations activities. Yet the line between appropriately persuasive communications and odious propaganda often is far from clear. Public relations practitioners must be cognizant of the dangers of crossing the line and setting off political consternation. This chapter guides the public relations practitioner in navigating the ambiguous border between appropriate and inappropriate activities. The chapter focuses on the U.S. federal government, as it exemplifies the diverse nature of the sorts of lines that practitioners can unwittingly cross. Description of the U.S. government's various legal prohibitions and related political norms, found in statutory and appropriations law and embedded in the larger legal context set by the U.S. Constitution, guides those who may not be at the federal level on what to look for and consider in their own unique governmental setting. The chapter includes several brief case studies that illustrate government public relations activities that avoid and breach these prohibitions along with questions posed to the reader for solving the dilemmas faced by government public relations practitioners.

In Chapter 11, Anne Zahradnik focuses on an important constituency for those tasked with public relations—the government organization itself. A government public relations practitioner who has researched, planned, executed, and tracked a strong communications program can still run into professional difficulties if he or she fails to communicate effectively with internal audiences. An ongoing program of educating internal stakeholders on the uses and value of public relations, and on the return on investment from public relations projects and programs, is an absolute necessity in a resource-constrained environment. Elected or appointed officials do not always understand or appreciate the important role of communications. They often consider communications a frill rather than a necessity, are understandably sensitive to accusations of wasting money, and may be quick to cut communications funding and jobs when resources become scarce. Zahradnik focuses on how to adapt and apply the external communications skills and tools covered in the earlier book chapters to ensure that internal stakeholders are aware of and understand public relations and the results it produces. This chapter gives practical advice that helps public relations practitioners apply the tools and techniques of public relations to their own work, improving funding prospects and making their job more secure.

Measuring the impact of government public relations is the focus of Chapter 12 by Maureen Taylor. She looks at moving beyond a simplistic accounting of the outputs of public relations efforts—a clipping file of news placement or anecdotes of success—toward a more deliberative process of documenting public affairs work and the resultant effects. This chapter discusses best practices in creating easy-to-use, systematic, and useful monitoring and evaluation (M&E) indicators that help us measure the impact of our efforts. This innovative approach is becoming an increasingly common and professional tool for measuring communication effectiveness, but it has not yet become widely used in the public sector. A brief discussion of the philosophy behind M&E is presented first, with the author offering a concise and practical explanation of how public affairs professionals can take traditional social science methodologies, such as content analysis, to show measurable outcomes of their efforts. The chapter concludes with specific examples and lessons learned of how public sector agencies (civilian as well as military) and nonprofit organizations have used this method to showcase their success and argue for additional resources.

The topics covered in this text are intended to provide the government public relations practitioner with the theoretical framework and practical tools for addressing current issues and demands in public communications. The reader is presented with a 360-degree approach to PR in government, looking at both the internal and external aspects from the start of a campaign or crisis, through implementation and eventually evaluation. Each of the authors brings a unique perspective in his or her area of expertise based on professional experience and academic research. The intent of this book is to help change the perception that government public relations is a tool made up of propaganda used to manipulate public opinion, and to develop a better understanding of how proper public communications can lead to more efficient, effective, and accountable public organizations.

Chapter 2

Government Public Relations: What Is It Good For?

Mordecai Lee

Contents

Just Your Routine Budget Hearing

It was supposed to be the usual boring annual budget hearing. The finance committee of your government's legislative branch (city council, county board, state legislature, or Congress) is holding a hearing on your agency's budget proposal for the next fiscal year. A boring ritual. The agency director makes a statement, hands out copies of a bunch of graphs and tables, and then answers questions from committee members. Going down the budget line by line and occasionally asking a question for clarification, the committee chair comes to an expenditure for salaries for the agency's communications and outreach office. The chair casually asks the agency director, "Does this office do public relations?" The other committee members, who seemed to be half asleep, suddenly jerk their heads up, their attention triggered. In a defensive tone, the head of the agency quickly answers that this is most definitely *not* a public relations office, but rather one that engages in public communication, as necessitated by the day-to-day needs of any government department. But it's too late. The other committee members rush in like a pack of wolves going for the kill. They clamor for the chance to denounce public relations in government. Some of their comments, camouflaged as questions, include:

Politician 1: It looks to me like you're trying to boast about what you do, trying to make yourselves look good. A government agency should never do that. This is purely a self-serving activity. Propaganda has no place in government. Good works should speak for themselves.

Politician 2: This is a waste of taxpayer money, spending it on press releases that nobody prints, brochures that nobody reads, public service announcements that nobody hears.

Politician 3: The editor of my hometown media outlet has been complaining to me about getting a blizzard of self-serving and duplicative releases from you. Stop wasting time and money.

Politician 4: One of my constituents, who uses your services, called me to complain. She said that an employee of your agency suggested she lobby me for more funding for your programs, otherwise she'll lose her eligibility. This is an outrageous meddling in politics. You're trying to make me look bad to my constituents. A government agency getting involved in politics is a violation of the basic principles of how democracy is supposed to work. You have lost my support forever.

The hearing goes downhill from there. A news reporter happens to be in the room, actually there waiting for the budget review of the agency which was next up and would likely be controversial. But she feels lucky to witness this unexpected uproar. The journalist quickly posts a blog on the blowup at the hearing, not too subtly reflecting how most reporters feel about government public relations. The lead reads, "The Finance Committee today gave a shellacking to an agency that was trying to renew funding for the half-dozen salaried flacks it has been carrying on its payroll, often with camouflaged job titles. Legislators expressed shock at such self-serving activities and denounced them as wasteful propaganda." The story is quickly picked up by many other news outlets and repeated frequently during afternoon drive time. By the end of the news cycle, it seems like *everybody* knows about it.

The agency's director gets back to the office and seems shell-shocked. She quickly convenes the senior management team for an urgent consultation and says, "We are never, ever, going to do anything that smacks of public relations. Never!"

The rest of the day is the usual humdrum public administration. A reporter calls the public information office wanting some information on one of the agency's programs. The director decides to call back personally and provides the information. The annual report for the previous fiscal year needs the director's signature on the cover page so that it could be posted on the agency's website. It is not an accountant's report with boring columns of numbers. Instead, it is an explanation, in plain English and lots of pictures, of what the agency did last year. Later that day, the agency head approves sending a notice to all the neighbors living near one of its facilities about a public session the following week to explain its plans for expanding the building. Finally, on the way home, she stops by a local TV station that has agreed to provide free studio time and technical support to tape a public service announcement. The agency director is at ease in front of the cameras. It does not sound like she is reading off the teleprompter. Using a conversational tone, as though she is having a one-on-one chat with a neighbor, she looks directly into the camera and says in a friendly way that the agency is starting a new program. If anyone in the audience knows of someone who might qualify, here's an easy-to-remember and catchy URL for more information or to sign up.

With her long day finally over, the agency head reflects on how bad the budget hearing had been and on her need to avoid doing public relations because it is so controversial with politicians. But, she feels she recovered. The second half of the day was well spent, just doing her job. Yes, the afternoon was satisfying—exactly why she chose a career in public service in the first place. Her favorite professor in the Master of Public Administration (MPA) program she had attended would be proud of her, she thinks, as she drifts off to sleep.

Public Relations as a Tool for Doing Public Administration *Better*

Is this scenario fanciful? Only a bit. It was intended to convey the netherworld in which government public relations exists. It is a red flag for elected officials, yet it is essential and integral to the day-to-day work of public administration. Given the hostility to public relations by politicians and the media, is it quixotic even to advocate for doing it? The authors and editors of this book respond with a resounding, "No!" We know that public relations is both inherent to public administration and a tool for helping an agency accomplish its mission. All of us will be making the argument in our respective chapters that there is much good that can come to a government agency from using public relations to do its job.

If there is only one idea that I could to convey to you, it is this: Public relations can help a public administrator do a better job by being better at (1) *implementing the agency's central mission* and (2) fulfilling the *democratic responsibilities* inherent in government.

This chapter presents an overview of the different *purposes* of government public relations. It focuses on public administrators who are implementing policies already adopted by elected officials, politicians, and political appointees. How can public relations help them do a better job? Many tools of public relations can help accomplish the agency's programmatic mission: delivery of services, customer relations, and so on. Also, public relations can help promote the democratic accountability of a government agency to the citizenry, an activity unique to public administration in contrast to business administration and nonprofit management.

Taking them up in reverse order, I suggest that there are, first, some reasons why public administrators *have to* engage in public relations, whether they like it or not. These are the democratic requirements of government management, closely tied to the *public* in public administration. A second cluster of benefits from public relations are optional. They help an agency do its core mission more effectively and, sometimes, less expensively. These are the pragmatic uses of public relations, focusing on the *administration* in public administration. Third, the most controversial category is the political use of public relations intended to advance the agency's autonomy and power.

Using that threefold typology, here is how the different purposes of government public relations (PR) fit together:

   I. Mandatory: Democratic purposes of government public relations
     1. Media relations
     2. Public reporting
    3a. Responsiveness to the public (as citizens)
  II. Optional: Pragmatic purposes of government public relations
    3b. Responsiveness to the public (as customers and clients)
     4. Increasing the utilization of services and products (Public outreach)

5. Public education and public service campaigns (Public outreach)
6. Seeking voluntary public compliance with laws and regulations (Public outreach)
7. Using the public as the eyes and ears of an agency (Public outreach)

III. Dangerous, but powerful: Political purposes of government public relations

8. Increasing public support

In general, this approach to public relations based on *purposes* is slightly different from the traditional action orientation of modern life. Yes, our culture seems to admire action heroes and action movies, but that is not a helpful mind frame for getting the most out of public relations. In fact, it is usually the opposite. For example, during a lengthy discussion at a meeting, some eager beaver pipes in and says enthusiastically, "Let's hold a news conference!" This might be wholly inappropriate in relation to accomplishing some purposes, while perfectly on target for others. In other words, *the purpose of the effort needs to be identified before any plan of action can be constructed.*

The focus on the *purposes* of government public relations also is helpful because once that particular goal has been identified, the specific communications techniques to use to accomplish that purpose will flow naturally from the purpose itself. For example, a news release might be useful for notifying the entire populace about a new regulation that affects the citizenry at large. However, if a new program targets, say, new immigrants from a specific country, then there are likely to be communication channels that are much more specialized to reach such a narrowly defined demographic.

Beginning with the next chapter, experts in their fields provide guidance on the practice of public relations: news releases, websites, social media, crisis communication, and so on. But first, it is important to identify *why* you're considering using news releases, social media, public information campaigns, and so on. What are you trying to accomplish? The various tools that will be presented in subsequent chapters are methods to reach specific goals that most government agencies have. Public relations can help accomplish the eight specific purposes listed above. They are clustered around the themes of stuff you have to do, stuff that might be a good idea to do, and finally, powerful stuff if you're willing to risk a lot as well.[1]

Mandatory for Public Administrators: The *Democratic* Purposes of Government Public Relations

First, public administrators need to recognize that some aspects of public relations are forced upon their agencies by dint of being in the public sector. As Young stated, "Communication is the basic prerequisite for democracy."[2] That means the communication obligations of a government manager include responding to inquiries from the news media, reporting to the electorate on agency activities, and generally being responsive to the public. These are not luxuries in the context of democratic governance. Rather, they are obligations that can't be ignored, even if and when a politician denounces them as self-serving and wasteful propaganda. The qualitative difference between public administration and business administration is the governmental context of agency management. In a democracy, public administrators must engage in certain activities that are expected as the sine qua non of government. For example, government managers must respond to inquiries from the news media, whether the particular issue would put the agency in a good light or a bad one. Similarly, given the central role of public opinion in a democracy, public administrators have a duty to report to the citizenry on the work of the agency and its stewardship of taxpayer funds. Again, these are part of the rubric of public relations. Hence, when focusing on these purposes, public relations is integral to public administration, not ancillary to it.

1. Media Relations

The link between public administration and media relations is practically a tautology. Government managers are public servants. They are accountable to the public, not quite like elected officials, but accountable nonetheless. One way that this accountability is operationalized is by the obligation of public administrators to work transparently, including the duty to respond to media questions, inquiries, and requests. "No comment" is not an acceptable answer from a civil servant whose salary is being paid by the taxpayers.

The First Amendment to the U.S. Constitution is chock full of rights that inure to each individual American citizen: speech, assembly, religion, petitioning government, and so on. Only one clause in the amendment grants a right to an *institution*: freedom of the press to what we now call the news media. Why the selectivity? In the eyes of the founders, journalism had to be independent of government so that citizens in a democracy could obtain information about what government and elected officials were doing from sources other than the government and the elected officials themselves. In that framework, the news media was an *instrument of democracy*, serving as the feedback loop of the democratic process. So, the tautology is that government agencies engage in media relations because government agencies in a democracy have the obligation to cooperate with the news media.

However, government–media relations tend to be stormy. Besides a built-in skepticism about "official sources" that is part of journalistic culture, there are several factors that specifically contribute to the difficulty of a public administrator having consistently good relations with the media. These factors include the following:

- The negative image of the bureaucrat in pop culture and public opinion
- The profit-making motives of the media

- The entertainment motives of the media
- The increasing competitiveness of old media versus new
- The fact that government agencies tend to generate inherently nonvisual and undramatic news that is often unattractive to the news media
- The built-in predisposition of reporters to archetypal stories that, by their very nature, put public administration in a bad light, such as a citizen being unfairly victimized by heartless bureaucrats, a government agency wasting money, or a government agency standing by idly (or incompetently) while a certain category of the population suffers
- The antigovernment strain within American political culture

In 2009, President Obama provided a trenchant critique of contemporary journalistic coverage of government (encompassing both politics and public administration). Speaking at a memorial service for Walter Cronkite, who had been the longtime anchor of an evening news program on an over-the-air TV network, he observed:

> Despite the big stories of our era, serious journalists find themselves all too often without a beat. Just as the news cycle has shrunk, so has the bottom line. We fill that void with instant commentary and celebrity gossip and the softer stories that Walter disdained, rather than the hard news and investigative journalism he championed. "What happened today?" is replaced with "Who won today?" The public debate cheapens. The public trust falters. We fail to understand our world or one another as well as we should—and that has real consequences in our own lives and in the life of our nation. We seem stuck with a choice between what cuts to our bottom line and what harms us as a society. Which price is higher to pay? Which cost is harder to bear?
>
> "This democracy," Walter said, "cannot function without a reasonably well-informed electorate." That's why the honest, objective, meticulous reporting that so many of you pursue with the same zeal that Walter did is so vital to our democracy and our society: Our future depends on it.[3]

Still, love 'em or hate 'em, the public administrator in a democracy *must* cooperate with the press. That is the price of working in the public sector. (For a detailed discussion of how to do media relations in public administration, see Chapter 3 in this volume, by Jerome Sadow.)

2. Public Reporting

By cooperating with the news media, a public servant is being held accountable to the citizenry *indirectly* through news coverage. However, the democratic obligation of public accountability should also be operationalized by *directly* informing the public at large. This is called *public reporting.* The purpose of public reporting is a generalized duty of the public administrator to convey information to the public on the agency's stewardship of its mission and its use of taxpayer funds. This is generally a post-hoc activity, focusing on the past—"here's what we did last year" kind of information. It is information for information's sake, not really *doing* anything tangible, but rather simply furthering the goal of an informed citizenry. Note that the concept of public reporting looks back. It is an over-the-shoulder, retrospective review. This is not to be confused with the slightly but distinctly different public relations activity of responsiveness to the public *as citizens* (Purpose 3a, discussed below). The latter is *prospective*; it focuses on looking forward and preparing to make decisions in the future—a kind of "help us decide what to do *next*." Public reporting is an aspect of governmental accountability to the public in a democracy.[4]

In a sense, public reporting is like the stereotypical scene of a parent standing in front of a grade school class on career day: "Hi, I'm a dentist and want to explain what I do all day, why this is important, and what you have to do if you want to become a dentist." Public reporting is a permutation of career day writ large for the public sector. "Hi, I work at the County Public Works Department. We build and maintain bridges, highways, and mass transit systems within the county limits, which is 400 square miles. We spent *x* million dollars last year. Here's what we did with all that money …."

The classic manifestation of public reporting is an agency's annual report. This is often issued by the chief financial officer (CFO), is crammed with incomprehensible accountant's jargon and statistics, and as one might expect, is unreadable except perhaps as the cure for insomnia. But the origins of such drudgery came from the duty of every government department to report on its performance to the citizenry. Besides annual reports, some other traditional venues for public reporting have included open houses, exhibits, displays at shopping malls or state fairs, tours, and a speaker's bureau.

The emergence of new communications venues of government-to-citizen e-government, and e-democracy have helped revolutionize public reporting. Now, agencies can post their annual (or semiannual, monthly, etc.) reports on their websites. The report can include pictures, video, and interactive features. Using plain language, it can efficiently help a citizen zero in on a particular topic of interest, rather than wade through everything the agency is involved in. Finally, the interactivity of these technologies can spur further communications between the citizen and the agency, such as feedback, surveys, and requests for information.

An example of how easily updated online e-gov communications have enhanced traditional public reporting is the posting of crime statistics. When a police department website includes information on "crimes in your neighborhood in the last 30 days," it is promoting public safety by providing information that helps citizens to engage in safe behavior (i.e., the central mission of the agency). (For a more detailed discussion, see the next section on optional but pragmatic uses of government public relations.) However, such a site is also making the department accountable to the public for its past record of performance. The citizen can then make an informed judgment—"I'm pleased with the Police Department" or "I'm unhappy with the Police Department" or anything in between. The methods and venues for public reporting are unlimited. The key is that the public administrator recognizes and implements the duty to contribute to an informed citizenry in a democracy.

3a. Responsiveness to the Public as Citizens

Government is different. It must be responsive to the public. If a business or nonprofit opts not to answer the complaint of a neighborhood organization, that's legal and OK. But government agencies can't. That's because their external relationships are not one dimensional, such as with customers or clients, and not even with stakeholders. Rather, for a government agency, everybody is a *citizen*. Even people who aren't being served by an agency have a claim on it. That's the difference between government and other sectors in the political economy.

To continue with this example, a business or nonprofit can (if it wishes) ignore criticisms coming from outside groups. A government agency cannot. It is expected to be responsive to the public at large. Nobody can be "blown off." Everyone must be treated with the respect that citizens have the right to expect from government. Another example: people don't have a right to attend meetings or see documents of a business or a nonprofit. Yet that is the presumption for government agencies. Transparency means open meetings (with certain justifiable exceptions) and freedom of information for documents (again, with certain justifiable exceptions). The *principle* is openness.

Therefore, one of the basic democratic purposes of public relations in public administration is *listening* to the public on multiple levels. Active listening then leads to modified agency behavior so that it can do a better job and be more responsive to the citizenry. This is different from being responsive for pragmatic and essentially marketing purposes, which is discussed in the next section.

In some cases, responsiveness to the public means gauging public opinion. Oddly, few government agencies engage in formal survey research. That's probably because conducting a poll might be susceptible to charges by politicians of wasting tax funds. But that's a shame. Private corporations spend gobs of money on survey research to be sure that they understand the views of the public. Some university-based polling institutes conduct research on satisfaction rates toward corporations and governments. These provide a real-time barometer of the standing that major government departments have with the public, such as the Internal Revenue Service (IRS), the Division of Motor Vehicles (DMV), the post office, or social security. Using public relations to improve the agency's satisfaction score is not something to scorn, as we would for so-called "PR," which is wholly divorced from reality and solely to manipulate the results by superficial or even misleading actions. Rather, doing a better job of serving the citizenry is a laudable effort that often results in improved scores. Yes, images and stereotypes change slowly, but they can change, whether up or down. An agency that is focused on being responsive to the public at large will gradually improve its satisfaction scores.

Another aspect of responsiveness relates to citizen participation in agency decision making. A reminder that the concept of public reporting (Purpose 2, discussed previously) is focused on past performance: "Here's what we *did*." Citizen participation is based on building on the record of the past: "OK, given what we did up to now, what should we do in the *future*?" The various techniques of citizen participation in public administration are, essentially, a way for the citizenry to influence agency decision making in addition to through their electoral choices. Citizen participation in public administration is a way to permit public opinion to influence agency decision making from *below* rather than only from above it.

There are many mechanisms for citizen participation in decisions about an agency's future path and programs. There are dozens of methods for an agency to avail itself of citizen input, including public hearings, advisory committees, drop-in centers, focus groups, surveys, facilitation, visioning, brainstorming, charettes (an architectural term for a workshop that involves active collaboration on design), fairs, newsletters, open houses, and booths. Readers interested in more details about citizen participation in public administration are directed to sources that focus solely on that subject.[5]

Optional, but Useful, for Public Administrators: The *Pragmatic* Purposes of Government Public Relations

The preceding section focused on the elements of government public relations that a public administrator has to do, like 'em or not. They are part of democracy, part of the complicated effort to mesh the inherently undemocratic process of organizational management with the basic requirements of democracy. This section focuses on how public relations can help an agency implement its goals better, faster, cheaper. This use of PR is, of course, optional. No one can make you do it. My argument is that the tools of public relations can help you do your job so much more effectively and efficiently. Unfortunately, the term *PR* has such a bad rap in modern society that over the last few decades public administration has tended to ignore what public relations has to offer. The key now is the revived recognition that public relations *is* public administration, that it helps *do* the central mission of the department.

The tools and techniques of public relations help reach potential customers and clients, notify the public of new laws and programs, promote the goals of the agency through public service campaigns that encourage (or discourage) certain behaviors, or increase public cooperation with the agency, such as through tip lines and websites. In all these examples, public relations is an inexpensive substitute for hiring more staff, increasing agency enforcement and regulation activities, or expanding field offices. Through public relations, an agency can extend its reach without necessarily increasing its size and costs.

This orientation of government public relations largely overlaps with marketing.[6] Yet like public relations, the term *marketing* in public administration has a slight whiff of the inappropriate, that somehow government should engage neither in marketing nor in public relations. It should just *be*. Sometimes it seems that's the position many antiquated politicians take. Whether you call it marketing or public relations, it is central to the modern delivery of public sector goods and services. For example, one could argue that government doesn't need to market or advertise because it is a monopoly. There aren't different organizations competing with one another that offer food stamps. Only one local government agency is the portal to obtaining them. So, why advertise? Aha, now we're getting somewhere. In a capitalistic system, marketing and advertising are used by private corporations to make their product more attractive to the customer than a competitor's identical (or nearly) product: Pepsi or Coke? Bud or Miller? Nike or Adidas? But that's an awfully narrow conceptualization of marketing. Getting back to food stamps: How does a citizen know what food stamps even are? If he or she qualifies? How and where to obtain them? The answer is through marketing and advertising, even in the context of government as a monopoly.

Let's look at it from the perspective of evaluating how good a government manager is. Let's say the director of the food stamps agency in City A has a budget of $1 million a year, a full-time staff of 100, and a *market penetration* (i.e., reaching the eligible population) of 75 percent. The director's counterpart in City B, with similar population size and composition, has a budget of $750,000 a year, a staff of 75, and a market penetration of 50 percent. Who would we judge as the more admirable and effective public administrator? Setting partisan political ideology aside, our professional management-based evaluation would probably rank Manager A over B. Why? Because Manager A got closer to fulfilling the public policy goal set for that subject matter (i.e., reducing hunger).

Given the constraints on public budgets, we want public administration to be cost effective. Are there marketing and public relations techniques that are relatively inexpensive and that can give a bigger bang for the buck in terms of market penetration? For a simplified example, one could hire door-to-door canvassers to locate families eligible for food stamps. But it would be much cheaper to engage in public service advertising to reach the easy-to-reach population on a lower per capita cost and only use canvassers for the harder-to-reach cases. In other words, government public relations as marketing is less costly because it usually uses a *wholesale* rather than *retail* approach to service clients and customers. Now, we'll proceed with a more specific discussion of the pragmatic purposes that public relations offers the public administrator.

3b. Responsiveness to the Public as Customers and Clients

This activity is government PR and is not a duplication of Purpose 3a. Responsiveness to the public was already covered in the preceding section, but remember that it focused on the mandatory and democratic obligation of a public administrator to be responsive to the public at large. The same purpose of responsiveness also belongs in the category of a public relations tool that can improve the pursuit of the agency's policy mission, the *doing* of public administration. For example, some governmental units have an ombudsman. This office is usually tasked with the duty to investigate complaints from clients and customers and then to correct authentic mistakes. This has the purpose of improving service delivery to enhance the central work of the agency, in contradistinction to the preceding purpose when responsiveness to public opinion was one way that public relations improves democracy in public administration.

Another aspect of using public relations to improve the central work of the agency is by trying to see the organization through the eyes of an outsider. Sometimes it's called an *experience audit*. In the private sector, it's sometimes called *secret shopper*. Is the organization's website easy to find in the first place? Once there, is it easy for a potential client or customer to find helpful information? To register or enroll? For in-person service delivery, is the facility easy to find? Is it near mass transit and does it have adequate parking? Is the signage clear, both outside and in? Are employees friendly, helpful, and polite? Is the wait for service relatively short even at peak times? What is the average wait for clients using a call-in phone service? These kinds of prosaic and mundane details, when gathered with dozens of others like them, provide each individual customer or client with a good or bad experience when interacting with the agency. This focus is sometimes called *clue management*, in the sense that every detail gives the customer a clue if the agency is trying to be customer friendly or not.[7]

4–7. Public Outreach

While the term *public relations* is usually viewed negatively by politicians, *outreach* has, inexplicably, been warmly embraced. Ibid for *public awareness*. Elected officials *expect* government agencies to engage in outreach with their stakeholders and to make the public aware of important information. Not doing so transgresses the essence of public administration in a democracy. The acceptability of outreach as a politically safe nomenclature for public administrators engaging in public relations can unintentionally obscure the important tangible meaning of the term. Government agencies can do a better job programmatically (as opposed to democratically) by reaching out to the people who need to be communicated with. This is not only a good thing, but central to the raison d'être of the agency. Doing outreach *is* doing public administration.

However, it is important to ask, outreach for what purpose? This author suggests there are four distinct public relations purposes that fall within the rubric of government outreach. Therefore, in an effort to identify with clarity the different goals that outreach can help accomplish, they are presented here as different purposes, even though all four are generically outreach and all relate to the pragmatic benefits of public relations to the government manager.

4. (Outreach:) Increasing the Utilization of Services and Products

A popular saying is "If a tree falls in a forest and no one hears it, did it make a sound?" Similarly, one could ask a public administrator, "If your agency offers a service, but no one knows about it, did you really *provide* that service?" Baldly put, a public servant managing a program is a *failure* if only a small percentage of eligible citizens utilize it. Part of public administration is to engage in outreach that informs potential customers and clients of services that they may be able to use. Opening your doors every morning is not enough. One must engage in multiple communication activities that are likely to reach the demographic you are seeking. People must *know* about your program if you want them to use it.

Again, there are many retail ways to reach these potential customers. But retail, reaching one person at a time, is expensive. Conversely, the multiplicity of techniques of public relations, marketing, and advertising are wholesale communication methods. They can help you target your message and reach your potential customers relatively inexpensively. Program managers need to be activists and initiators of informational efforts that maximize the utilization of governmental services intended to help segments of the public.

5. (Outreach:) Public Education and Public Service Campaigns

By using paid and free media coverage, an agency can accomplish its mission and reduce its expenditures by encouraging behavior that has broad social approval and reflects widely held values. These are sometimes called *public service campaigns*. Whether it's about using seat belts to save lives ("click it or ticket"), washing hands frequently during flu outbreaks, or reducing consumption of junk food, these government agencies are reaching out to the public as a way of accomplishing their public policy goals. In these instances, there are more service-intensive and expensive ways to pursue those objectives, such as more law enforcement officers focusing on seat belt violations, more public health nurses to deal with the effects of flu, or more obesity-related health service projects. The most widely recognized example of a public education campaign is the effort by the U.S. Forest

Service to reduce fires in national forests through its Smokey the Bear campaign. By encouraging a change in public behavior regarding use of fires while camping, the Forest Service was able to reduce the demand on its fire suppression infrastructure.[8] (For a more detailed discussion of public service campaigns, see Jenifer E. Kopfman and Amanda Ruth-McSwain's coverage of the topic in Chapter 5 of this book.)

6. (Outreach:) Seeking Voluntary Public Compliance with Laws and Regulations

Agencies can reduce their regulatory costs by engaging in public relations to encourage voluntary compliance with the new laws, regulations, and programs they have been assigned to enforce. This is a cost-effective approach to the implementation phase of the policy process. A common example is the effort by the U.S. Postal Service to inform the public about an increase in postal rates as a way to reduce the percentage of items that have to be pulled from the mail stream and returned for insufficient postage. (Similarly, its "forever stamps" helped reduce the problem for first class mail.) Another example was an effort by prosecutors to notify the public about a new aggressive policy of increasing criminal charges for crimes committed with guns. One of the prosecutors was quoted as explaining, "If those people don't know about it, how's it supposed to serve as a deterrent to them?" In 2009, the U.S. Treasury Department announced a "name and shame" publicity effort as a way to encourage greater compliance by banks with new programs to reduce mortgage foreclosures.

7. (Outreach:) Using the Public as the Eyes and Ears of an Agency

Government agencies can encourage citizens to serve as their eyes and ears, thus reducing the need for staffing. For example, when a person chooses to call 911 in an emergency, he or she has been co-opted effectively by the police and fire departments to serve as a member of its informal organization. This is sometimes referred to as co-production of government services. Incentives for participation can vary from self-interest to self-satisfaction to rewards. The key to the success of this function is that citizens are familiar with their potential role as an extension of the agency, an awareness accomplished through public relations. Cell phones have helped permit citizens to report the location of a pothole and then to expect that the local public works or highway department will respond promptly to their report. Other agencies have created tip lines, abuse reporting lines, and websites for anonymous citizens to report wrongdoing. One sheriff said that he could not afford to put deputies to patrol for drunk drivers all the time. Instead, he created a public relations program called Mobile Eyes. It informed drivers that they could receive $100 for calls that resulted in arrests for drunk driving.

Dangerous, but Powerful, for Public Administrators: The *Political* Purposes of Government Public Relations

Generally speaking, government agencies desire autonomy.[9] Then, they can operate more as they wish and with less political interference from legislators and the elected chief executive. In what is now a classic quote, political scientist Francis Rourke described the benefits of an agency having a good image with the citizenry:

> Because public opinion is ultimately the only legitimate sovereign in a democratic society, an agency which seeks first a high standing with the public can reasonably expect to have all other things added to it in the way of legislative and executive support. Power gives power, in administration as elsewhere, and once an agency has established a secure base with the public, it cannot easily be trifled with by political officials in either the legislative or executive branch.[10]

Therefore, good public relations can enhance the power of an agency and help it grow and thrive.

8. Increasing Public Support

One of the political red lines of government public relations is that agencies cannot directly appeal to the public for help against the elected overseers of the agency. This is considered propaganda, a forbidden activity. For example, an agency might not like a bill that the legislative branch is about to pass, but it would be a cardinal sin to issue press releases, hold news conferences, and send out speakers to give public talks on the need for the public to tell lawmakers not to pass the bill. Politicians take great umbrage when agencies try such end-runs. They feel such behavior interferes with the legislators' own institutional powers. In the eyes of elected officials, public administrators are supposed to passively implement whatever these elected institutions set for it. This so-called politics–administration dichotomy was a long-time premise of American public administration. In the fancier jargon of our times, this is a principal-agent view of how the executive branch is supposed to operate. Agencies are to be seen, but not heard. (For a more detailed discussion of the "rules of the game" imposed on the public relations activities of federal departments and agencies, see Kevin R. Kosar's Chapter 10 in this volume.)

However, politicians are not helpless in a slightly different scenario. An agency might have a high level of public support not because the agency overtly pursued this goal, but rather as a consequence of its bread-and-butter activities, including the implementation of public relations Purposes 1 through 7, described previously. So, for example, if *as a result* of its Smokey the Bear campaign, the public thinks well of the U.S. Forest Service, well, the politician can't complain about it. Similarly, the politician would likely avoid a major public fight with the Forest Service. Elected officials want to be associated with popular agencies as much as they want to be viewed as critics of unpopular ones. Furthermore, one person's propaganda can be another's information. If propaganda is in the eye of the beholder, then agencies have much more maneuvering room in their public relations activities than may be initially apparent. Therefore, one implicit reason for public administrators to engage in effective public relations is to help, *indirectly*, improve their organization's popularity with the citizenry. Much good flows from such public support—just as long as it's not obvious that this is what the agency is seeking. Benefiting from the political consequences of good public relations is not the same as actively pursuing it.[11]

Summary and Conclusions

As a prelude to a practical and pragmatic discussion of government public relations for practitioners, this chapter summarized the *purposes* and *benefits* of such activities. With the rapid expansion of the digital age and the information explosion, the importance of managing external informational relationships in the twenty-first century is certain to increase. Public administration practitioners can broaden their scope of attention to embrace the practice of public relations. It is a useful, helpful, and important aspect of managing government agencies. They can use public relations to (1) accomplish the democratic responsibilities associated with the public sector, (2) implement the central missions of their agencies on a cost-effective and efficient basis, and (3) contribute to public support for their agencies.

I hope this chapter has confirmed that public relations can help you, as a practitioner, do your job—namely, public relations is interwoven into doing public administration. Now that the subjects of the *why* and the *what* have been addressed, the remaining chapters in this book focus on the *how-to* of government public relations.

Endnotes

[1] For a more detailed discussion and readings regarding these purposes of public relations, see Mordecai Lee, *Government Public Relations: A Reader* (Boca Raton, FL: CRC Press/Taylor & Francis, 2008).

[2] Sally Young, "Introduction: The Theory and Practice of Government Communication," in *Government Communication in Australia*, ed. Sally Young (Melbourne, Australia: Cambridge University Press, 2007), p. xxiii.

[3] "Remarks by the President at Memorial Service in Honor of Walter Cronkite," White House, Office of the Press Secretary, September 9, 2009, accessed March 3, 2010, http://www.whitehouse.gov/the_press_office/Remarks-by-the-President-at-Memorial-Service-in-Honor-of-Walter-Cronkite/.

[4] For a broader discussion of the larger topic, see Mark Bovens, "Public Accountability," in *The Oxford Handbook of Public Management*, ed. Ewan Ferlie, Laurence E. Lynn, Jr., and Christopher Pollitt (Oxford, UK: Oxford University Press, 2005), chapter 8.

[5] See, for example, Nancy C. Roberts, *The Age of Direct Citizen Participation* (Armonk, NY: M. E. Sharpe, 2008). This book is a compilation of the quality articles on the topic published in *Public Administration Review* and other leading journals sponsored by the American Society for Public Administration (ASPA).

[6] For a discussion based on the marketing orientation, see Philip Kotler and Nancy R. Lee, "Marketing in the Public Sector: The Final Frontier," *The Public Manager* 36:1 (spring 2007) 12–17. (Note: Ms. Lee and the author of this chapter are not related.)

[7] Lou Carbone, "Engineering Experiences That Build Trust in Government," in *The Trusted Leader: Building the Relationships That Make Government Work*, ed. Terry Newell, Grant Reeher, and Peter Ronayne (Washington, DC: CQ Press, 2008), chapter 10.

[8] For more general information, see Janet A. Weiss, "Public Information," in *The Tools of Government: A Guide to the New Governance*, ed. Lester S. Salamon (New York: Oxford University Press, 2002), chapter 7; and Ronald E. Rice and Charles K. Atkin (eds.) *Public Communication Campaigns*, 3rd ed. (Thousand Oaks, CA: Sage, 2001).

[9] This generalization is based on the work of Daniel P. Carpenter, *The Forging of Bureaucratic Autonomy: Reputations, Networks, and Policy Innovation in Executive Agencies, 1862–1928* (Princeton, NJ: Princeton University Press, 2001).

[10] Francis E. Rourke, *Bureaucracy, Politics, and Public Policy*, 3rd ed. (Boston: Little, Brown, 1984), p. 50.

[11] Brian Friel, "Toot Your Horn?" (Management Matters column), *Government Executive* 42:2 (February 2010) 37–38.

REACHING THE CITIZENRY: THE TOOLS OF GOVERNMENT PUBLIC RELATIONS

1

Chapter 3

Media Relations

Jerome Sadow

Contents

For government agency media relations practice, or for that matter for all kinds of media relations, there are few laws or statutes, regulations or rules (outside of your own agency) that you must follow or must obey—unless, of course, you step over the line into criminal activity. The practice of media relations is not like the practice of law with statutes and court decisions or math with geometric and trigonometric proofs. What you have in media relations in order to succeed are parameters of good and empirical public relations (PR) knowledge, of good media relations writing and practice, and of good and acceptable approaches of working with the media.

There are no absolutes here—only one way to write a news release, only one way to speak to a print reporter or a TV news editor, only one way to handle an agency crisis that has become public (even if you know how a very similar crisis was handled before by your or another government agency), or only one way to respond to media criticism, valid or unfounded.

Understand that precedent is not king, that every situation is somewhat different, and that relativity is what you must follow and practice and carry out. In the profession and career of media relations, you must deal individually with the reality of the current and new situation without relying totally on past experience or actions. The media is constantly changing, and to succeed as a public affairs practitioner, you must adapt and be flexible, making the wisest possible decisions based on your knowledge of the media, on your media relations writing skills, and on the best crisis management approaches, if necessary, as applied singularly to perhaps unprecedented situations and events. What follows is an overview of information and recommendations that you can use, hopefully successfully, to carry out many of your functions and assignments with intelligence, knowledge, and foresight.

PR Strategies, Tactics, and Objectives

There are shelves of books on media relations and speechwriting, and there are also numerous volumes on PR strategies and tactics and lengthy chapters specifically dealing with government agency public relations. This is not the place to describe overarching PR models, such as the Two-Step Flow Theory and the Concentric Circle Theory, and how you can apply them to your PR approach. But it is the place to mention that following how previous situations, perhaps similar to yours, were handled by high-level government agencies or by elective offices in Congress, state legislatures, or city mayors, may not result in PR success by merely copying their actions. As you know, the best and the brightest, fully informed on PR methodology, can make bad judgments. Past precedent and practice may in actuality have little or no relevance to your unique circumstances.

It should be your goal as a public affairs director to communicate superbly your agency's policies, positions, and regulations to the diverse audiences that you must confront with your information—not only the media, but also special interests from large corporations to local businesses, community-based and nonprofit organizations, influential constituents and the public at large. Your agency's communications success will depend on the good public opinion and wholehearted support of these audiences, not your cleverness with public relations operations or your knowledge in employing what are called the *tools of communication*.

Good agency communication strategies and tactics require an agreed-upon approach with your top administrators of how you are going to act in both planned written and interview media opportunities and in unplanned sudden critical situations. In this regard, timing can mean everything to your overall public relations approach. You should be fully aware of local, state, and national news and actions by other government agencies and the private sector that may occur on a given day that will cloud, impede, and reduce to irrelevance your "important" message.

With all of your professionalism and the release of what your top people consider as real news or the considered "excellent" response to spontaneous negative happenings, you may not succeed in your communication goals because of what have been characterized as barriers to effective communication. Public apathy to and suspicion of the credibility of your statements in print or on TV, a lack of public knowledge and interest, or a lack of understanding of your agency's complex issues and programs may defeat your good media-smart intentions. Your best efforts may be dismissed by the media and public if on specific issues your agency's words and actions are interpreted as "spin" or even outright propaganda. (Remember Lee's opening case study in Chapter 2?)

Realize as you instinctively should that the work of government public affairs and of the media are entwined in an adversarial relationship. You serve different masters, from the White House to a town Board of Selectmen on one side, and from the *New York Times* to a small town weekly on the other. Mutual distrust and mistrust is real from claims by the media that government officials mislead and lie and by government claims that the media has a hostile agenda, exaggerates, and is only interested in selling papers and increasing TV ratings. You, your actions, and words can define for your agency, as perhaps no one else possibly can, how this natural adversarial relationship will affect your entire agency's PR strategies and tactics—friendly with mutual respect and understanding of whom you and the media representative serve, or hostile with disrespect and personal dislike and continual grievance.

With this knowledge, in order to compete with the voluminous news releases and publicity seeking by other organizations, you should consider releasing your information to the media on a "slow" news day (Monday afternoon is a good time) in an expected uneventful week, even though you can't prepare for totally unexpected national and international events. And you certainly can advise that unfavorable but must-be-made-public information should be released on Friday or Saturday night, or just on the web, even though the media is well aware of this timing "trick."

As "the person in the middle," your credibility, personality, writings, and verbal responses are central, in part, to good or bad news coverage, the public image of your agency, and the successful execution of your public relations.

Knowledge of Print, Broadcast, and Online Media

You should know not merely the publications, major TV stations, and online nonmedia news and opinion sites by name, but also the ownership and syndicate groups that interconnect newspapers and broadcast outlets, especially if you're a public affairs officer for an agency on the national or state level. You should also be aware of the most influential and important editors, columnists, and reporters by name in the print media, and of the names of the anchors, editors, and program producers for the broadcast media. There are plenty of media relations sources to give you this information.

For a handy overview of the entire media scene, you should have at your desk a current Bacon's or Burrelle media directory. These books, in separate volumes by daily and weekly papers, by broadcast stations, by magazines and periodicals, by Internet sites, and by advertising/marketing, give you very informative lists not only of names but also the relevant media information associated with those names— title or position, e-mail address, phone number, fax number, and so on. In addition, these directories help you organize media lists for any form of communication and give you the contacts for PR Newswire, Business Wire, Internet News Bureau, Medialink, and others, all with accompanying web info.

These days a lot is made of the newest and "hottest" news and political websites not tied in directly with major media such as Politico.com, Pro Publica.com, The Huffington Post, Slate.com, Salon.com, and individually known blogs that may be geographic or substantively focused. Even though mainstream media may on occasion refer to and quote from their articles, there is no doubt that all of these electronic sources, and also TV networks and local stations, scavenge heavily, and on a daily basis, the news articles, opinion pieces, editorials, and op-eds published by the most comprehensive and influential newspapers, print news syndicates, and current event periodicals. That is why, from your government media relations, media coverage, and influencing public opinion perspective, you should know well the print media influence beyond the individual *New York Times, Washington Post, Los Angeles Times, Chicago Tribune, Wall Street Journal*, and so on. Depending on your agency's geographical sphere of influence, you may need to understand the major print corporations: Gannett, Tribune Co., McClatchy, Copley, Cox, Hearst, Pulitzer, News Corp., Knight Ridder, Scripps Howard, Newhouse, and Thomson Reuters, among others. Scan these news groups by state to visualize the connective news operations that can influence not only general news coverage but also the use and play of your agency's news releases, speeches, and other types of communications.

Radio stations, including the so-called 24-hour news stations, today have minimal coverage of their own except for reporting on local on-the-scene police, fire, and accident situations. They also will attend some of the most important local press conferences and record for one-minute news excerpts. Most of the news you and the public hear is from syndicated sources. Stations "rip the wire" from the Associated Press (AP) feed, which sends across every hour the top 10 to 12 stories in one- or two-paragraph form. Yes, part of your news release also may be included in the top-of-the-hour 5-minute newscast (less time with commercials and promos) along with police, fire, and political and celeb briefs, but don't expect your news release to dominate unless it is of truly major news import from your agency and for the specific locale. The exception here is National Public Radio (NPR) with its own editors, reporters, and on-air talent, which frequently makes its work in local news segments available for national distribution. Each news market ordinarily has at least one NPR station and you should be in direct contact with NPR headquarters in Washington, DC, New York City, and Los Angeles, and in your locality because its listening audience is among the most attentive and concerned about issues in the country.

It's your job, of course, to seize the opportunity to get your agency and top administrators positive coverage in feature and human interest articles in daily and Sunday papers, in "left" periodicals such as *The New Republic* and "right" periodicals such as *The National Review*, on appropriate TV, radio talk, and interview programs, and in commentary on relevant nonmedia websites and blogs. Your full knowledge of print, broadcast, and online media sites will assist you greatly in preparing written and verbal briefings and background material for your agency heads. They will be impressed and rely on you and on your judgment of media operations, government and political leanings, and media personalities.

For your own information and to keep current, you should also subscribe to or scan PR, government, and journalism periodicals for articles that may bear directly on your work. By no means a definitive list, such journals as *Public Relations Review*, *Public Administration Quarterly*, *Public Relations Quarterly*, and *Columbia Journalism Review* may prove insightful and provide helpful hints about current agency problems. Media relations buzzwords online and at Google can quickly narrow your periodical research.

Control of Interactions with the Media

Take a moment to realize that you are in control—or should be. As the public information officer (PIO), you know far more about your agency/office programs, regulations, functions, personnel, and not-to-be-made-public information than virtually any media operation or inquiring reporter. Whether on the federal, state, or local level, very few, or a tiny percentage, of media people really know how your agency works and all the ramifications of its public outreach. Today the media that you deal with most likely does not have the time, the interest, or the staff to carry out in-depth and day-by-day coverage of your agency. Print, TV, and online reporters no longer stay on the same beat for very long, leave their current job, or are unwillingly reassigned by their employer.

That being said, the caveat is, of course, the following: If your agency in a particular circumstance is embroiled in a major crisis, controversy, or scandal, the media at your agency level will pull out all investigative resources to report on it and try to outflank the competition. Chances are, like most PIOs, you will rarely confront such a situation unless your agency is constantly in the news or handles national security matters.

So you have the advantage in knowledge. You also have the advantage if you have done your media homework, to respond to media in myriad ways. If given authority as the PIO, you can limit or increase access to agency people and to news that is not printed or distributed to all media, even to the extremes of outright favoritism or freezing out certain media. You can bypass influential media regularly covering your agency to give stories to smaller papers and TV stations, thereby hopefully gaining more favorable coverage that will then be picked up by major mainstream media.

You can recommend what information to leak and to whom, and when to use the Internet or social media. You can arrange for "exclusive" human interest and feature pieces with the media of your choice. You are the one, not the media, to determine when and if a press conference will be held, when official statements should be released, and if an event should be planned at a strategic time to draw attention away from negative or critical agency news. Even if the media realizes at the time that it is a non-news pseudo-event, they still would have to cover it.

In other words, by being attentive, you can set the media agenda, frame and shape the message to the media, and in a diplomatic and likeable way, control the flow of agency information rather than have even the more experienced and knowledgeable reporters intimidate you by implied threat of a potential damaging report. All of these steps relate to what you can or are allowed to control. Spontaneous, unexpected, and unknown-to-you agency decisions and statements, and sudden external events are of course uncontrollable by you and your public affairs operations, yet you will be the ones to deal with the resultant media attention, all the more reason for your inclusion in high-level meetings and contingency planning.

This information for your "control" of the media relates to elements of media relations, not to government control of the media. I'm referring to, for example, claims of executive privilege, what is a public record, access to government documents under the Freedom of Information Act (FOIA) on the federal level and public records laws on the state and municipal level, and control of broadcast media by communication acts and by Federal Communications Commission (FCC) regulations.

Still, from a town Board of Selectmen or mayor's office, from state agencies to state legislatures to the governor's office, from federal agencies to congressional offices to administration executive offices, you can set intelligent information parameters that are respected and accepted by the media, however reluctantly. Further, you can employ situational media relations techniques that will gain the praise and maybe even admiration of your top elected or appointed official, upper-echelon administrators, and other employees in your agency.

Guidance on Responding to the Media

At the outset of this chapter I indicated that there is not simply one way to handle a PR situation or write a release or to rely on precedent because something "worked" in the past. The same holds true for responding to the media. When and how do you respond to criticism of your agency and its leaders? When do you not respond at all? How much do you have to tell the media about internal matters or decision making or controversy in your agency or office that has not been publicly vetted?

First, realize that most persons working for the media are not dopes, that they are skeptical and even cynical about government actions and statements, and that they have access to most news sources and their related high-tech electronic operations. Most importantly, know that when they ask you a specific question on a specific issue, they already have researched information about their query and may be looking for verification and to test your personal and agency credibility.

Expect to be pressured by informed media to have you respond right away to questions, to allow interviews and quotes from your top officials, and to provoke answers and controversy by their citing other news reports and rumors that are "in the air." Your knowledge of your agency's position on an issue and your knowledge of the media and how it will report a situation is absolutely crucial and central to the kind of response you will make or recommend making by your elected or appointed agency head.

If it is serious and valid criticism (from the media point of view), it may be your judgment to respond immediately to counter, neutralize, or discredit that criticism because the 24-hour news cycle will demand it, and because once agency or office criticism is reported by any one respected news source, it will be picked up by the AP and other news syndicates, headlined on TV news broadcasts, and become a national story if it so warrants. On the other hand, in your judgment, you may determine that there is "time" to respond to this particular criticism, that it's more important to gather a lot more information and facts to give the media a well-informed perspective on this issue. Therefore, you will tell the media your response will come "as soon as possible." Try not to panic. Ask for their deadline, gather the information you need, and respond by their deadline if possible and practical. Remember that the news cycle has shortened; if you do not respond with some information, you run the risk of "not available" for comment or appearing evasive.

A rule of thumb that I recommend is, if the criticism is valid, factual, and may have "legs," respond right away to get your agency position in the middle of the report, to contradict the criticism, and to muddle the overall effect of the story so that the reading or viewing public will not be able, for most of these complex and complicated pieces, to conclude clearly and unequivocally that the agency media criticism is in fact valid. You want to disprove that your agency is "wrong" on the issue, that your agency actions or decisions can be considered outrageous, and that your agency's image deserves the negative fallout in public opinion. You definitely want to try to prevent that outcome.

Of course there will be situations where the criticism cannot be denied, where your personal and agency credibility is at stake, where the "truth" of the information overwhelms the "power" of the government. In that case, your best decision may be not to respond at all to the criticism, to let it play out in the media and let it be superseded inevitably and quickly by a host of other major government and private sector news stories and controversies, foreign and domestic.

When agency criticism by the media is incorrect, invalid, or outlandishly wrong, when the information supplied to the media by organizations and institutions or individuals can easily be knocked down and contradicted, you can decide in your judgment to purposely not respond for a day and then come back with a full frontal media assault of news releases, a press conference, and TV appearances by top agency officials. This time delay will give your agency a chance for a clear channel to the media to completely refute this criticism, to disparage the sources of this criticism, even to ridicule the charges being made. Holding your media fire for a day may well vindicate your agency's position on an issue and give pause to future potential critics.

A lot of different opinions exist of what an *off-the-record* response to the media really means. When you talk to the media in person or on the phone, what are the guidelines for information that is on the record, for background only, for deep background only, or for off the record only? Based on prearranged and mutually understood ground rules, *background* generally implies that the media can name the agency or office as the source, but not the precise organizational division or administration within that agency, and can refer to an agency individual as a source but not by name or position title. *Deep background* usually implies upon agreement that even the agency or office can't be named, forcing the media contact to use clauses such as "it is understood that ...", or "it has been learned that...", or "because the source was not authorized to speak to the media...", and so on.

This puts the burden for credibility with the public squarely on the media to justify and back up its source(s). Totally and absolutely *off the record* means by agreement that any and all information discussed is only for more perspective and fuller understanding of a controversial matter, not to be written about or broadcast any time soon.

More important than these word designations or interpretations is to use your best judgment in choosing who in the media to discuss this behind-the-scenes subject with and in gaining top official approval of what is to be discussed. This off-the-record device can be a very beneficial tool for explaining and justifying an agency action and for changing media attitude. But it is the trust that you have placed on your chosen reporter and the particular media that will determine the success of this oft-used government media ploy.

You are under no obligation to the media to volunteer additional agency information that is not specifically requested. You do not have to discuss or reveal anything to the media that you feel or believe may be detrimental to your agency and its officeholders, unless of course the decision is made that nonrequested information made public would be beneficial to your agency. Filibustering and leaks on purpose will be discussed soon. Your loyalty is to your agency, not the media. Force the reporter or any media operative to pinpoint precisely the information that he or she wants. Then you can determine how to phrase your answer, provide the requested information, and emphasize the positive points of the agency's position.

Relationship with Agency/Office Leadership

Your relations with your elected official, administrator, or executive—whatever the nomenclature of the person who heads your office—can determine your success as the public affairs or information officer, whether your work is respected, and whether you are "in the loop" not only on media matters but also on all important agency issues, controversies, and decisions. Nothing can limit your effectiveness more than being excluded from meetings regarding important agency decisions affecting the agency image and public relations.

Personal relationships, not merely your skill in writing a news release, can directly affect how you and your office are viewed in the agency and by all the top managers and execs who invariably will take their cue from their leader. This type of one-to-one relationship varies widely from government agency to agency, and it is the luck of the draw when your personality meshes perfectly with the personality of the agency head. I say *luck* because personality and situations can and do change suddenly and unexpectedly to your detriment as the employee.

To help make your role indispensable, make sure that you are the one to provide the essential verbal and written briefings to agency execs on media and media-related issues, for press conferences, for PowerPoint presentations, for background "talking point" memos, and that you are the one turned to for question and answer (Q&A) setups when it comes to suggesting how to deal with both positive and negative aspects of matters that affect personal and agency reputation.

You should make and maintain contact with other government PIOs for potentially valuable and helpful relationships at all government levels. These staff contacts, whether federal, congressional, state or municipal, will invariably assist you on some future crucial situation. See Anne Zahradnik's Chapter 11 in this volume for more a more in-depth discussion of planning and managing your internal public relations.

Who Is the Agency or Office Spokesperson?

Virtually nothing is more important in media relations and PR terms for your agency's overall image and credibility than the "face" of your agency. Who should, and who should not, appear on TV to respond to media questions, and at press conferences and one-on-one interviews? Who, and what kind of agency staff, should be authorized to speak to the media and be quoted in print, broadcast, and online? *Appear* is the operative word here because on-camera appearance and speaking fluency and articulation, and quotes in print that are believed to be sensible and reasonable by readers are, many times, far more important for making a good impression on the public than the intellectual cogency of what is being said. Style rather than substance rules in this public arena.

Beyond that is the decision of how much and when should you, as perhaps the top public information officer in your agency, be the spokesperson to initiate or follow up on statements involving agency procedures, policy, controversy, and crisis management. The media is well aware that you do not set policy, that you are not the ultimate decision maker, and that you are there to act as a buffer for your agency head, to deflect and minimize criticism, and to defend decisions and positions in a smooth media-smart way. Thus, the media will do what it can in many situations to avoid and circumvent you.

That being the case, an authoritative and respected voice, the top elected or appointed official, or a high-level administrator or knowledgeable issues specialist should be the one to respond to the media. Of course there are many variables concerning who that person should be. You and the agency should have an intraoffice memo via email prepared for how to handle both planned and spontaneous media interaction. It is your job to brief that person fully on the parameters of what is expected to be discussed at a press conference or one on one, on setting up Q&A briefings and practice sessions, and on how best to respond to "trick" and confrontational inquiries. You should supply the background and known political leanings and prior issue comments of the publication, and if possible of the reporter, whether from print, TV, or online, and be responsible for arranging media meetings with agency staff experts (you will sit in).

For TV at a press conference or other media event, you should provide advice on length of statements, on the importance of opening with newsy sound bites, on talk pacing, on looking at the camera, on making eye contact with the questioner and using his/her name if known, on diplomatically correcting a reporter's incorrect facts, on when to start a brief filibuster to insert information not requested but helpful to agency explanations, and on how and in what circumstances to go off the record with a media rep. You should provide advice, if there is a choice, of when and where such media meetings should take place, on the time of day or night, on the backdrop and lighting for the speaker (visualize the difference between Nixon and Kennedy, or McCain and Obama).

Unless specifically requested you, as a public relations professional, should hold your volunteered print and online quotes, and your TV and radio appearances, to a minimum. You're not a press secretary to the president, and no one in the public or private sector outside of your agency and your immediate media circle knows your name or position. Your ambition for public notice and a few lines or seconds of fame should be severely circumscribed. However, there are going to be times and circumstances when your agency head not only wants you to speak to the media, but so directs you. These are usually negative-type situations—commenting on "bad" news, dealing with and responding to harsh media criticism, telling you to say that he or she was misquoted (even if that's not true), using you for deniability to say that he or she never saw or approved that news release from you or that policy statement from one of the top associates, and even asking you to lie to the media and therefore the public about what was said, for example, in recent past agency meetings.

What to do when as "the man in the middle" both your job in the agency and your credibility with the media may be threatened? For perspective, these unfortunate occurrences ordinarily adhere only to those government agencies and personalities that are frequently in the news. Hopefully you won't be forced to make a painful and career-shortening decision either to carry out what you consider as unacceptable behavior or resign. One way to defend yourself later against charges of "who was responsible" if such circumstances should arise, is to always write an extensive note to your file detailing these requests and actions ordered by a superior—it's called CYA, or "cover your ass." See Chapter 9 by Shannon Bowen and Chapter 10 by Kevin R. Kosar for further discussion on the ethics and legality of government public relations.

Media Relations Writing

After the meetings, the decision making by your agency's top elected or appointed official, by inner-circle aides, and perhaps also by you, in most cases the communication is in the form of writing to the media and therefore the public whether for print, broadcast, or online. Who is going to do this for a federal agency, congressional office, governor's office, a state agency, a mayor or selectmen's office? Not the top officials, and not some engineer, or accountant, or operations analyst. You or someone like you with journalistic skills and media knowledge is going to have to sit down and start typing, from initial draft to media-ready final copy.

This is not a tutorial on how specifically to write for a government agency about ten very frequently used types of media relations writings. These writings may seem diverse, but they all have common threads that will help you be successful in getting the media to use, quote, elaborate on, and refer to your information. The media today are not merely skeptical, but downright cynical of what is pushed on them by government agencies—and with good reason. For those agencies that seek publicity, there are too many exaggerated claims, non-news "news," unworthy press conferences, indulgent puffery, withholding of important information, misinformation, and misdirection. So my advice is to be as credible, authoritative, and factual as possible in all of your writings, especially those that have your name on them as the agency contact. We will come later to the situation when your superior tells you purposely to give out half-truths, leave out pertinent information, or even lie.

Wait a minute, you say—not my agency! You may be right, because many federal, state, and municipal (local) agencies and offices do not seek daily or even frequent publicity. They say, "Leave us alone to carry out our mission and work." There are even many congressional offices, both House and Senate, whose office holder is virtually unknown to the rest of the country until casting a nationally strategic vote or a personal scandal hits. In fact, many agencies by their functions are not hounded by the media, are afraid of the media, and are fearful of making public missteps leading to embarrassing criticism. But when you do have to respond to criticism or employ damage control, you will most likely follow and use the media relations writing techniques and approaches employed by those agencies that seem to be in the news, wanted or not, all the time, even every day.

A note on timing of your interactions: In order to compete with the voluminous news releases and publicity seeking by other organizations, you should consider releasing your information to the media on a "slow" news day (Monday afternoon is a good time) in an expected uneventful week, even though you can't prepare for totally unexpected national and international events. And you certainly can advise releasing unfavorable but must-be-made-public information on Friday or Saturday night, or just on the web, even though the media is well aware of this timing "trick."

So here are some parameters and insider advice that hopefully will lead to positive media coverage that enhances the image of your agency.

News releases: Newspapers and other print outlets, no matter how good your release is—newsworthy, well written, and factual—the odds are it will not appear the way you wrote it in major and influential mainstream media. Publications invariably determine what they want to emphasize for their reading audience, and reporters and editors have their own egos and say to themselves, "I'm not going to accept this release from some flack the way it was written and plant it in my paper verbatim." This does not, however, reflect the reality at minor dailies, weeklies, narrowly directed periodicals, and news-oriented magazines. Due to smaller staffs, they may very well use most of what you have written as long as it is not libelous or of questionable veracity.

TV and radio: Because of broadcast writing and reading style, with opening "hooks" and short declarative sentences, it is rare when a national or local TV station lead-in on regular network or cable starts with a conventional PR-style paragraph. For radio stations, with perhaps one or two reporters (not on-air talent), most of the news you and the public hear is from syndicated sources. Stations "rip the wire" from the AP feed which sends across the 10 or 12 top stories in one- or two-paragraph form every hour. Yes, part of your news release also may be included in the top-of-the-hour five-minute newscast (less time with commercials and promos) along with police, fire, political, and celeb briefs, but don't expect your news release to dominate unless it is of truly major news import from your agency and for the specific locale.

Online news media sites, nonmedia news sites, websites, and new social media with audio-video components: If your agency issues a lengthy newsy release, chances are local and national media sites will use even more of your paragraphs than the print edition. Online mediums have more space and the readers are interested in all of the information they can get. Well-known commentary and opinion sites such as The Huffington Post.com, Politico.com, Slate.com, Salon.com, and others may well incorporate information from your release as part of a longer piece. You and others from your agency will determine, based on the subject matter, which individual websites, blogs, and social media (covered in other chapters) will be included on your distribution lists.

Writing government PR news releases: Play it straight. You want to pack in as much media-usable information in the lead and first three paragraphs and use the "who, what, when, where" approach. The writing should be strong on verbs and moderate on adjectives, with no self-indulgent puffery. The length of sentences and paragraphs can vary—one to three sentences per paragraph with no run-ons or "ands" that go for ten or more lines. Ease of readability of the typed page is important for journalists and all readers, especially when word appearance can be blurred via fax and e-mail.

For the lead paragraph, you are going to choose, many times with your agency or office head's approval, what is in your judgment most newsworthy or unprecedented, even dramatic if it so warrants. For the second and third paragraphs you are going to add, via quote or not, information that expands or explains what was in the lead. After that, at least in a one-subject or one-theme release, you will continue to the end with what you hope is good journalistic style writing with the least important information, again in your judgment, coming at the end.

However, when you have more than one release topic—perhaps two, three, or even four—it is your job to incorporate these topics if possible into your opening paragraphs. This allows you to get all or most of the newsworthy information to the media right away. In a longer release you can then augment, in later paragraphs, each topic via facts, quotes, or perspective information. The question of length is vital in a fragmented and distracted media environment. Most news releases should be no longer than two single-spaced pages, double-spaced between graphs; three pages if spacing is space-and-a-half; and three-and-a-half pages if text is double-spaced. This is, of course, after your masthead or logo, contact information, headline, and subhead if desired.

Media advisories: A media advisory is used as a one-day-before or even same-day reminder of a press conference or event or happening that your agency or office is holding. It can be e-mailed or faxed to the media as a first notice if something suddenly arises or as a follow-up to a previously sent news release. The format is brief and eye-catching. In vertical order with first word(s) in big bold type in capital block letters: WHAT, then WHEN, then WHERE. There is no mandatory one-size-fits-all appearance. You can write an intro headline and each section should be no more than a few sentences. Be sure to follow up with media phone calls to TV news directors or producers after their morning postshow meetings to try and "reserve" video cams, a few hours before the event for print and online media.

Fact sheets: Most government agencies have a plethora of written, photo, and graphic material to be disseminated to the media, special interest groups, agency staff, the general public, and visitors to their offices. We're talking here about information without a deadline that has a sense of permanence until personnel, regulations, agency functions, and facts or data have to be changed, which can now be accomplished with a few clicks of the mouse. Multipage fact sheets, agency regulations, newsletters, annual and/or periodic reports, slide and video presentations, website referrals, and diverse handouts are usually available.

The significant advantage of an agency information one-page fact sheet, aside from easy e-mailing, mailing, webbing, and faxing, is that it can be useful not merely for all media but also for all your audiences—your fellow employees, other government agencies, special interests, the private sector from corporations to community groups, agency visitors, and the general public (see the Appendix for a fact sheet example). They all will thank you for your brevity, your cogent writing, and your skillful use of the most essential information about your agency.

Pitch letters: If successful, this is one government agency media writing area that will really make you look good as a PIO. Pitch letters ordinarily are sent via e-mail, fax, or mail to print media and are designed to result in a lengthy feature or human interest piece, invariably positive, placed in a major daily or city/town weekly anywhere from page 1 to a very noticeable inside page, in a Sunday paper magazine or feature section, or in a subject-appropriate magazine or periodical published weekly, biweekly, monthly, or quarterly. And last, but not to be forgotten, you can pitch to news syndicates such as the AP, the *New York Times*, and large multipaper ownership groups like Gannett. And of course you would hope the chosen news outlets would automatically also place it on their websites.

For pitch letters for TV, whether regular broadcast, cable or special pay groups such as HBO, try to induce news or "magazine" pieces about the good works of your agency and of your top elected or appointed officials and administrators.

Your previous interaction and personal contact with the selected media recipient, extensive or nonexistent, will determine whether the written pitch is a follow-up to prior discussions or a "cold call" first communication missive. In either case, you want to make it immediately known, in writing or not, that your proposal to the media outlet is an exclusive and not to appear in a truncated version in any same-media outlet.

After the usual inside address format in the top left corner, the pitch should be single-spaced with a double space between paragraphs on one page. O.K., you can extend it to one to two short graphs on a second page if necessary. One of the best ways to write it is the following: Open with a paragraph or two providing some background and perspective on your subject or issue and its current relevance; then, no later than the third graph, comes your pitch—"I propose a feature article on ...," or "a Sunday magazine piece on...," or "a TV interview with —— on ...," or "a taped video segment on ...."

The next one or two paragraphs should provide more background on and justification for the topic appearing in the chosen publication or TV program and why it would strongly appeal to its reader/viewer audience. Next, write about what you can provide à la documents, photos, computer software, and so on. Your closing paragraph should contain words such as "I will take the opportunity to contact you in (a week) ...; thank you for your consideration of my request for ...." Naturally, the writing style should be as direct and concise as possible with no redundancy.

Your tone is one of being well informed on the proposed topic, on its newsworthiness, and confident and assertive of its public interest without being aggressive or condescending.

Public service announcements (PSAs): As a public affairs or public information officer for a government agency, your involvement and centrality with PSAs should be in their writing and script, and in what you determine as their most effective placement and timing on selected TV channels and radio stations. You probably will not have the background or the time to involve yourself in the video and audio production and technical requirements for professional broadcasting of these spots. In any case, many agencies go outside of their staff and hire specialists to produce the PSA.

This is a media area where you control the message and on which, as a nonprofit entity, your agency pays absolutely nothing for the air time whether your PSA(s) is a one-timer or repeated over a period of time. Your agency does have to pay, of course, for the video and/or audio production. The FCC defines a PSA as "any announcement ... for which no charge is made and which promotes programs, activities or services of federal, state or local governments ... or the programs, activities or services of non-profit organizations ... and other announcements regarded as serving community interests."

The message in most PSAs relates to health, safety, security, education, and agency regulations and programs. When the opportunity arises for such legitimate purposes, you should recommend taking it. PSAs enhance your agency's image by showing the public your interest and concern for its well-being, by providing needed educational and even emergency information. Best of all, it is a cost-free way to gain for your agency positive broadcast publicity that will be picked up by print and online media as news and as a public service.

PSAs usually run from 60 seconds (60 s) to as short as 10 seconds (10 s), and depending on your arbitrary deadlines, can be repeated in weeks-long campaigns to campaigns as short as a few days. Typically, if they start at 60 s, to avoid repetition and hold viewer and listener attention, they can be revised and then also shortened to 20 or 30 s.

In brief, a PSA's first sentence should open with a broadcast "hook" to get viewers/listeners out of their doldrums: "How would you like to start your own small business?" "This is information you should know for your family's safety and security." "Here's an easy way to help plan your monthly finances and save money." The rest of that first paragraph and the second and third graphs should add pertinent message facts in succinct declarative sentences. A PSA windup should give directions: "For more information, call (contact/e-mail/mail) ...," giving the agency name, phone number, e-mail address, and whatever else is necessary to carry out the directive.

It's your job to make contact with the channel or station PR director, tell the person what the PSA is about, the importance of the message for the public, how long you'd like the PSA to run, and how many times a day and at what hours, and the level of PSA exclusivity. You can ask for all these "wants" but there's a good chance you may not succeed based on regular program schedules and other PSA competition for the limited minutes made available. After first contact you will submit all relevant video/audio tapes and a script timed to the precise second. Professional broadcast quality from your agency's chosen studio is an absolute given.

Look at the "split screen" appearance of vertical video/audio parallels on the broadcast page to see how newscasts, voice-overs, and PSAs are printed out and presented. The next phase, in person or by e-mail or fax, is to negotiate (you may need some agency help here) changes in the tape or script, which broadcasters invariably request. Finally, of course, you or someone in the agency should be designated to make sure the agreed-upon video/audio contract actually occurs.

Speeches and speechwriting: For many of you working in communications on any government level, this is an area that can test your ego and provide plenty of frustration. As a PIO or press secretary, you may be asked to write an entire speech for your administrator or elected official, but more likely your role will be to assist in the writing, to edit and comment on someone else's first draft, to participate in inner-circle discussions, or to write a news release topping a speech to be distributed to the media. Be prepared that in many cases your words, strongly felt and that you believe should definitely go out to the media and public, will be revised, rewritten, or taken out entirely, not only by the head of your agency but also by other staff whom you have no respect for, who "don't know a thing about the media," and who have no idea of the impact or interpretation that certain positions or issues stated in the speech will have on news judgment by influential media. Pick your fights carefully here, be selective, and determine on which speeches and positions you want to "go to the mat." Your agency head will be watching closely.

To assist you in speechwriting, for speeches that are designed to inform, persuade, or entertain, I offer this practical and time-tested outline and semblance of order for your consideration:

- Begin with an introduction, opening setting, greetings, and welcoming remarks.
- Use humor and appropriate joke(s).
- Ease into the main points, use some attention-getting statements, and build a rapport with your particular audience.
- Steadily build your argument or positions for the main points in the speech.
- Determine how many major topics you want to mention and how much space to allow for each.
- Include personal knowledge and personal experience of the speaker.
- Use quotes from relevant authorities to buttress your own positions.
- Write a smooth transition of topics from paragraph to paragraph.
- Use facts, data, and statistics for support, but don't overload the audience.
- In building the speech, use the past, present, and potential future of your issues, positions, and situations.

- Isolate your more dramatic and most important statements in short paragraphs.
- End and conclusion: summarize the main points, near-future situations, what you expect will result from your positions, what will happen in certain situations, and a final statement that is memorable, if possible.

Websites

Chapter 4 will deal extensively with a government agency's website use and contents, but from a media relations point of view and your role as a PIO or public affairs director, you have a responsibility to update, for the media and other users, changes that have to be made on those entries you have initially included on the website. You must ensure that any news releases, fact sheets, or bio sketches quote up-to-date and accurate information.

On a strategic PR note, your website can be used, if necessary, to "bury" controversial and negative news about your agency that must be released to the media, but only made available in this way, not in any other written, verbal, or broadcast form. You notify the media that this "release" is on the website and leave it to them to make the effort to find it. You may also further bury uncomplimentary news by releasing it on a Friday or Saturday night.

Crises, Crisis Management, and Damage Control

All government agencies and offices should have written crisis plans for distribution to all top officials that anticipate possible emergency situations. The procedures for who is allowed to speak to the media, executive crisis meetings, and methods to inform all agency and office employees should be predetermined. But when it comes, what will the "crisis" be? That is the key question that may be unanswerable for your particular agency relating to its programs, functions, issues, and personalities.

Whatever the media devices used, two areas will define your role and potential success in limiting the crisis—credibility in responding to media and public criticism and the drawing up of as many positive points as you can muster to neutralize and mitigate the crisis when the criticism is valid. Your recommendations concerning the type of media options to be used can be one of your most vital PIO functions. You can also recommend, based on the seriousness and newsworthiness of the crisis, in your judgment, not to have any official agency position relayed to the media.

This last option is usually employed if you believe that agency responses to the media will only prolong the crisis in the public arena, that the crisis will just go away in a matter of days, or that the charges and criticism that will be exposed by the media itself are without merit, and not sustainable or believable. Not responding is the option when "the elephant in the room" relates to the exposure of perhaps "unacceptable" personal behavior of a top agency official. Chances are that you will not be well informed of aspects of a leader's private life, but you may be asked how best to limit damage and provide an acceptable credible statement if such a decision is made. The conventional wisdom in dealing with so-called sex scandals, which have entangled high-level government and political figures in recent years, is "get it all out, tell everything right away and absolutely completely; don't let this damaging information drip out day after day; don't give your enemies time to add to the juicy details, the cover-up is far worse than the crime," and so on.

In virtually all other types of agency crises, your voice should be influential, maybe even decisive, in how and what media relations strategies and tactics should be used. But the decision of what crisis information to release and how much will invariably be decided by agency policy makers. However, in agency meetings you should speak up about the political dangers in withholding essential crisis-related material if and when a major media outlet finds out that the whole story was not released. Your crisis role can prove invaluable when, in addition to agency statements that the media may consider as self-serving, you propose how to buttress your agency's position by gaining allies, accepted as more impartial and independent, from other government agency heads, from businesses and the private sector, from acknowledged public opinion leaders, and from scientific, technological, and cultural experts and specialists. Gaining such public backup is definitely good PR in turning media opinion at a difficult moment. Brooke Fisher Liu and Abbey Levenshus provide more strategies for crisis, emergency, and disaster public relations in Chapter 6 of this book.

Leaks and Leaking

Leaks and leaking are just about as controllable as sex and sexing—not very. Stopping leaks of information that an agency really and perhaps desperately wants to withhold has truly been forever a losing battle. And when it comes to agency leaks, *battle* is an important descriptive word in two public affairs areas that have not been highlighted as yet—civilian agencies centering on national security such as the Central Intelligence Agency, Federal Bureau of Investigation, the National Security Agency, and information that is classified with designations, among others, of *top secret*, *secret*, or just *classified*.

Those government agencies and the voluminous data they control may be more vital to our national well-being than the hundreds of other civilian federal, state, and municipal agencies, but the role played by you and your counterpart public affairs officers and the interplay with all media on leaks and leaking contain remarkably similar functions. Obviously the media and government agencies need and want one another for news and publicity. For leaks, official, accidental, or unofficial, this mutual dependence is much deeper and needier because of the limited

Table 3.1 Type of Leak and Purpose

Leak Type	Purpose
Ego Leak	To give importance and self-importance to the individual via name recognition and publicity
Goodwill Leak	To gain favorable coverage and personal mention from the selected media on a future occasion
Policy Leak	To associate an individual with the accepted final decision on an important policy made public; or alternatively, by a disgruntled official who disagrees with an agency final decision and feels this is the only way to make public the "minority" report that he/she supports
Animus Leak	To get revenge on a coworker and make him/her look bad
Trial Balloon Leak	To see if an issue or position will fly or fall flat in public opinion
Whistle-Blower Leak	To expose agency corruption, deceit, or "misguided" behavior; sometimes motivated by getting a substantial reward for saving the government lots of money in any settlement
No-Purpose Leak	For "honesty" or personal satisfaction without regard for any publicity or money

Source: Adapted from Hess, Stephen. *The Government/Press Connection.* (Washington, DC: The Brookings Institution, 1984).

number of times they occur and are used in comparison to the everyday flow of news, the relative scarcity of this type of information, and the somewhat illegal and daring nature of the contents.

PIOs and other agency officials leak far more government information that gets to the public than the media finds through its own independent research, digging, and nongovernment sources. Why, for what purpose, and who does it? Hess (1984) provides a labeling of information leaks from agencies in Table 3.1.

You may not be involved or have knowledge of an agency leak, or who did it, but virtually all of the competitive media without the leaked information will beat a path to your door as the PIO for verification of the facts and to find out if the source was within your agency. Know that if even one media outlet prints or announces a leak that is deemed credible, it is fair game for all media to publicize it. Be prepared, after discussing the matter with your top officials, to respond using precisely what words they want you to say, and only those words. I am reminded of a former State Department official who, commenting on a leak said, "There is no evidence that reporters were told anything we didn't want them to know."

That approach is fine if the leaked information relates to only one subject or issue, is relatively complete and straightforward, does not contain obvious factual ambiguities, does not provoke the media to ask for a lot of additional information, and does not raise speculation of a cover-up, incompleteness, or purposeful disinformation. But you will earn your pay and have your judgment tested if the leak hits the papers and TV before the official agency announcement on a matter is released. Consider that leaks may be comprised of multiple statements with varying degrees of accuracy. What is your response if: (1) the leak contains totally false information, and is fabricated by an outside source to create alarming headlines about your agency or one of your top officials, (2) the leaked information is only partly accurate and truthful, (3) the leak is about half complete and half accurate on the issue, or (4) the media has virtually the whole story, but some essential and agency-favorable information is omitted?

As a PIO you have to consider and recommend, based on this particular situation, several options. The first says, in effect, "I can't confirm or deny this report. We'll have an official statement soon and release at that time all of the information allegedly related to this report." Second, when the leak is partially or half accurate but contains substantial errors of fact and misinformation, you may no longer be able to deny the overall substance, but you want to knock down and dissuade the media from continuing to use "wrongs," thereby getting a course correction and guiding the follow-up reports so that any agency damage is restricted. Finally, if more than half of the unofficial story is out, you may determine that "the cause is lost" and advise your top officials that the agency should actually give the media even more of the heretofore secret stuff, and thus hopefully get new and favorable angles in updated reporting.

For so-called *official leaks*, your leadership may determine that someone else or you should make public this information so as to obtain exclusive and lengthy coverage in a paper or on a TV station or on an Internet website, and to use a trusted media connection who will not reveal the source and thereby avail the agency of deniability. "What? How did this material get out? I don't know who did it. Why should we leak this? We're going to start an agencywide investigation and find out the source." The person who says these things to the media should be angry, unsmiling, with not a hint of smirking. Are you ready for your acting role?

Most, but certainly not all, real internal investigations of agency leaks by a high or regular staff official have come to naught. If caught, that person could be fired immediately, suspended without pay for a designated time period, or even criminally charged. Investigations by the government to get the media to disclose its government source(s) are among the most contentious actions an agency can take, leading to, as you know, subpoenas, civil and criminal court appearances, or rulings by judges that have resulted in imprisonment of reporters. The media—its owners, publishers, broadcasters—never want to reveal any information source and are united in supporting the work of its employees in any court. Only the threat of a prison sentence and jailing of a reporter forces a media executive to ultimately decide to hand over documents and reporters' notebooks.

Epilogue

If all of this background, insight, and recommendations on media relations, on diverse media relations writings, on required knowledge of various media, on how to respond to the media, on relationships with your boss and government PIOs, on spokespersons, on PR strategies and tactics, on managing crises and damage control, on leaks and leaking, and on control of the media does not cover or provide the best way to handle a major public affairs situation that developed in your agency or office, it is evidence that you have to act, write, and recommend based on the singular and unique circumstance, not on precedent or case study.

This narrative is informed by personal experience and readings. It does not recapitulate the narrative in books or reflect the near-copying of passages. Therefore, I wish to offer a short selected list of books that may be very helpful in augmenting your knowledge and practice of media relations in government.

References and Further Reading

Aronson, Merry, Don Spetner, and Carol Ames. *The Public Relations Writers Handbook*. (Jossey-Bass, latest).

Bennett, Lance. *News: The Politics of Illusion*. (Longman Classics).

Caywood, Clarke L., ed. *The Handbook of Strategic Public Relations & Integrated Communications*. (McGraw-Hill, 1997).

Graber, Doris A. *Mass Media and American Politics*. (CQ Press [Sage], 2011).

Graber, Doris A., Denis McQuail, and Pippa Norris, (Eds.) *The Politics of News, the News of Politics*. (CQ Press [Sage], latest).

Hall, Kathleen Jamieson, and Karlyn Campbell. *The Interplay of Influence: News, Advertising, Politics*. (Wadsworth Publishing, latest).

Hess, Stephen. *The Government/Press Connection*. (Washington, DC: The Brookings Institution, 1984).

Iyengar, Shanta, and Jennifer A. McGrady. *Media Politics: A Citizens Guide*. (New York: W. W. Norton & Company, 2007).

Wilcox, Dennis L., and Glen T. Cameron. *Public Relations Strategies and Tactics*. (Allyn & Bacon, latest).

Appendix: The John A. Volpe National Transportation Systems Center

Mission and Purpose: The John A. Volpe National Transportation Systems Center is a unique fee-for-service organization within the U.S. Department of Transportation's (DOT) Research and Innovative Technology Administration (RITA) located in Cambridge, MA. It supports all agencies within DOT with strategic national research on air traffic management, highway and rail safety, environmental assessment, security, planning and economic analysis, and transportation logistics.

History: The Volpe Center, named after former DOT Secretary and Massachusetts Governor John A. Volpe, was established in 1970 to provide analytical, scientific, and engineering support to the newly established Department. Since its opening, the Center has successfully carried out vital national transportation research and development for the Office of the Secretary and all modal Administrations.

Funding: The Volpe Center differs from most Federal agencies in that it receives no direct appropriation from Congress. It is fully client funded for its project work, mostly by DOT but also by other federal/state/local government agencies, academia, and industry, with an annual budget of about $200 million.

Workforce and Project Organization: The strength of the Center as a world-class transportation resource lies in its more than 500 highly skilled and professional Technical Experts. Its projects on present and future transportation challenges are organized around Centers of Innovation which include:

- Multimodal Systems Research and Analysis—transportation system mobility needs for goods and people.
- Safety Management Systems—analyzes systems data in order to take action to reduce transportation deaths and accidents.
- Environmental and Energy Systems—technical and analytical support for decision-making on climate variability, air quality, noise, hazardous materials.
- Communication, Navigation and Surveillance (CNS)—analyzes and applies CNS capabilities to enhance the capacity, safety and security of next-generation transportation systems.
- Advanced Vehicle and Information Network Systems—provides systems engineering and operations research to deploy advanced technologies.

Technology Transfer: The Volpe Center technology transfer among government agencies, Federal laboratories, and the public and private sectors is accomplished through Cooperative Research and Development Agreement (CRADA) activity, and the Center's website, conferences, and seminars. The Center also coordinates DOT's Small Business Innovation Research (SBIR) Program.

Contact Information: Address: The John A. Volpe National Transportation Systems Center, 55 Broadway, Cambridge, MA 02142. Telephone: 617-494-2222. Website: www.volpe.dot.gov.

* Special thanks to the Department of Transportation, Volpe Center.

Chapter 4

Government Websites

Napoleon Byars

Contents

Better Websites, Better Government

Step into the shoes of a taxpayer worried about the current state of affairs. The first recession of the twenty-first century has the nation in its grips and unemployment is a continuing problem. On television, network and cable news media continue to highlight the disconnect between government policies and the lives of every-day people. You've had enough with government bureaucrats and empty promises about creating jobs. It's time to take action and write a letter to the president of the United States. After all, it's your citizen duty to voice concern about national economic policies and their impact on you and your neighbors.

The first thing to decide is what to put in the letter. As a taxpayer, you'd like to know how much money the IRS collects each year in income taxes—taxes you believe are too high. You recall reading a story in the newspaper about a State Department program to substantially increase aid for developing nations. You wonder about the effectiveness of foreign aid and want more information to help frame a question about national priorities.

As you sit down to write, the roar of four military fighter jets can be heard overhead. It's a flyover for the local college football game. What a waste of taxpayers' dollars. How much does the U.S. military spend on all these flyovers anyway? You would like to include that fact, too. It's going to be a heck of a letter—one that really highlights government waste and inefficiency. All you need is a few minutes to research the facts online.

Now, flashback to the pre-Internet world without websites or e-mail and the time required to research the facts could easily grow to a few months or even years.

The current explosion in communication technology allows unprecedented access to information about government—from policies and budgets to programs and activities—and much of it via government websites. Federal, state, and municipal government websites now afford communicators an opportunity to inform, educate, and interact with stakeholders in ways never before considered. Websites can help disseminate important information about programs and policies, increase stakeholder support, and even mitigate citizen dissatisfaction. Government websites are also valuable as communication tools during organizational crises, contingencies, and special events. Additionally, communicators can also gain valuable insight into the profile of web audiences through the use of analytical tools. For example, audience demographics and media consumption habits are all available online. One thing is certain—the public's appetite for information is increasing.

A University of California research consortium found that average Americans consume 34 gigabytes of information each day—the equivalent of 340 yards of books on a shelf. Additionally, Americans spend 16 percent of their information hours on the Internet, much of it in two-way communication exchange.[1]

According to the Pew Research Center, 70 percent of Americans expect to be able to get information or services from a government agency website. In fact, nearly four out of five Internet users have visited government websites to do just that. More importantly for communicators, nearly 80 percent of Internet users expect government websites to provide what they need.[2] By some estimates, Americans have access to more than one billion Web pages, including those belonging to government agencies at the local, state, and federal level.

How did all this happen? Specifically, who or what is behind the effort to make government information more accessible to the public? You may be surprised to learn that the very government so often criticized for resisting change is in the forefront of using websites to make government more responsive.

The federal government has its own dot-gov domain where it operates more than 24,000 websites. Many of them are cataloged at the government's official portal, *USA.gov*. For nearly a decade USA.gov has been the catalyst for a growing electronic government.[3] Local governments have become e-government savvy, too, and in some areas set the standard for excellence when it comes to web operations. Collectively, government websites are now essential to the practice of public information and public administration.

In an online society, government websites help agencies carry out their primary mission while maintaining positive relationships with stakeholders. Contrary to the belief that an Orwellian future awaits us on the web, the public is increasingly logging on to get information, request services, and interact with government officials. This digital information exchange is part of an evolving discourse between government and citizens. With so much at stake, the development and management of websites is not being left to chance. Specifically, a group of federal web managers is charting the course for the future. The objective is to improve online interaction between citizens and ultimately, all levels of government.

Web Managers Council

The Office of Management and Budget (OMB) established the Federal Web Managers Council or Web Council in 2004. The purpose of the Council is to improve online delivery of government information and services and facilitate better public administration. The goals of the Council are threefold:

1. Help the public quickly and easily accomplish its most critical tasks online.
2. Improve online content so it's on par with the best content in the world.
3. Support and expand the community of government web managers nationwide.

This interagency group of government web managers collaborates and shares common challenges, ideas, and best practices. Members include all federal cabinet agencies as well as congressional support agencies.[4] As a result of their efforts, the old way of communicating with government—snail mail, phone calls, and personal visits—is being replaced by the online experience.

The Web Council's original mission was to recommend policies and guidelines for federal websites to comply with the E-Government Act of 2002.[5] Specifically, the law covers the operation of government websites, categorizing of information, and public access to information including federally funded research.

The move to improve government websites coincides with a shift in information consumption trends. An annual survey conducted by the University of Southern California revealed that 80 percent of Internet users age 17 and older consider the web to be a more important information source over all other media, including newspapers and television.[6]

Proponents of digital governance point to the growing acceptance of the web, particularly government websites. However, the push toward digital governance is not without detractors. Critics warn that a networked society could facilitate the creation of unintended political authorities within government or beyond the influence of the state. They also caution that digital governance could change the nature of democracy itself in unintended ways.[7] For example, citizens in rural communities without Internet access or with slower connectivity could be left out—and what about economically disadvantaged populations or senior citizens who may be less apt to go online?

Criticism notwithstanding, the Web Council seeks to improve the methods by which government information on the Internet is organized, preserved, and made accessible to the public. Making web content accessible to individuals with disabilities, including the blind and hearing impaired is a priority. Multilingual initiatives are also under way to improve access for people with limited proficiency in English.[8] In fact, a number of government websites already have content in Spanish, Korean, Mandarin, and other languages. Following the Web Council's lead, some local government sites offer expanded menus of translation from English to more than a dozen languages. In doing so, they seek to improve outreach to diverse local populations as well as international tourists.

Over the years, the Web Council has evolved into much more than a compliance body and now offers training and seminars. It also sponsors conferences for web managers through its very own Web Manager University (WMU). Additionally, a Content Manager Forum of 1,600 federal, state, and local web managers affiliate online to improve government websites at all levels.

The upshot of this extensive collaboration effort is a phenomenal growth in website traffic and the requirement to deliver e-government services better. Among other goals, the Federal Web Council hopes to establish web communications as a core management function. Additionally, the Council wants to make certain that underserved populations can access critical information on the Internet. These are daunting objectives. Nonetheless, the very future of responsive government rests on the shoulders of government administrators and communicators responsible for managing websites.

Best Practices and Oversight

Web managers can find a Best Practices Checklist at WebContent.gov. The list, which includes everything but the kitchen sink, identifies the essential elements of a first-rate government website.[9] Table 4.1 pares the checklist down to a Top Ten Best Practices to make it more useful for communicators who want to evaluate their current websites, or are in the process of creating new ones. High on the list is the requirement for an online strategic plan that provides for change and corrects problems with web content. In addition to managing web content effectively and

Table 4.1   Best Practices and Oversight Table

Top Ten Best Practices of Government Websites [10]
1. Decide on a strategic plan to accommodate changing organizational and stakeholder requirements as well as the evolving nature of the Internet.
2. Maximize branding by selecting an appropriate name and domain identification, i.e., .gov, .org, .com, etc.
3. Create a design that is functional, reader friendly and easy to navigate.
4. Incorporate a *Contact Us Page, About Us Page* and *Site Map.* Include a *Search Box* on every page and provide search hints and recommendations.
5. Keep content current, audience driven, and use plain language free of acronyms.
6. Decide on which forms and publications to include and how to provide for download of data files.
7. Avoid duplicating material from other websites and link to relevant cross-agency portals when appropriate.
8. Adhere to federal laws, regulations and directives concerning web content, operations and the protection of personal information. Incorporate transparency features, i.e., a privacy policy, security protocols and guidelines on linking, disclaimers and advertising.
9. Institute a process for continually improving web operations by conducting formal evaluations using online surveys and usability testing.
10. Establish emergency operating procedures and protocols for taking the site off-line for system maintenance and other contingencies.

efficiently, government communicators are encouraged to formally evaluate their websites. Ensuring that the public can find desired information by creating search-friendly web pages is equally important.

A series of laws, regulations, executive orders, and policies govern federal website operations and content. For example, web managers must guard against any direct or indirect lobbying in accordance with Title 18, Section 1913 of the U.S. Code. They must also comply with copyright, trademark, and patent laws, and agree to post agency content in the public domain.

In the area of confidentiality, government web managers work to protect the privacy and identity of individuals as they interact online. Each government website is required to post a Privacy Act Statement that spells out an agency's authority for collecting personal data and how it will be used. Identity theft is a major concern, too. According to the Federal Trade Commission, more than 9 million citizens have their identity stolen each year. In fact, identity theft is

America's fastest growing crime, amounting to more than $40 billion in losses annually.

Government web operations are constantly being targeted by identity thieves.[11] Initiatives such as the Federal Trade Commission FTC.gov's Identity Theft Web page and the President's Task Force on Identity Theft are dedicated to informing citizens about the problem. Understandably, the Social Security Administration is sensitive to concerns about protecting citizens. The nine-digit Social Security Number (SSN) that identifies every U.S. citizen requires special handling in terms of encryption, firewalls, and other security measures. The Social Security Administration (SSA) website, SSA.gov, includes a comprehensive privacy policy written in plain language explaining how it handles personal information collected over the Internet. Additionally, the SSA discourages the sending of SSNs and other personal identifying information in e-mail.

Governmentwide, federal agencies have established guidelines to address how to implement firewalls to protect network servers containing treasure troves of data. Furthermore, cyber security, which involves protecting websites, computers, and computer systems, is no longer the concern of a single agency. All web managers must consider the security aspects of websites during the planning stages of web operations.

Government departments large and small are daily under constant attack from domestic and international hackers, and even foreign governments. Hackers routinely use spyware and malware in attempts to penetrate computer networks and gain access to personnel data, classified documents, and sensitive source codes. Several government agencies, including the Pentagon and State Department, have come under persistent cyber attack in recent years. Recognizing the seriousness of the matter, the Pentagon has taken the unprecedented step of elevating cyber space on par with air, land, sea, and space as a potential conflict zone.[12] Ironically, unauthorized intrusion into federal government computer networks has touched off "a bidding war among agencies and contractors for a small pool of special talent: skilled technicians with security clearances."[13] To protect itself, the Defense Department is in the process of assembling a corps of cyber experts to defend web operations and more than 15,000 computer networks it operates worldwide.

President Barack Obama is concerned about cyber security, too. Speaking from the East Room of the White House he said:

> It's the great irony of our Information Age—the very technologies that empower us to create and to build also empower those who would disrupt and destroy. And this paradox—seen and unseen—is something that we experience every day.
>
> It's about the privacy and the economic security of American families. We rely on the Internet to pay our bills, to bank, to shop, to file our taxes. But we've had to learn a whole new vocabulary just to stay ahead

of the cyber criminals who would do us harm—spyware and malware and spoofing and phishing and botnets. Millions of Americans have been victimized, their privacy violated, their identities stolen, their lives upended, and their wallets emptied.[14]

Seven months after making these remarks, President Obama announced the new position of White House Cyber Security Coordinator (or Cyber Czar) to oversee cyber security activities across the government. In fact, cyber security figures heavily in the operations of government websites. Creating opportunities for web users to interact with the government in a secure environment is the Holy Grail of e-governance. From Web Manager University to Cyber Czar, the federal government is breaking new ground in website management and operations. Nowhere is this better illustrated than by logging on to the websites of the Big Four—the Department of Defense, Department of State, Department of the Treasury, and the White House. And not to be left out, state and local governments are innovating, too. For example, the City of Virginia Beach, located in the Hampton Roads area of Virginia, operates one of the best local government sites on the web.[15]

What follows is an analysis of various governmental websites that serve as models for various best practices in communication, management, and design.

The Military and the Internet

It is only fitting that the agency whose research helped create the Internet is a leader in exploiting it for public information purposes. The Pentagon runs one of the most vast and sophisticated websites in the form of Defense.gov. In reality, Defense.gov is a labyrinth of websites that fall under the management umbrella of the Assistant Secretary of Defense for Public Affairs. The four military service branches (Army, Navy, Marines, and Air Force) along with the National Guard and Reserve each link to Defense.gov. Collectively, Department of Defense (DOD) installations, agencies, and arsenals make up the most powerful military force, and online defense information source, on the planet.

Defense.gov and its multiple components all have one goal in common—to address the informational needs of the U.S. military and its various audiences. The Pentagon, with an annual budget of more than $600 billon, is a big operation, and its list of stakeholders is imposing. Key among them is the 2.6 million members of the Armed Forces and their families, Congress, the public, the news media, as well as allies and enemies of the United States.[16] Each stakeholder group has unique informational requirements but all share a common desire to access information and data 24/7, 365 days a year.

Defense.gov is a top 10,000 website attracting more than 230,000 Americans monthly. Approximately 59 percent of its visitors are males ranging in age from

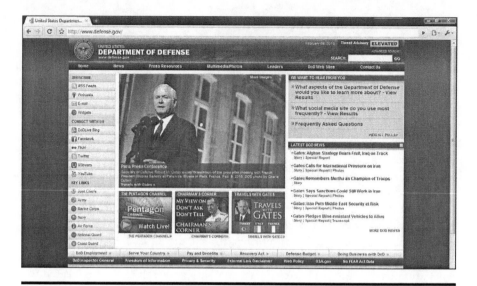

Figure 4.1   U.S. Department of Defense. www.defense.gov

18 to 49. Additionally, they are less affluent, with 62 percent earning from $0 to $60,000 annually. All in all, more than 12 million people visit Pentagon-affiliated websites each month.[17]

The information the public is able to access is both vast and specific. Visitors can get the latest news concerning DOD operations and activities, search endless archives of photographs, and view video footage and graphics. There are even surveys to find out what visitors want to see on the site. To keep the troops informed, there are fact sheets, speech archives, and links to more than 100 websites for additional information. Defense.gov also links to information on pay and benefits and ways to join the Armed Forces, or apply for any one of more than 33,000 U.S. government job openings worldwide.

The complete annual DOD budget is available too, in Portable Document Format (PDF). A taxpayer researching the costs of flyovers of football games will discover that they generate millions of advertising impressions and are important to military recruiting. For contractors, there is information on doing business with the military along with procedures on how to bid for government work.

Defense.gov has literally something for everyone and anyone with Internet access. Want to look up the meaning of a military acronym? Just click on the DOD Dictionary of Military Terms link. News reporters and the public can access press releases and advisories, contract announcements and awards, and a wealth of defense news from the press resources page. There is also a quick-reference listing with links to the top DOD websites from A to Z. Daily casualty updates from Iraq and Afghanistan are available along with official documents in English and Arabic detailing the charges against terrorists held in custody.

In the spirit of transparency, the Defense.gov home page features a tool bar with links to the web pages of the Freedom of Information Office and inspector general. There are also links to information on privacy policy and security, and DOD's web policy.

The military is seriously into the practice of pushing information out to keep the public informed. At Defense.gov, the public can easily subscribe to Really Simple Syndication (RSS) feeds, link to podcasts, Defense News Widgets, and e-mail. The Pentagon is also a leader in merging television and Web-based content. Using a video-on-demand capability, the public can access *The Pentagon Channel* 24/7 on YouTube. The convergence of television and online platforms allows individual stakeholders a personalized web experience as they consume DOD news and information.

The Pentagon is adapting to social and interactive media and the evolving communication reality of the Internet world. Public information officers know full well the importance of information accuracy and its relationship to stakeholder trust. User-generated content and the potential for damage to the military's brand are areas of great concern. The DOD lives and dies by command and control and good order and discipline. Consequently, DOD web policy seeks to eliminate any possibility of a rogue blogger wreaking havoc in the ranks. Balancing creativity and caution, the Pentagon has jumped headlong into the new media era and today has its own *DODLive* blog along with Flickr, Facebook, and Twitter pages.

The future of the marriage of the military and the social media movement depends on the ability of Pentagon leaders to adapt to the expanding capabilities of websites. For now, the DOD Twitter page invites the public to join it online with the following banner:

> **Get short, timely messages from DoD.**
> Twitter is a rich source of instantly updated information. It's easy to stay updated on an incredibly wide variety of topics. Join today and follow @DeptofDefense.[18]

Across the military establishment, public administrators have been encouraged to embrace interactive media and websites. In a policy letter to all military departments, the Deputy Secretary of Defense wrote, "Interactive Internet activities are an essential part of DOD's responsibilities to provide information to the public, shape the security environment and support military operations."[19] The policy further requires that Internet activities be true in fact and intent, and highlights the essential roll of communicators in dealing with the news media. Specifically, the policy directs military commanders to ensure that "only public affairs personnel engage in interactive Internet activities with journalists employed by media organizations including new websites, online bulletin boards, and blog sites affiliated with news organizations."[20]

World Affairs on the World Wide Web

The U.S. State Department's forward-looking website features a "Smart Power Meets Smart Design" video on its homepage. More than 2 million Americans visit State.gov each month making it a top 1,000 website.[21] Audience demographics reveal a 50:50 ratio of males to females with annual incomes from $60,000 to $100,000 and up. The site proudly promotes its new look and functionality. State.gov also makes use of twenty-first-century statecraft to educate, listen, and engage.[22] Click on the homepage video and the Secretary of State welcomes you:

> We're working hard to make this website as accessible and useful as possible. Here on State.gov you can find important information for travelers, including how to apply for a passport or visa. You can also learn about US foreign policy and our diplomatic and development efforts around the world. On our blog, Dipnote, you can read the stories posted by our diplomats and aid workers in overseas missions, and then share your own thoughts and opinions. No one person or country has a monopoly on good ideas. So I hope this website will be a forum for learning, discussion, and collaboration. And there are more exciting changes coming to State.gov, so please stay tuned, and thanks for stopping by.[23]

In no uncertain terms, the State Department recognizes the communication value of a website that is intuitive and easy to navigate. The site loads quickly and features red, white, and blue in its design graphics. A series of rollover menus allow visitors to look around without leaving the homepage.

State.gov has a "search the site" function and a first-rate search engine for additional ease of use. A "browse by topic" feature allows visitors to conveniently search by topic, speaker, publication, country, or date. Want to know the latest concerning Antarctic Treaty Consulting Meetings? Then go to "A" in topic search and there it is. Need to research remarks made by the Special Representative of the President for Nuclear Nonproliferation? Click on the speaker link, select the name, and the transcript appears.

The complete archive of op-eds written by the Secretary of State can be accessed from the publication page along with interviews, congressional testimony, background notes, communiqués, and daily appointment schedules. Moreover, each web page banner is branded with the official seal of the State Department along with the slogan "Diplomacy in action."

State.gov is more than an archive of information. The website includes the who, what, when, where, and why of each State Department program.

In a tough economy, taxpayers want to know whether foreign aid dollars are effective. The State Department recognizes this and uses State.gov to provide

Figure 4.2   U.S. Department of State. www.state.gov/media

answers and constant reminders that foreign assistance programs are important to overall national security.

In short, State Department communicators use their website as a teaching tool. For example, how does the government measure the effectiveness of dollars invested abroad? The answer is easy to find on State.gov. Go to the "Framework for Foreign Assistance" web page for the following explanation:

> The *Foreign Assistance Framework* is an analytical tool aimed at targeting limited U.S. Government resources efficiently and effectively within countries and at the regional and global level. It categorizes each country receiving U.S. foreign assistance based on common traits, and places them on a trajectory of progress, with the ultimate intent of supporting recipient country efforts to move from a relationship defined by dependence on traditional foreign assistance to one defined by full sustaining partnership status.[24]

There is something for younger audiences, too. Click on the link to FutureState. gov and a web page created for recruiting future diplomats appears. Click on the link to Careers.State.gov and a recruiting video extolling smart power and the virtues of serving in the Foreign Service plays. There are also links to student-focused programs, fellowships, internships, and career opportunities along with a narrated invitation to browse.

Visitors can register for the Foreign Service Officer Test and order the study guide. They can also begin the process to apply for a new or replacement passport. Travelers can sign up for travel advisories, alerts, or research country-specific requirements for visa applications. The engaging and transactional nature of State. gov, together with its easy navigation, makes it a benchmark for interactive government websites.

A Treasury Trove of a URL

Treasury.gov, the U.S. Treasury Department's website, comes without the bells and whistles of its Defense and State Department counterparts. It features no fancy rollover menus, no voice-on-page instructions, and no video archive. There are no links to social networks, blogs, or RSS feeds. Its Web pages are, for the most part, text heavy with few graphics and photographs. When it comes to eye appeal, Treasury.gov violates nearly every guideline for an attractive website. However, it does satisfy the key requirement for an effective website—complete accuracy of the information it publishes.

In fact, Treasury.gov is the authoritative source on virtually all matters relating to the finances of the federal government. Its stakeholders include nearly every branch and level of government, financial entities of foreign governments, Wall Street, and 138 million taxpayers. Approximately 47,000 Americans visit the site each month. Analysis of Treasury.gov traffic reveals that its audience is mostly well

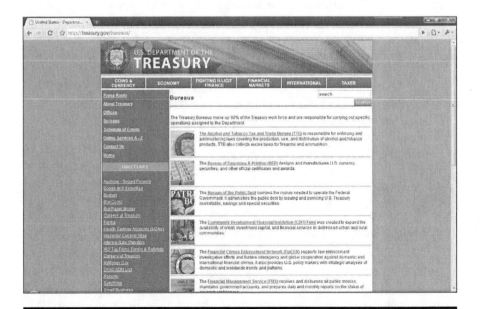

Figure 4.3   U.S. Department of the Treasury. www.Treasury.gov/bureaus

educated, comes from high income brackets, and is more inclined to invest in the stock market.[25]

Treasury.gov does what it must do first and best, which is to be an effective communication tool in helping the Treasury Department promote economic stability and manage the government's finances.[26]

Although the look and feel of the site is stiff, it is not unlike foreign counterpart websites in Canada, Japan, Germany, and other nations. Treasury.gov is a repository for information on taxes, coins and currency, the economy, financial markets, international financial agreements, and efforts to thwart illicit finance. The site links to the web pages of 12 bureaus belonging to the Treasury Department, including the U.S. Mint, the Alcohol Tobacco and Trade Bureau, and the Internal Revenue Service. A news release on IRS.gov states that $2.3 trillion personal income taxes were collected in 2008. What taxpayers may not know, but also stated on the website, is that $270.4 billion was returned in tax refunds. By linking to the IRS's website, Treasury.gov is a portal for more than 80 million Americans who file their taxes electronically.[27]

The takeaway from visiting Treasury.gov is that it is a well-organized and authoritative financial website. Photographs and graphics notwithstanding, it has a firm grasp on the expectations and needs of the stakeholders who depend on it. Moreover, Treasury.gov provides a secure environment in which to retrieve financial information and conduct online transactions. For example, citizens can buy, manage, and redeem electronic U.S. Savings Bonds directly while online. They can even convert paper bonds to electronic bonds for convenience and accounting purposes. As part of the security protocol, information is collected on anyone who visits Treasury.gov. Its privacy policy includes the following notice:

> If you visit the *Treasury.Gov* Web site to read or download information, we collect and store only the following information about you: the name of the domain from which you access the Internet; the date and time you access our site; and the Internet address of the Web site from which you linked directly to our site. We will not obtain personally identifying information about you when you visit our site unless you voluntarily choose to provide such information to us by e-mail, by completing a comment form, forum registration site, or other on-line form.[28]

Treasury.gov is clear in its communication to all visitors and puts would-be hackers on notice:

> Unauthorized attempts to upload information and/or change information on these Web sites are strictly prohibited and are subject to prosecution under the Computer Fraud and Abuse Act of 1986 and 18 U.S.C. §§1001 and 1030.[29]

Defense.gov, State.gov, and Treasury.gov, each in its own way, are examples of websites leading the way in making government information more accessible to the public. They are also setting new benchmarks in web operations.

The White House Online

The clear leader among federal government websites is White House.gov. From arms control to jobs programs to seniors and social security, the White House uses websites to inform and educate the public and solicit stakeholder input. White House.gov is a top 1,000 website and attracts a more educated, affluent, and younger audience. A record-setting 6.3 million Americans visited the site during President Barack Obama's first month in office. Approximately 1.7 million visit the site monthly.[30]

To browse White House.gov is to look into the future of government websites and e-government itself. In addition to highlighting administration policies and programs, White House.gov serves as a role model and portal to thousands of federal government websites that seek to interact with various stakeholders.

Information that was once inaccessible to the public can now be retrieved in seconds. White House.gov does an excellent job of pushing information out as well. Visitors can access and subscribe to receive speeches, reports, photographs, or podcasts. They can also choose to receive notices of live streaming videos. Additionally, they can e-mail the president directly, or ask questions of the White House staff and cabinet officials.

Gone are the days when the only way of sending a letter to the president was through the U.S. Postal Service. Today the White House receives approximately 100,000 e-mails daily. Each is read, screened, and categorized, along with snail mail, by issue. Ten letters are forwarded to the Oval Office in an effort to foster a direct dialogue between the president and concerned citizens. The mammoth task of collecting and processing e-correspondence is made manageable through the operations of White House.gov. The sophistication of its e-mail system recognizes the fact that the modern-day commander-in-chief is by necessity the communicator-in-chief, too.

White House.gov reflects the personality of the president and extends the reach of the bully pulpit. Its home page is focused on individual visitors and at the same time has the efficiency of a Fortune 500 company. White House.gov visually portrays the image of a fully engaged executive branch. It features photographs of the president and first lady, cabinet meetings in progress, press conferences, and exterior views of 1600 Pennsylvania Avenue. Click on any picture and you are taken to a video highlighting one of the administration's top issues. White House.gov pushes the interactive envelope and allows citizens to participate in virtual town hall meetings, or watch and take part in discussions of national issues via Facebook, Twitter, MySpace, and other social networks.

Figure 4.4   The White House. www.whitehouse.gov/

Recognition of the power and reach of blogs is evident, too. There are individual blogs dedicated to the Middle Class Task Force, Council on Environmental Quality, Open Government, Office of Management and Budget, and an Office of Public Engagement blog. The latter is an attempt to allow the public to be in direct dialogue with the administration and make government more accessible to citizens. Blog topics run the gamut from the importance of math and science to the nation, to the award of the Congressional Gold Medal to the Women Airforce Service Pilots (WASP) of World War II.[31]

White House.gov visitors can find someone to dialogue with, in English or in Spanish, on almost any topic that involves the federal government. And there are ample links to other government websites on everything from arms accords to urban policy to flu prevention—and yes, there is even a Flu.gov. Furthermore, the White House website is handicap friendly, allowing people with disabilities to browse for information and interact online. For example, images have tags that allow the disabled to listen in to content using a screen reader. Closed captioning of videos is also available along with written transcripts of the president's speeches.

White House.gov is the leader in advancing e-government as well as digital democracy. It is also working to speed the pace of improving government services online. Michael Marolis and Gerson Moreno-Riano captured this sentiment in *The Prospect of Internet Democracy:*

> E-Government is a sophisticated, efficient, and customer sensitive manner in which to provide public services to all citizens. Citizens can now

connect online and schedule trash pick up, file and pay taxes and bills, acquire important public information, and suggest to governments improvements and commendations regarding the performance and delivery of public services.[32]

After considering a number of factors such as security, cost, and performance, White House.gov was relaunched on October 24, 2009, using an open-source program content management system (CMS). The move allows White House web managers to more easily publish, organize, and manage a variety of content. The switch to open source software is a sea change in the administration of government websites. As reported by The Huffington Post.com on the day of the announcement, "The online-savvy administration on Saturday switched to open-source code—meaning the programming language is written in public view, available for public use and able for people to edit."[33]

The move to open source signals a significant challenge to proprietary software. Another big advantage of popular open-source software is that basic website installation and administration requires no programming skills. The genie is out of the bottle with White House.gov and open-source software is sure to attract the attention of other government web managers.

The changing of the guard in citizen communication is evidenced in the growth, sophistication, and person-to-person interaction of government websites. White House.gov allows citizens to navigate around the once stalwart battery of government bureaucracy and brings them face to face with decision makers. Taxpayers can get answers to questions about national policies, including economic policies to ease unemployment or access data directly. For example, White House.gov includes information about the American Recovery and Reinvestment Act of 2009. The Act provides for the investment of $787 billion to create jobs, spur economic activity, and bring transparency and openness to government.[34]

How do citizens find out exactly where the money has gone and to what purposes? Answers are easy to find. Just click the Recovery Act Web page on White House.gov and there is a list of frequently asked questions (FAQs) along with answers. Want to know more about contracts awarded or up for bid? Click on the link to Recovery.gov and a map displays information on projects by zip code along with the amount of specific contracts and jobs created. There are other web initiatives that illustrate transparency and innovation in government.

Data.gov is another by-product of executive branch efforts to change the paradigm of public access to government information and data. The idea behind the site is to make collections of data or datasets generated by the government publicly available online. The hope is that individual entrepreneurs, researchers, and corporations will create new web applications and uses for the data. This, in turn, will stimulate greater innovation and productivity.

Data accessed through Data.gov are restricted to public information and do are not include national security information or violate individual privacy. More

Figure 4.5   Data.gov. www.data.gov

than 168,000 datasets are now online and more are being added as the catalog of data continues to grow. The commercial potential of datasets is catching on and individual states have begun launching data sites with California, Utah, Michigan, and Massachusetts leading the way. The United Kingdom has launched its own Data.gov.uk and made available datasets that include crime maps, renewable energy projects maps, and population obesity data. Other countries are considering launching sites, too. If the goals of Data.gov are met, it could well signal the start of a twenty-first-century renaissance online.

In addition to Data.gov, the federal government is expanding citizen participation and oversight with other websites. For example, USASpending.gov is a performance dashboard that tracks billions of dollars in IT investments throughout the government. Website dashboards are yet another way of providing a window on government expenditures.

White House.gov, Recovery.gov, and Data.gov, along with other federal websites have brought about a remarkable level of transparency never before seen in government, a development not lost on the media. Moreover, government is embracing web technology in the quest for better solutions as noted in a CNN report on the Top Tech Trends:

> Government has a reputation for lagging behind the technological curve. But in 2009, the Obama Administration tried to prove that bureaucrats could be hip and tech-savvy, too. The administration launched *Data.Gov*, a clearinghouse of information on how the federal

government works and how tax money is spent. It also backed digitizing health care records, held the country's first online town hall meeting and moved toward the more efficient cloud-computing model, which essentially outsources some storage and processing of government files to companies such as Google.[35]

The Growth of Local Municipal Websites

As federal government websites have grown in sophistication and popularity, so have citizen expectations for local government websites. State and local government sites number more than 11,000 and new ones are added daily.[36] In fact, local municipal websites are now indispensable tools for city managers and other administrators seeking to better serve and connect with local communities. Municipal web operations are often smaller in size in terms of content and staffing than federal counterparts. Nonetheless, the frequency with which local citizens visit municipal websites is increasing. Moreover, local sites such as Virginia Beach's VBgov.com are setting a new standard of excellence. VBgov.com serves a community of 400,000 plus residents and is an information source for millions of tourists including families who are attracted to Virginia Beach and its many recreational activities.

VBgov.com is first and foremost an online resource where Virginia Beach residents can locate and apply for the services they need most from local government. From the homepage of VBgov.com, citizens can apply for building permits or business licenses, city employment, volunteer in the community, or register for food stamps and other assistance programs. In the how-to category they can find out where to vote, become a foster parent, bid for city projects, or request public utility service. Residents can also pay for parking tickets and property taxes, and use e-check services to pay water bills. Additionally, they can interact with library officials on the availability of books or get information concerning fines and fees.

Public information practitioners and administrators use VBgov.com to effectively expand the reach of municipal services by enlisting the help of the community. For example, citizens can use the site to report a pothole problem, a street light outage, or storm damage. Using VBgov.com they can also report problems with graffiti, traffic signs, and stray animals. Additionally, the site provides human services information about financial assistance programs to help citizens in need. It also provides information about how residents can report child abuse or neglect.

The demographics for VBgov.com reveal a slightly female and more youthful audience. Approximately 49,000 people visit the site monthly with 54 percent earning annual incomes from $60,000 to $100,000 and up.[37] VBgov.com is one of the best organized and designed local government websites. Its home page makes use of the F-shape design by positioning the most sought after information in the upper left quadrant of the web page. Research has shown that visitors usually read

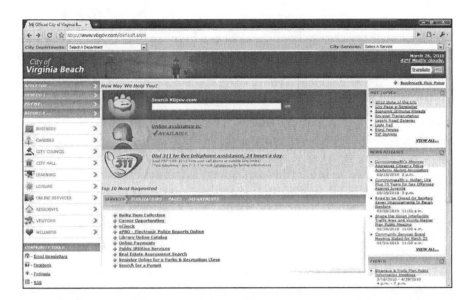

Figure 4.6   City of Virginia Beach. www.vbgov.com

across the top portion of a web page first, then down and horizontally, and finally vertically along the left side completing the F pattern.[38]

In addition to an efficient organization and page design, VBgov.com includes the information local residents desire most. Its most popular pages are its home page, followed by the Parks and Recreation page, the About VBgov page, and the Virginia Beach Police Department Annual Report page.[39] Also included on the VBgov.com home page are links to the city's economic development plan, the convention center and visitor's bureau, the center for the performing arts, and city public schools.

VBgov.com's privacy policy is straightforward concerning the use of IP addresses and cookies. Moreover, it plainly states that the purpose of the site is "To provide accurate, non-editorial content and information about the functions, services, activities, issues, operations and projects of the City of Virginia Beach municipal government."[40] Overall, VBgov.com is a comprehensive and interactive website intended for city residents and visitors alike. The site makes use of best practices for page design and content. As a result, VBgov.com joins its federal counterparts in breaking new ground in web operations and citizen interaction.

Summary and Conclusions

Such is the promise of the brave new world of transparency and interaction with government websites. From White House.gov to Data.gov to much smaller and local municipal websites, e-government is taking hold—and spreading to other nations. Globally, the United States ranks second behind South Korea in a 2010 e-government survey conducted by the United Nations. The survey measures the capacity and the willingness of the public sector to leverage information and communication technology to better inform and deliver services to all citizens.[41]

Some sociologists predict that ninety years from now we will look back on the growth of the Internet as the most important phenomenon of the twenty-first century. Only time will tell if that prediction holds up. Still, two things are apparent about the nature of the Internet. First, it abhors the middlemen who stand between researchers and data, consumers and producers, readers and the news, and citizens and elected officials. Second, the Internet is forcing hierarchal organizations, including government, to adapt to the new reality of direct citizen-to-government communication. Communicators should take full advantage of this by using websites to free themselves from the often time-consuming task of dispensing routine information.

Government websites have unlimited potential to enhance public trust by the very nature of their transparency. Additionally, their functionality allows administrators and communicators to dialogue with citizens in real time. With a $7.2 billion program in the works to expand broadband throughout the United States, the government is betting big on the Internet. But what does the crystal ball reveal about the future of government on the web?

Websites can also be helpful in sampling stakeholder sentiment and trend spotting for issues that could impact organizations in the future. Almost everywhere one looks the Internet is accelerating the pace of change. Even the source code behind government websites is becoming less proprietary and web managers would do well to take notice.

Public information, administration, and web operations will continue as natural allies in the quest for better government. More government websites are surely on the way. Moreover, the look and functionality of older sites will require constant updating to keep pace with changing requirements and new technology. Having a strategic plan for web operations will remain an important first step to better government websites. Accuracy of web content is a must too. Public information practitioners and administrators can also find help by joining the online dialogue of web managers.

Additionally, the sheer volume of web content alone can help achieve a better website as evidenced by Defense.gov, which literally has something for everyone. Communicators must also continue reaching out to a world audience. State.gov demonstrates how to do just that, with engaging conversation and intuitive navigation to welcome multiple stakeholders. Creating a secure online environment that protects personal and financial information will also remain critical for web operations such as Treasury.gov.

Volume of content, online conversations, and security are also necessary for effective government web operations. However, what distinguishes an innovative website is the degree to which it communicates transparency, openness, and encourages stakeholder interaction and input. White House.gov fits that description. It is continually pioneering new initiatives in Internet democracy and charting the future of e-government.

Collectively, federal government agencies are pointing the way for administrators and communicators at all levels to create better websites. Citizens who may perceive little connection between their lives and the policy and programs of government could well discover it on the Internet. As that happens, the goal of better government via better websites will edge closer to reality.

Endnotes

1. Roger E. Bohn James E. Short, "How Much Information? 2009 Report on American Consumers," January 2010, USCD.edu. Retrieved March 27, 2011: http://hmi.ucsd. edu/pdf/HMI_2009_ConsumerReport_Dec9_2009.pdf
2. Lee Rainie, Leigh Estabrook and Evans Witt, "Information Searches That Solve Problems," December 30, 2007, Pewinternet.org. Retrieved January 23, 2010: http:// www.pewinternet.org/Reports/2007/Information-Searches-That-Solve-Problems/04-Americans-in-contact-with-their-government/3-78-percent-of-internet-users-have-visited-government-Websiteswebsite.aspx?r=1
3. "About USA.gov," March 7, 2011, USA.gov. Retrieved March 27, 2011: http://www. usa.gov/About.shtml
4. "Federal Web Managers Council," March 14, 2011, USA.gov. Retrieved March 27, 2011: http://www.USA.gov/webcontent/about/council.shtml
5. "E-Government Act of 2002," State.gov. Retrieved December 19, 2009: http://www. archives.gov/about/laws/egov-act-section-207.html
6. "Annual Internet Survey by the Center for the Digital Future Finds Shifting Trends Among Adults About the Benefits and Consequences of Children Going Online," DigitalCenter.org, 2009. Retrieved January 19, 2010: http://www.digitalcenter.org/ pdf/2008-Digital-Future-Report-Final-Release.pdf
7. Hans Krause Hansen and Jens Hoff (eds.) *Digital Governance://Networked Societies—Creating Authority Community and Identity in a Globalized World* (Samfundslitteratur Press, Frederiksberg, Denmark, 2006), Chapter 11.
8. "E-Government Act of 2002," Archives.gov. Retrieved March 27, 2011: http://www. archives.gov/about/laws/egov-act-section-207.html
9. "Requirements Checklist for Government Web Managers," June 25, 2010. Retrieved March 27, 2011: http://www.usa.gov/webcontent/reqs_bestpractices/checklist.shtml
10. Ibid.
11. "About Identity Theft," FTC.gov. Retrieved March 27, 2011: http://www.ftc.gov/bcp/ edu/microsites/idtheft/consumers/about-identity-theft.html
12. "U.S. Faces Shortage of Talent to Fight Cyber-Attacks," December 23, 2009, Allbusiness.com. Retrieved March 27, 2011: http://www.allbusiness.com/government/ government-bodies-offices/13646439-1.html
13. Ellen Nakashima and Brian Krebs, "As attacks increase, U.S. struggles to recruit computer security experts," *Washington Post*, December 23, 2009, A01.

14. Barack Obama, "Remarks by the President on Securing Our Nation's Cyber Infrastructure," May 29, 2009, WhiteHouse.gov. Retrieved December 23, 2009: http://www.whitehouse.gov/the_press_office/Remarks-by-the-President-on-Securing-Our-Nations-Cyber-Infrastructure

15. "Virginia Beach city, Virginia," November 4, 2010, Quickfactscensus.gov. Retrieved March 27, 2011: http://quickfacts.census.gov/qfd/states/51/51810.html

16. David Silverstein, "Pentagon Channel Starts Mobile Streaming Service," American Forces Press Service, May 13, 2010, Defense.gov. Retrieved Retrieved March 26, 2011: http://defense.gov/news/newsarticle.aspx?id=59158

17. "Defense.gov.," March 2011, Quantcast.com. Retrieved March 27, 2011: http://www.quantcast.com/defense.gov

18. "Department of Defense twitter Sign Up," March 2011, Twitter.com. Retrieved March 27, 2011: http://twitter.com/DeptofDefense/dodleaders

19. Gordon England, "Policy for Department of Defense Interactive Internet Activities," June 8, 2007, Dtic.mil. Retrieved December 19, 2009: http://www.dtic.mil/whs/directives/corres/pdf/DTM-08-037.pdf

20. Ibid.

21. "State.gov.," March 2011, Quantcast.com. Retrieved March 27, 2011: http://www.quantcast.com/state.gov

22. Hillary Rodham Clinton, "Secretary of State Hillary Rodham Clinton," December 1, 2009, State.gov. Retrieved December 24, 2009: http://www.state.gov/video/

23. Ibid.

24. "Director of U.S. Foreign Assistance," December 2009, State.gov. Retrieved March 26, 2011: http://www.state.gov/s/crs/c38150.htm

25. "Treasury.gov.," March 2011, Quantcast.com. Retrieved March 27, 2011: http://www.quantcast.com/treasury.gov

26. "Site Policies and Notices," January 7, 2011, Treasury.gov. Retrieved March 27, 2011: http://www.treasury.gov/SitePolicies/Pages/privacy.aspx

27. "IRS Releases 2008 Data Book," March 13, 2009, IRS.gov. Retrieved January 30, 2010: http://www.irs.gov/newsroom/article/0,id=205235,00.html

28. "Security and Privacy Notice," January 2009, Treasury.gov. Retrieved December 30, 2009: http://www.ots.treas.gov/?p=SecurityPrivacyNotice

29. Ibid.

30. "WhiteHouse.gov.," March 2011, Quantcast.com. Retrieved March 27, 2011: http://www.quantcast.com/whitehouse.gov

31. "Office of Public Engagement Blog," July 9, 2009, WhiteHouse.gov. Retrieved March 2011: http://www.whitehouse.gov/blog/2009/07/09/one-could-not-help-be-touched

32. Michael Margolis and Gerson Moreno-Riano, *The Prospect of Internet Democracy* (Ashgate Publishing Company, Burlington, Vermont, 2009), p. 154.

33. Philip Elliott, "White House Opens Web Site Programming to Public," October 24, 2009, HuffingtonPost.com. Retrieved January 28, 2010: http://www.huffingtonpost.com/huff-wires/20091024/us-obama-web-site/

34. "The Recovery Act," November 2009, WhiteHouse.gov. Retrieved January 15, 2010: http://www.whitehouse.gov/recovery

35. John Sutter, "The Top 10 Tech Trends of 2009," December 23, 2009, CNN.com Retrieved December 29, 2009: http://www.cnn.com/2009/TECH/12/22/top.tech.trends.2009/index.html

36. "State Government Offices, Local US Government, City Government and Federal Government," 2009. Retrieved March 30, 2010: http://www.statelocalgov.net/index. cfm
37. "VB.gov.," March 2011, Quantcast.com. Retrieved March 27, 2011: http://www. quantcast.com/vbgov.com
38. Jakob Nielsen, F-Shaped Pattern for Reading Web Content," April 17, 2006, Useit. com. Retrieved March 29, 2010: http://www.useit.com/alertbox/reading_pattern. html
39. "VBgov.com SmartViper Website Analysis," January 2010, Markosweb.com. Retrieved March 30, 2010: http://www.markosweb.com/www/vbgov.com/
40. "Terms of Use and Privacy Policy," January 2010, VB.gov. Retrieved March 30, 2010: http://vbgov.com/vgn.aspx?vgnextoid=954b340df304c010VgnVCM1000006310640 aRCRD&vgnextchannel=55ab7e192ca49010VgnVCM100000870b640aRCRD&vg nextparchannel=55ab7e192ca49010VgnVCM100000870b640aRCRD
41. "E-Government Overview," January 2010, 2UNPAN.org. Retrieved February 4, 2010: http://www2.unpan.org/egovkb/egovernment_overview/index.htm

Chapter 5

Public Information Campaigns

Jenifer E. Kopfman and Amanda Ruth-McSwain

Contents

Introduction

"Click it or ticket." "Only YOU can prevent forest fires." "Friends don't let friends drive drunk."

For decades, governments have informed, persuaded, and motivated the public to buckle their seat belts, practice safe sex, prevent forest fires, get vaccinated, and designate a sober driver. These ubiquitous messages have resulted in some of the most familiar and successful communication efforts in recent history, with tag lines that many of us remember all too well. Now your office needs to produce a public information campaign, but you may not know how to get started. This chapter will provide a guide through the process of developing and evaluating your public information campaign.

The Public Information Campaign

Utilized by both government and nonprofit organizations to create social change, public information campaigns are designed to reach a widely varied audience. Their purpose is to benefit society by disseminating information intended to enhance the well-being of the audience. From the early eighteenth century to the present day, public information campaigns have provided many societal benefits and facilitated social change to support the reform goals of various publics and policy makers. With the purpose to inform, persuade, or motivate behavior change, public information campaigns have ranged in scope from personal issues (e.g., heart disease) to societal issues (e.g., global warming), and these information dissemination efforts have been used by the federal government, government agencies, nonprofit associations, foundations, mass media, and corporations alike.

Although direct involvement of government agencies in public information campaigns was once atypical, the government's current use of public information campaigns to cultivate awareness for social issues and secure participation in federal programs is prolific for several reasons. First, an increase in information resources, supported in part by the technological revolution, has provided individuals with a personal fountain of knowledge. These increased information resources also have given communicators additional tools to reach publics with valuable information. Second, as a result of increased access to information, individuals are more educated and engaged in public decision making, causing a heightened demand for information as well as an expectation for government information and transparency. This increased participation has prompted government agencies and organizations to communicate information that informs the public decision-making process. Elite decisions can no longer solve societal issues, but rather public support and participation is now required for effective change, and this public support and participation can only be acquired through an open flow of communication and dialogue, providing the rationale for the use of a public information campaign. Third, the increased sophistication and effectiveness of contemporary communication campaigns have revealed that the use of a public information campaign is not only efficient but valuable in achieving government goals. From generating AIDS awareness to eradicating crime, public information campaigns have impacted public policy as well as societal reform. This has been accomplished through many communication opportunities that have improved the accuracy and influence of targeted communication efforts.

Commonly referred to as public information campaigns, this label does not accurately reflect the varying approaches to communication efforts today. In fact, much of the contemporary literature makes a distinction between information campaigns and communication campaigns. The information campaign resembles early efforts to inform various publics and is unidirectional in nature, providing information rather than focusing on a two-way communication effort. On the other hand, the communication campaign is more participative and interactional in nature, establishing a dialogue between the sender and receiver of the information. It is important to note that the communication campaign closely resembles the model of dialogic communication that is ideal for most public relations efforts today. However, regardless of the campaign approach—information or communication—*all* campaign efforts should include specific elements to ensure successful outcomes. For the ease of discussion throughout this chapter, we will consider the public information campaign and communication campaign as one and the same when planning campaign efforts.

So often a communicator is overwhelmed with the campaign process, resulting in the question, "Where do I start?" We believe that the success of a campaign fundamentally relies on the communicator's knowledge of the campaign process as well as campaign principles; therefore, providing a simple, useable summary of these processes and principles is the focus and foundation for this chapter.

Building the Campaign Foundation

Before embarking on the development of a communication compaign, it is important to take a step back and establish the foundation for it. Three stages of a public information or communication campaign help an organization facilitate the accomplishment of desirable outcomes. Those three stages are: planning, implementation, and evaluation.

The campaign planning stage is the phase of the campaign that includes the strategic development of campaign efforts; we view this phase as developing the blueprint for the campaign, which includes conducting formative research, setting campaign objectives, identifying target audiences, developing campaign strategy, creating campaign tactics, and establishing a campaign timeline and budget. This stage lays a strong foundation for the creation of an effective campaign.

The implementation stage of the campaign process includes making a decision on how and when to execute the campaign. We consider this phase of the campaign process to involve expanding the blueprint to include elements like the use of specific communication sources and media, message appeals, frequency and timing of message dissemination, and considerations for increased campaign credibility. This stage includes the steps that most people think of when considering public information campaigns—message development and presentation—but also includes several other steps that many forget. We won't let you forget those in your campaign.

Evaluating the campaign, the final stage of the process, is often overlooked yet increasingly important in today's economic environment. Sitting back and enjoying your perceived success can be satisfying and liberating; however, without research-based methods to measure campaign efforts, you will never realize the extent of your accomplishments and the true impact of your campaign. Have you constructed an effective campaign from your blueprint? Have you been successful in reaching the desired publics with your strategic message? Have you created the social change that you anticipated? Determining if the campaign has been successful should include the use of systematic evaluation methods and a focus on collecting data specific to the achievement of campaign goals and objectives. This is not a step to be overlooked! This is where you prove to yourself (and the powers that be) that your campaign worked.

It is through these three stages that a communicator lays the groundwork for successful public communication efforts. To help illustrate this process, we will examine the stages of planning, implementation, and evaluation of a government public communication campaign that received national recognition. The *Don't Be That Guy Alcohol Reduction Campaign* developed by the United States Department of Defense (DOD) has been recognized by the Public Relations Society of America as an outstanding public communication effort and exemplifies the stages involved in the campaign process. From developing the campaign plan, to evaluating the campaign results, the campaign has achieved remarkable results as well as created health behavior awareness and change within the target audience. This campaign will be used throughout the chapter to provide an example of each stage of the campaign process. A brief summary of this public communication campaign will provide background for our review:

The Don't Be That Guy Alcohol Reduction Campaign was created by the U.S. Department of Defense (DOD) to bring awareness to the alarming rate of binge drinking taking place within the junior levels of all branches of military services as well as to reduce the abuse of alcohol among members of the military. In collaboration with Fleishman-Hillard International Communications, the DOD developed a campaign grounded in social science research called the *That Guy* campaign.

The primary goal of the campaign was to deliver a cautionary tale about excessive drinking—*Don't Be That Guy!* The process that may be used to develop each of the three stages of this campaign will be discussed in the rest of this chapter.

Developing a Campaign Plan

Although campaign literature provides several different and valuable procedures for developing communication campaigns depending on the purpose of the campaign, we consider the RACE model to be a simple, practical way to remember the important components for designing and implementing a successful public communication effort. RACE, a four-step model developed by John Marston (1963), outlines a public relations management process commonly used by public relations practitioners to provide straightforward guidance for the communicator in campaign planning efforts. RACE stands for the following elements in the campaign process:

R = Research
A = Action
C = Communication
E = Evaluation

Following this model, the starting point for the campaign planner should be *research*, or assessing the situation using several forms of formative assessment. Using both primary and secondary research methods to fully investigate the issue will provide the communicator with a clear picture for moving forward with campaign development. Following a thorough analysis of the situation, the communicator is ready for *action*, or formulating a practical strategic plan for the campaign process. This phase requires the communicator to make many decisions regarding campaign goals, audiences, messages, channels, resource allocation, and timing for message delivery. Next, the *communication* phase primarily focuses on the execution and placement of messages based on existing communication theories, principles, models, and best practices. Finally, the last phase of the campaign process includes the *evaluation* of campaign efforts; conducting outcome research will help answer many questions about the campaign's effectiveness aside from the obvious goal attainment. Evaluation can answer questions such as was the campaign adequately planned, were the communication messages received and understood, did efforts remain within the initial budgetary constraints, and how can future campaign efforts be improved. In recent years the evaluation phase of the campaign process has become increasingly sophisticated in systematically evaluating campaign efforts to demonstrate impact.

The remainder of the chapter will provide detailed explanations of each phase of the campaign process, RACE, as well as essential considerations to ensure campaign success.

Research: Assessing the Campaign Situation

Most communicators recognize the need for a campaign without conducting extensive research; however, to truly understand the present issues, organizational involvement, as well as the relevant publics, the first step in the planning process is to conduct an analysis of the situation requiring various forms of assessment. It is important to stress that both formative and outcome research should be conducted throughout the entire campaign process. Marking the start of the campaign process, formative research should be conducted to create a thorough understanding of the situation; this research process is often referred to as *situation analysis.*

The formative research conducted to analyze the campaign situation can include many different methods of research; however, it is important that the communicator identify the most appropriate research methods to answer questions that will help formulate the campaign strategy. For example, in the Don't Be That Guy Alcohol Reduction Education Campaign, the DOD employed survey methods and discovered a 44 percent binge drinking rate among junior military personnel. Clearly this behavior could negatively impact members of the military, military families, and the contribution and readiness of military personnel, and as a result the DOD recognized the need for a public communication campaign. This information was just the start of its research process. It would not be able to create an effective campaign based on a few statistical facts. Rather, the DOD needed to first fully analyze the situation before developing a plan to raise awareness of the issues of alcohol consumption among military members. The situation analysis should answer questions like these: What is binge drinking? Why is binge drinking a problem among junior military? How do junior military perceive this problem? How have other organizations handled the issue of binge drinking? And, how can the change of alcohol-related behaviors best be accomplished?

Considered an integral step before moving forward, the DOD conducted both primary and secondary research to answer the aforesaid questions as well as effectively analyze the current situation. The DOD team first conducted extensive *secondary research* (or investigation of existing information) in these three steps:

1. First, they conducted further analyses on the DOD survey that revealed the binge drinking issue. In addition to the 44 percent binge drinking rate, the data indicated that the problem was worst among young enlisted men ages 18 to 24.
2. Next, they reviewed scientific and popular literature relevant to binge drinking.
3. Finally, the team evaluated current alcohol abuse prevention programs in the military.

Using the findings of the secondary research, the DOD team conducted *primary research* (involving active data collection) to determine the messages and concepts that would resonate with the target audience. The primary research consisted of eight focus groups with military members representing all branches of the U.S. military. This research of the situation provided many valuable insights for campaign planning, including the fact that social consequence messages, such as loss of control or embarrassment among peers, resonate very well with this target audience. Results also suggested that the target audience would not respond well to campaigns that promote abstinence and that they preferred humorous appeals when receiving communication about negative implications of excessive drinking.

Gathering this valuable information helped the team avoid several potential mistakes. Secondary research allowed the team to focus on a specific target audience (enlisted males ages 18 to 24), and primary research opened their eyes to the fact that they should *not* use an abstinence campaign but *should* use humor. The data were used to formulate the campaign strategy and identify the most effective campaign tactics to achieve the campaign objectives.

Although the research phase of the campaign process can prove somewhat costly in both time and resources, the benefits of this part of the process far outweigh the costs. Research provides the credibility, accountability, insight, and most importantly, a strong foundation for campaign planning. We strongly suggest that every communicator utilize the most appropriate research methods available to them as the first step in their campaign endeavors whether it is through the review of existing literature or the use of survey, interview, focus group, or observation methods.

Research Part Two: Linking Theory to Practice

Complementary to the formative research phase and often missing in the communicator's campaign toolbox is the understanding and use of theory as a basis for base campaign development. Once a sound understanding of the situation is acquired, identifying a theoretical foundation to guide campaign efforts can be extremely beneficial. In fact, linking appropriate theory to the situational factors present before jumping into the tactical brainstorming for the campaign can equip the communicator with a valuable framework for understanding audiences, developing messages, and choosing appropriate mediums for message dissemination. The use of communication theory as well as proven campaign principles can be the difference between a successful campaign strategy and one that fails to accomplish desirable outcomes.

Although there are numerous communication theories that inform both the input and output processes of communication, the campaign planning stage primarily uses input processes of communication (how messages are constructed and how messages are communicated) to inform campaign efforts. The input process of campaign development involves: (1) the source of the message, (2) the communication of the message, (3) the channel that delivers the message, and (4) the receiver of the message. Each element of the process plays a large role in the success of the communication effort. For example, the sender and receiver play an important role in the delivery and receipt of the message, while the message and channel determine what information is communicated and how. Communication theory can provide a deeper understanding of one or all of these input variables to campaign development. For example, the DOD's Don't Be That Guy Alcohol Reduction Education Campaign utilized reliable social science research as a basis for strategic campaign efforts; the use of Prochaska and DiClemente's (1984) Transtheoretical Model (sometimes called the Stages of Change Theory) provided a roadmap for campaign development by offering a possible explanation of the receiver variable relevant to this process.

Predominantly used for communication efforts when a health behavior change is desired, the Transtheoretical Model (TTM) describes how individuals transform a health problem or adopt a positive health behavior. In the case of the DOD campaign, the desired behavior of reducing alcohol consumption and curbing binge drinking was best examined through the five stages of change outlined by the TTM: (1) precontemplation, (2) contemplation, (3) preparation, (4) action, and (5) maintenance. These stages provided the campaign with a framework for understanding the gradual progress made by individuals who experience a change in behavior. These stages are briefly described here:

> **Stage 1:** Precontemplation: The individual is not aware or is underaware that a problem exists and there is no intention to change in the immediate future.
> **Stage 2:** Contemplation: The individual thinks about making a change and sorts through the pros and cons of changing his or her behavior.
> **Stage 3:** Preparation: The individual trials the behavior to answer the "how to" question, and gets a feel for what it feels like or looks like to change or adopt a new behavior.
> **Stage 4:** Action: The individual commits to the behavior and develops a plan to take action.
> **Stage 5:** Maintenance: The individual continues the behavior while anticipating and planning for relapse.

Although the TTM provided a strong theoretical framework for the development of the Don't Be That Guy Alcohol Reduction Education Campaign, it is certainly not suitable for all public information campaign efforts. Additional theoretical frameworks common to public information campaign development include the Elaboration Likelihood Model (Petty and Cacioppo, 1986), Theory of Reasoned Action (Ajzen and Fishbein, 1973), Diffusion Theory (Rogers, 1995), Expectancy

Value Theory (Fishbein, 1963), Cognitive Dissonance Theory (Festinger, 1957), Source Credibility (Hovland, Janis, and Kelley, 1953), Attribution Theory (Heider, 1958), Uses and Gratifications Theory (Blumler and Katz, 1974), and the Health Belief Model (Becker, 1974). If the use of a fear appeal (a message that scares the recipient into changing his or her behavior) is being considered, the Extended Parallel Process Model (Witte, 1992) certainly should be considered. Having an understanding of these and other communication theories can facilitate the analysis of the situation as well as establish additional guidance for the development of the campaign blueprint.

Armed with ample knowledge and research, as well as the selection of a theoretical foundation, it is time to begin the next phase of campaign planning—action.

Action: Developing the Campaign Plan

Following the research phase of campaign development, the action phase includes the strategic development of campaign components; as previously mentioned, we consider this phase the development of the campaign blueprint. This phase of campaign development includes six components: (1) setting of campaign goals and objectives, (2) creation of the audience profile, (3) formation of campaign strategy, (4) development of campaign tactics, (5) construction of the campaign timeline, and (6) compilation of the campaign budget. Each of these components is described below.

Campaign Goals and Objectives

A first and very critical step in creating the blueprint for the campaign is to establish campaign goals and objectives. Many practitioners consider the two synonymous; however, there are marked differences between the two and both are important elements of the campaign. Campaign goals compose the broad intentions for the campaign by providing a campaign vision; goals are intangible and abstract and most times cannot be measured. Objectives differ from goals in that they are narrow, precise, tangible, and as such, can be measured through evaluation efforts. For example, a common goal of a public information campaign is to educate individuals about the consequences of a negative behavior, while the campaign objective is to reduce the number of individuals participating in the negative behavior through education efforts within a desired time frame.

It is critical to develop strong objectives; the strong objective is specific, measurable, achievable, relevant, and time-stamped (SMART). Most importantly, SMART objectives, an acronym coined by George Doran in 1981, are the standard for monitoring campaign progress, providing campaign targets for accountability, and evaluating campaign success.

Demonstrating the relationship between goals and objectives, the DOD crafted goals and objectives that provided direction, accountability, and valuation for their campaign efforts. For example, the goals of the Don't Be That Guy Alcohol Reduction Education Campaign included the following: to raise awareness of the negative effects of excessive drinking and help reduce alcohol abuse among active-duty military. The specific objectives were twofold: (1) raise awareness for the That Guy campaign and the negative effects of excessive drinking, and (2) motivate 50 military installations to implement the campaign in the first year of the program while leveraging results to set the stage for increasing engagement among additional installations in 2008.

Setting SMART objectives early in the process allows for a more thorough evaluation of the campaign later in the process. Be sure campaign objectives are SMART!

Audience Profile

With most public communication efforts, understanding the target audience is one of the most important components of the planning process. Since the purpose of the public information campaign is to provide valuable information that seeks to benefit some segment of society, it is the communicator's responsibility to understand the cognitive and behavioral attributes of the target audience in order to best communicate the beneficial information. Research can help reveal important audience demographic and psychographic characteristics like age, gender, education level, socioeconomic status, attitudes, opinions, and experiences. Various campaign decisions can be based on this information; effective message appeals, source choices, and the type of media employed are all critical decisions for which a thorough audience analysis can provide direction.

Simply, an audience analysis includes assessing the characteristics and interests of the audience and then tailoring the campaign efforts to fit audience needs and wants. An analysis of the campaign's primary audience is essential; however, the campaign may have more than one audience, meaning there is a secondary audience that also requires thorough analysis. The primary audience of a campaign is the audience segment that is deemed the primary user of the campaign, more specifically, the audience that will be directly impacted by the information. The secondary audience is the audience segment that might be affected by the campaign information and the decisions or actions made by the primary audience following campaign exposure. For example, the DOD's Don't Be That Guy Campaign targeted both a primary and secondary audience. The primary audience included active-duty enlisted military personnel across all branches of service, males 18 to 24 years old, and the secondary audiences included the DOD and military leadership.

From the audience analysis, a thorough audience profile can be developed. Sometimes both primary and secondary research are required to develop a comprehensive the audience profile. Many times reviewing academic and trade publications, organizational archives, census data, national polls and surveys sponsored by market research companies like Gallup, Nielson, and Cision can provide information sufficient for understanding the campaign audience(s). However, there are times when descriptive information does not exist for audience members. Therefore, primary research is helpful in gathering audience-specific information. Through surveys, focus groups, interviews, and even observation, informative information can be collected regarding audience demographics and psychographics. A sample audience profile developed for the DOD's communication campaign for alcohol reduction is included in Box 5.1. This sample profile provides an excellent example of the level of detail that should result from an ample audience analysis.

BOX 5.1   SAMPLE AUDIENCE PROFILE

ALCOHOL REDUCTION EDUCATION EFFORT

Primary Audience: Active Duty, Enlisted Military Personnel

- **Demographics:** These men are aged 18 to 24. They have an average income of $38,000 per year. About 54% are married (70% have an employed spouse), and 47% have children. Over 61% are White, 21.8% are African American, 10% are Hispanic, and 7% are classified as Other (Native American, Pacific American, Asian American, and others). Approximately 98.6% have a high school diploma or high school equivalency degree. More than 40% are from the South, the largest region for military recruits, and contrary to popular belief, a disproportionate majority come from high-income neighborhoods. Of those that indicate a religious preference, the majority are Roman Catholic, followed by Christian (nondenominational) and Baptist.
- **Value Systems:** These enlisted men value service, family, and personal sacrifice. They are committed to the "Don't Ask, Don't Tell" policy of the armed forces. They value respect, recognition, and reward.
- **Knowledge about Binge Drinking:** The majority of the audience understands excessive alcohol consumption but is confused over the term *binge* drinking. Further, the bulk of this group does not consider themselves as binge drinkers and instead define themselves as social drinkers.
- **Major Barriers to Adoption of the Desired Behaviors:** Alcohol fact and traditional health messages are inconsequential to this audience. They have a negative response to abstinence messages or militarylike messages and materials, especially military recruiting messages and materials. They face deployment, combat, and peer pressures that can overshadow intent to participate in desired behaviors.

- **Preferred Media Channels/Media Use:** Peer-to-peer viral communication is most preferable. In addition, social networking sites like Facebook, MySpace, and select chat rooms are highly accessed, as well as web-based material, movies, men's magazines like *Maxim* and *Playboy*, video/computer games, and pop/country/classic rock radio stations.
- **Sources That Audience Trusts and Finds Credible:** Peers and family are the most trusted sources; it is important to avoid messages from military chain of command to provoke a positive response.
- **Behavioral Determinants of Desired Behaviors:** Social consequences like loss of control and embarrassment resonate with this audience. They hold negative thoughts and feelings toward the "person who drinks to excess and loses control." They feel the need to distance themselves from those who are socially out of control, unpredictable, and humiliating due to excessive drinking. This audience responds best to humor when dealing with the disapproval of social and health behaviors.

Campaign Strategy

Once the goals and objectives of the campaign are developed and a thorough audience analysis has been completed, it is time for the communicator to brainstorm campaign elements. Although commonly confused with tactics, campaign strategy establishes the campaign's direction and thematic application. In short, the campaign strategy needs to first and foremost answer how the campaign objectives are to be achieved; strategy provides the big picture, themes, feelings, and ideas that the campaign should embody.

Strategy statements can include action strategies like audience participation, sponsorships, or organizational performance; communication strategies like media endorsement, paid placement (advertising), or transparent communication; message strategies like emotional appeals, slogans, and power words; or distribution strategies like repetition, use of multiple channels, and timing in association with calendar year.

The DOD's Don't Be That Guy Alcohol Reduction Education Campaign used many different strategic initiatives including the use of humor and focus on short-term, social consequences that grab attention and resonate with audience; the creation of a "surround-sound" approach using multiple channels of communication and multiple levels of influence; the use of viral, peer-to-peer media to reach the target audience; the use of the cautionary warning campaign theme "Don't Be That Guy"; and the development of turnkey campaign resources for contacts to use in support of campaign implementation. The DOD campaign strategy clearly materialized from the situation analysis research results as well as considerations borrowed from social science theory. This example demonstrates that thorough research leads to well-developed campaign strategy, which in turn will provide the direction for the campaign tactics employed.

Again, the difference between campaign strategy and tactics can be somewhat confusing. However, it might help to consider the strategy as providing the big picture for the campaign, and the campaign tactics as the objects, people, and scenery in the picture. It is important to establish strategy before developing the specific tactics that accomplish that strategy.

Campaign Tactics

Campaign tactics are the nuts and bolts of the campaign that facilitate the execution of the campaign strategy. Example tactics are websites, billboards, town hall meetings, media kits, online contests, brochures, social media, television and radio public service announcements (PSAs), and special events. The specific mediums that will distribute the campaign strategy, the exact events that will encourage audience participation, and the detailed documents that will pitch the story to media outlets make up the campaign tactics. It is vital that the tactics chosen to carry out the campaign strategy relate to the campaign's big picture. For example, if the campaign strategy was to create an interactive opportunity for the target audience to experience the campaign message, then a tactic that allows for two-way communication or a participative interface is necessary (an example would be a chat room or message board hosted on the organization's website).

The Don't Be That Guy Alcohol Reduction Education Campaign utilized a pilot program to initially launch and test its campaign tactics. The following tactics were used to carry out the aforementioned campaign strategy and were first implemented at four military facilities:

- Highly interactive, flash-driven website (www.ThatGuy.com)
- That Guy MySpace profile as well as advertising on MySpace to drive traffic to the profile
- Banner ads placed on online ad networks to increase site visits
- That Guy billboards in areas of high audience frequency like bars, restaurants, and recreation centers, advertisements on shuttle buses, in convenience stores, and in newspapers
- Posters in bathrooms at popular bars and clubs
- Radio station promotions including radio PSAs, on-air contests, and humorous promotional items such as posters, coasters, stickers, and temporary tattoos
- Thirty-second PSAs prior to movies that are shown at military theaters, reminding viewers, "the buzz is temporary, the humiliation is forever—Don't Be That Guy!"

Following the pilot program, additional tactics were developed to assist the launch of the campaign globally. These tactics included the following:

- Road shows to military facilities in order to distribute a program toolkit to aid in the implementation of the campaign tactics
- Additional campaign materials, including coasters, playing cards, and additional posters
- The "Buzz Kill" interactive web game that showcased the legal consequences of becoming That Guy were developed

By reviewing the tactics from the DOD campaign, the relationships among the objectives, audience, strategy, and tactics are apparent; it is important to note that each component of the campaign should build on the previous component.

Timeline

Although seemingly simple, the campaign timeline is an important element to campaign success. The timeline consists of the scheduling of campaign tactics by carefully considering how the execution of campaign tactics relate to one another. There are many different approaches related to scheduling patterns and message frequency that complement the campaign strategy and that require advanced planning. For example, the campaign may be best implemented using a seasonality approach, meaning that campaign tactics should be implemented in association with the calendar year or seasonal trends. Another approach to scheduling may be pulsing, which means that there is limited communication with the target audience on a year-round basis except for determined peak periods for the campaign when the communication efforts are at an all-time high. Some communicators may even be interested in roadblocking to ensure audience exposure to the campaign message at a certain point in time. *Roadblocking* is the placement of campaign messages in all major television networks, radio stations, or print publications in the same period of time; therefore, regardless of media choice, an audience member has the opportunity for message exposure with this approach. Regardless of approach chosen, careful planning and consideration needs to be given to the scheduling patterns and message dissemination of the campaign.

The campaign timeline is commonly organized using a Gantt chart. The Gantt chart, developed by Henry Gantt (1903), uses a common bar chart format to illustrate the important dates and deadlines through project completion. The Gantt chart can be organized by day, week, month, or any other time frame that is relevant to the campaign. Figure 5.1 provides a sample Gantt chart for the DOD campaign for alcohol reduction.

Budget

Equally important to the campaign timeline, the campaign budget details the financial resources needed to implement the campaign tactics and achieve campaign

Tactical Activity	Month 1	Month 2	Month 3	Month 4	Month 5	Month 6	Month 7	Month 8	Month 9	Month 10
				December 2006–September 2007						
				Pilot Phase						
Launch ThatGuy.com										
MySpace Profile										
Banner Ads										
Billboards										
Ads/Posters										
Radio Contests										
Movie PSAs										
				Propagation Phase						
Road Shows										
Program Toolkit										
Password Portal										
Campaign Promotions										
Interactive Web Game										

Figure 5.1 Sample Gantt Chart: Don't Be That Guy Alcohol Reduction Education Campaign.

objectives. There are commonly five categories to a campaign budget: (1) personnel costs, (2) materials costs, (3) media costs, (4) equipment and facility costs, and (5) administrative costs. One or all of these categories may be relevant to the campaign budget; nonetheless, it is essential that the campaign budget accurately reflects the resources needed to implement the campaign or the success of the campaign may be compromised. For example, the accuracy of the budget for government communication efforts can be especially important because of the way in which fiscal resources are allocated. If the campaign budget reveals an approximate campaign cost of $750,000, many times that is the exact amount of financial resources allocated for the campaign, not a penny less or a penny more.

Although not itemized by campaign expense, the campaign budget for the Don't Be That Guy Alcohol Reduction Education Campaign demonstrates the total cost for a successful public information campaign effort. The DOD campaign totaled $1,814,527 in fees and expenses for one year of campaign implementation. Obviously, great expense was needed to pull off a campaign of this magnitude, but very effective campaigns can be executed on a much more limited budget, especially if they are local in focus.

Communication: Implementing the Campaign

After all the research and planning, it is finally time to develop the campaign messages. The main goal in this stage of the process is to develop a message that resonates with the audience. There are many factors to consider when designing effective messages. Not all of them can be reviewed in one short book chapter, so we'll point out some of the important considerations that need to be addressed, but please be aware that this is *not* a complete list of all the communication variables that may affect message design.

Some of the issues to consider in designing a message are discussed in the following sections.

Message Goal

The first decision that needs to be made has to do with the response desired from the target audience. Is the goal of the public information campaign awareness, instruction, or persuasion? In other words, is the goal simply to make the audience aware of the issue/information/topic so they seek out additional information (awareness), or is the goal to educate the audience so they have knowledge about what to do and how to do it (instruction), or is the goal to change the attitudes or behavior of the audience by convincing them of the validity of the argument (persuasion)? The goal the communicator is trying to achieve will influence the content that needs to be included in the message, as will the tactics chosen in the previous action step. Consider what types of messages will work best given the goals and the methods and tactics chosen to distribute them.

The goal of the That Guy campaign was twofold. Some of the initial materials, such as billboards, posters, and radio PSAs, were designed simply to create awareness and provide the audience with the curiosity to find more information by providing a web address. Other aspects of the campaign, including the longer video PSAs and the website itself, were designed to persuade. Providing more information in these formats allowed the campaign to convince the audience members that they needed to change their behaviors so that they would not be viewed as "that guy."

Credibility

Messages should be perceived as credible by the target audience. Recent research suggests that there are three primary dimensions to credibility: the first is that the message needs to be competent or show expertise, the second is that the message needs to be perceived as trustworthy, and the third is that the message needs to demonstrate goodwill rather than self-interest. Credibility is akin to beauty in that it most certainly is in the eyes of the beholder. Just because the communicators believe a message is credible does not mean that the target audience will see it the same way, so we strongly suggest using the audience research obtained in the previous steps to determine what will be perceived as credible by those who will be receiving the message.

The Don't Be That Guy Alcohol Reduction Education Campaign used the results of the research phase to determine what would be perceived as credible to the 18- to 24-year-old enlisted men who comprised their audience. Abstinence messages were shown not to be trustworthy, and messages that had the look and feel of military recruiting materials were not perceived to have goodwill. Rather, the use of humor was perceived as competent for delivering peer-to-peer messages; it was trusted and viewed as being concerned with the best interests of the men. Credibility was key in creating messages for the DOD's That Guy campaign, and the communicators made sure that their messages would be seen as credible.

Attractiveness and Relevance

Campaign messages should be engaging and use features that are both attractive and relevant to the intended audience. This is true for the visual and image-based aspects of the message, or what the audience *sees*, as well as the language and text-based aspects of the message, or what the audience *reads*. Attractiveness means that the visual images used in the message and language used to convey the desired information should be interesting, appealing, or pleasant for the message recipients. Relevance suggests that the audience should see how the message can be applied to their own situation and needs, making it personally involving. Just as we suggested with credibility, it is important that communicators use the audience research obtained in the previous steps of this planning process to figure out what images and phrases will be perceived as attractive and relevant to the members of the intended audience.

The reason that both the images and the text of campaign messages must be viewed as attractive and relevant is that different audience members are going to pay attention to different aspects of the message. Some people are going to pay attention to the words of the message. Message processing scholars call this *central* or *systematic processing*, and people who do this are likely not only to read the information in a message but also to do some "issue-relevant thinking" in which they compare and relate the new information to similar information they already know. This type of processing is very persuasive, and usually results in longer-lasting behavior change if individuals are influenced to change their behavior consistent with the message recommendations.

Although some people will process messages this way, other individuals are likely to ignore the words and pay more attention to the visual images in the message. When this happens, these individuals are doing what scholars call *peripheral* or *heuristic processing*. This means that they are *not* likely to be thinking about the message content, but instead they are likely to be using simple decision rules to make choices related to the message. These individuals may be influenced by things like the attractive woman in the skimpy bikini or the muscular man wearing no shirt, the pleasing scenery, or the popular or dangerous activity portrayed in the message. Other things may also trigger the simple decision rules, such as the number of arguments presented (even though they aren't really reading the arguments, the fact that there are so many can be persuasive). These factors can be somewhat persuasive, but any persuasive effects are likely to be short-lived. So to be most effective, communicators want to be sure their messages appeal to audience members using both types of processing. Those people processing the words are likely to be persuaded more quickly, but the people processing the images can still be persuaded by the message. Sometimes with repeat exposures, those repeated simple decision rules will lead to the issue-relevant thinking that is needed for longer-lasting persuasion. So to be sure you have something to offer both types of message processors, pay attention to both the visual appeal and the verbal appeal of the messages being designed.

Attractiveness and relevance were important in creating the That Guy campaign. Planners wanted actors and models who would portray "that guy" to be attractive, but not overly attractive, since they wanted audience members to be able to picture themselves in similar situations, thus showing that they could relate to the character in the message. To be sure that they chose appropriate actors and models, the planning team conducted some focus groups. The participants said they found the people in the messages to be both relevant and real, and that these communication vehicles were effectively delivering the campaign's messages. Similarly, at the same time the ads were being developed, the campaign planners also created a website (www.thatguy.com) containing both textual information and visual images. Once again, attractiveness and relevance were key components in designing the web pages, resulting in an interactive, flash-driven site that was both visually pleasing and full of important, relevant information.

Emotional Appeals

A common strategy in public information campaigns is to motivate behavior change by threatening the audience with unpleasant outcomes that could occur if members do not comply with the message recommendations. These types of messages are called *fear appeals*. The "Click it or ticket" campaign is an excellent example of a fear appeal, because it clearly lets the audience know that if they are caught driving without wearing a seat belt, they could face some unpleasant consequences like having to pay a fine. However, it also offers a clear method for avoiding these unpleasant consequences—to avoid a traffic ticket and the associated fine, all one needs to do is wear a seat belt when driving. This campaign has been quite effective at increasing seat belt usage.

Fear appeals can be very effective in persuading audiences, but not all campaigns should use fear appeal messages. Communicators should think very carefully about whether scaring individuals into complying with their message recommendations is an appropriate way to reach their particular audience. However, if it is decided that a fear appeal would be a desirable message choice, there are four steps that must be followed to produce an effective fear appeal. First, the message must contain a clear threat, such that the consequences of not following the message recommendations must be obvious and fearful. In the seat belt campaign, the threat in the message is that people who don't wear seat belts will receive a ticket and pay a fine. Second, in addition to being scared by the threat, audience members must perceive themselves as vulnerable to this threat. If they see that something bad might happen, but they don't think it could happen to them, then they won't be persuaded by the message. Showing the likelihood of the negative outcome happening, or showing its immediacy rather than distance, can increase this sense of vulnerability. Third, the message must show the audience that there is an action they can take to prevent the negative consequence from happening. Obviously, this step is the goal of the campaign, and shows the desired behavior the communicators are trying to produce. Fourth and finally, the audience members must perceive that they are capable of performing the desired behavior. Even if they know it can prevent the negative consequence, if they feel they cannot do whatever is recommended in the message, then they will simply experience fear and not be able to take steps to prevent the bad outcome from happening to them. Thus, if people felt like they were incapable of fastening a seat belt when driving, they might constantly be fearful of getting caught and having to pay a fine. Including these four elements in any fear appeal should produce the desired responses.

The "That Guy" campaign is an excellent example of a fear appeal. Ads clearly showed someone who had been binge drinking and experienced loss of control or embarrassing situations. In this example, the threat was the possibility of overdrinking, behaving like "that guy," and losing control or embarrassing oneself. Anyone who drinks even a small amount of alcohol, and particularly those individuals who have experienced similar situations either as an observer or a participant, will be likely to feel vulnerable to this threat. While the ads did not specifically state that the desired behavior was responsible drinking, messages clearly implied that responsible drinking was the key to not being "that guy." Finally, the campaign tried to provide efficacy, or provide the audience with the perception that they could perform the recommended behavior. This was enhanced with messages like "The buzz is temporary, the humiliation is forever. Don't be that guy!" Emphasizing the lasting consequences of humiliation made it easier for audience members to feel like they were capable of drinking responsibly. All four critical components of a fear appeal message were present, thus producing an effective emotional appeal.

One-Sided or Two-Sided Messages

A decision that the communicator must make is whether to use a one-sided message or a two-sided message. A *one-sided message* presents only the case favoring the desired behavior, without mentioning the opposing side or any of the drawbacks associated with the desired behavior. A *two-sided message* strategically raises the opposing side's arguments and then refutes these arguments, showing why the desired behavior is most preferred. Most of the research evidence suggests that two-sided messages are more persuasive and perceived as more credible than one-sided messages in most situations. In other words, it usually is best to address the "other side" rather than ignore it. The only exception is if research shows that the entire audience is already favorable toward the recommended behavior; only in this case should a one-sided message be used.

Messages in That Guy ads demonstrate a very creative use of two-sided messages. They show the "other side" by portraying That Guy as having fun while drinking, but then focus on his embarrassing behaviors to show why no one should want to be "that guy." Similarly, the PSAs that included a more detailed text message used the statement "The buzz is temporary, the humiliation is forever. Don't Be That Guy!" While this is a fear appeal, as discussed in the previous section, it is also a two-sided message because it addresses the fact that the "other side" of responsible drinking is the buzz that many people seek. It acknowledges that many people drink to enjoy the buzz, but it encourages people to focus on drinking responsibly rather than focusing on getting buzzed. In doing so, this message refutes the undesirable behavior and shows why the desirable behavior is better.

Summary

Considering each of the five issues listed previously should provide a solid foundation for beginning the message design process. Each campaign is going to find different aspects of these issues important at different times, so we cannot provide specific recommendations that will be the "right" answer for everyone. Instead, we raise these issues for each communicator to refer to during the message design process in each individual campaign. Only the research and action phases of RACE campaign planning can dictate how each of these issues will influence this communication phase.

A final thought regarding the communication phase: Although it helps to have a communication expert in house when designing campaign messages, it is not absolutely necessary. Many campaigns that have been produced by governmental agencies were created by individuals who were biology, history, or social work majors when they were in college. However, if some expertise is desired, but the budget does not allow for hiring such a person, we have a suggestion: Recruit a communication intern from your local university or college! Depending on current needs, it may be worthwhile to consider a student majoring in communications, marketing, visual design, or any number of other students. Since the authors of this chapter are communication professors, we can attest that our students learn how to design messages for various audiences using effective, appealing communication strategies, but we are certain that students in other relevant majors may provide some helpful expertise.

Evaluation: Measuring Campaign Effectiveness

Once the campaign has been implemented and the target audience is beginning to pay attention to the message, it could be very easy to sit back and enjoy the "success" of all the planning and effort by everyone involved. But work on the campaign is not yet finished! Evaluation is a critical component of this process. Evaluation involves the use of research procedures to determine whether the campaign was effective, how it did and did not achieve its objectives, and the efficiency with which it achieved them. In other words, the campaign's "success" cannot be concluded until evaluation research has proven it.

Three main findings should result from the evaluation phase in the form of answers to the following questions:

1. To what degree did the campaign reach its objectives?
2. How or why did the campaign work?
3. What lessons can be learned for future public information campaigns?

Two different types of research help examine the effectiveness of the campaign: process research and outcome research. *Process research* usually involves collecting data on when, where, and for how long the campaign is broadcast. For example, the evaluator might want to listen to the radio at prespecified times to verify that the ad was played the number of times it was supposed to be played. *Outcome research* is conducted by collecting data to measure the program's impact. This data collection could be done using quantitative measures such as surveys, or qualitative methods such as interviews or focus groups, but no matter which method is selected, it is important to include both people who have been exposed to the campaign *and* those who have *not* been exposed to the campaign in the evaluation research. This control group provides a comparison and allows the evaluator to determine just how effective the campaign has been.

Some of the critical variables that should be assessed during the evaluation phase include the following:

- *Campaign exposure.* This is the extent to which the targeted audience has seen, can recall, and/or can recognize the campaign materials. Process evaluation can help determine the level of possible exposure to the campaign, but only outcome research can provide information about whether members of the target audience recognize or recall the campaign message or components of the campaign.
- *Interpersonal communication.* Public communication campaigns can be very effective at stimulating interpersonal communication. If a target audience member sees one of the campaign tactics, it may or may not change his or her behavior. But frequently this target audience member is quite likely to mention what he or she saw to a friend, coworker, or family member. Now the information in the campaign has spread even further even though this next group of people has not yet seen any campaign materials. When these friends, coworkers, and family members are actually exposed to one of the campaign messages, research suggests they are more likely to pay attention because they had previously heard some of this information. Outcome research can help the evaluator determine if interpersonal communication played a role in the campaign's effectiveness, and if so, how.
- *Campaign impact.* Clearly, the goals of a campaign are to change the audience's knowledge level, attitude, and behavior, so it is critical to measure changes in these variables. Assessing any other variables that comprise the theory selected to guide the campaign development also is recommended.

A good way to approach evaluation is to consider each objective separately. The Don't Be That Guy Alcohol Reduction Education Campaign used this approach in its evaluation. Its first objective was to raise awareness for the That Guy campaign and the negative effects of excessive alcohol consumption. Process research provided the campaign evaluators with some initial information. For example, it was noted that the www.ThatGuy.com website recorded 235,082 different visitors who spent an average of six minutes visiting the site and viewed a total of 954,798 pages. The That Guy MySpace profile registered 1,800 friends, over 167,750 promotional materials were distributed, and specific counts were obtained for how many times the video PSA ran in movie theaters, the radio spots were aired, and the streaming website ads were run. This information provided evaluation of the campaign exposure, but outcome research was needed to demonstrate campaign impact.

The DOD conducted two types of outcome research to assess the first objective: focus groups and a web survey. The focus groups allowed the evaluators to determine several important evaluation outcomes. First, it was found that there was a high level of awareness of the campaign among the target population. Focus group participants not only knew about the campaign, but indicated that the That Guy messages were relevant and real. Second, evaluators were able to determine that the communication vehicles they selected were effectively delivering their messages. Third, the focus group participants indicated that the campaign was helping service members be more cautious regarding what they do when they drink. While the focus groups provided evaluators with valuable information about campaign effectiveness, another important component of the evaluation was a web survey featured on www.ThatGuy.com that collected additional data. The survey indicated that 37 percent of those who visited the site and viewed campaign messages were likely to think twice about their actions so they don't become That Guy, thus demonstrating an impact on behavioral intentions. The respondents also provided information indicating that the campaign's strategy of using humor and entertainment to reach the audience was working. Finally, many of the survey respondents reported that they visited the website at a friend's recommendation, which showed that interpersonal communication was contributing to the success of the campaign by making it viral.

The second objective of the campaign was to motivate 50 military installations to implement the campaign in the first year of the program while leveraging results to set the stage for increasing engagement among additional installations the following year. Process research indicated that by the end of the first year, 145 military installations were engaged in the campaign, well over the stated objective. At the same time, 900 military sponsors in more than 40 states, the District of Columbia, and 9 foreign countries also were promoting the That Guy campaign, so that the increased engagement was achieved within the first year of the campaign. Building on the campaign's first-year success, the DOD created and aired a suite of six additional public service announcements on American Forces Network, generating a total of nearly 120 pro bono airings per week on three different stations. Their success also allowed them to formalize partnerships with many different military organizations as the campaign grew even larger.

Only by collecting all of the evaluation research, both process and outcome, and both quantitative and qualitative, could the DOD reach the conclusion that the That Guy campaign had met both of the specified objectives, and therefore, was successful. The evaluation research also allowed communicators to revisit the theory they selected at the beginning of their campaign process to determine if progress had been made. Based on the information obtained, many members of the target audience clearly had moved from the precontemplation stage of the TTM into other stages. While many of the enlisted men had moved to contemplation or preparation, some had progressed to action and maintenance stages. Revisiting theory is another important component of the evaluation process that allows the campaign planners to assess their success.

When evaluation shows that campaigns have been successful in achieving their objectives, everyone involved is pleased. But what happens when evaluation does not demonstrate success? Most importantly, if this happens, remember not to panic. This outcome should be used as a learning opportunity to discern which parts of the campaign process need more attention the next time. Questions to be asked include: Was more research needed to gain a more comprehensive picture before moving to the action phase? Was the theory selected appropriate for guiding campaign development or might a different theory be better? Were the goals and objectives reasonable and achievable? Did we have enough information about the target audience? Were the strategies and tactics effective in achieving campaign goals? Were the time and budget allocations sufficient for what we were trying to accomplish? Was the right message used in the campaign? Did our evaluation assess all important aspects of the campaign? Answers to these questions will allow planners to be better prepared for the next adventure in public information campaigns.

Chapter Summary

Public information campaigns involve detailed planning, creative execution, and careful evaluation. Following the RACE model for campaign planning will result in campaigns that effectively deliver the desired message to the appropriate target audience. Always begin with *research* that describes the situation and the target audience, and select a theory that will help guide your campaign planning. Take *action* by setting clear goals and objectives, creating an audience profile, developing specific strategies and tactics, and constructing guidelines for timeline and budget. Develop *communication* that is appropriate for the target audience and clearly expresses the messages of the campaign. Finally, conduct a thorough *evaluation* to determine the success of the campaign. Following these steps, your campaign may be the next memorable slogan to get stuck in people's heads and produce the behavior change you want to see. Please allow us to conclude this chapter with our best wishes for success in your next public information campaign!

Endnotes

1. Don't Be That Guy Alcohol Reduction Education Campaign, Public Relations Society of America, 2008. http://www.prsa.org/awards/search?pg=1&saYear=2008& sakeyword=6BE-0813C03&saCategory=&saIndustry=Government+-+Public+ Affairs&saOutcome=

2. Doran, G. T., "There's a S.M.A.R.T. Way to Write Management Goals and Objectives," *Management Review* 70, no. (1981): 35–36.
3. Klingemann, H. D., and A. Römmele, eds., *Public Information Campaigns and Opinion Research: A Handbook for the Student and Practitioner* (Thousand Oaks, CA: Sage, 2002).
4. Marston, J. E., *The Nature of Public Relations* (New York: McGraw-Hill, 1963).
5. Rice, R. E., and C. K. Atkins, eds., *Public Communication Campaigns*, 3rd ed. (Thousand Oaks, CA: Sage, 2001).
6. Wilcox, D. L., and G. T. Cameron, *Public Relations: Strategies and Tactics*, 9th ed. (Boston: Allyn & Bacon, 2008).

References

Ajzen, I., and Fishbein, M. (1973). Attitudinal and normative variables as predictors of specific behaviors. *Journal of Personality and Psychology, 27,* 41–57.

Becker, M. H., ed. (1974). The health belief model and personal health behavior. *Health Education Monographs, 2,* 324–473.

Blumler J.G. and Katz, E. (1974). *The uses of mass communications: Current perspectives on gratifications research.* Beverly Hills, CA: Sage.

Festinger, L. (1957). *A theory of cognitive dissonance.* Stanford, CA: Stanford University Press.

Fishbein, M. (1963). An investigation of relationships between beliefs about an object and the attitude toward that object. *Human Relations, 16,* 233–240.

Heider, F. (1958). *The psychology of interpersonal relations.* New York: John Wiley & Sons.

Hovland, C.I., Janis, I.L., and Kelley, H.H. (1953). *Communication and persuasion.* New Haven, CT: Yale University Press.

Petty, R.E., and Cacioppo, J.T. (1986). *Communication and persuasion: Central and peripheral routes to attitude change.* New York: Springer-Verlag.

Prochaska, J. Q, and DiClemente, C. C. (1984). *The transtheoretical approach: Crossing traditional boundaries of change.* Homewood, IL: Dorsey Press.

Rogers, E.M. (1995). *Diffusion of innovations.* New York: The Free Press.

Witte, K. (1992). Putting the fear back into fear appeals: The extended parallel process model. *Communication Monographs, 59,* 329–349.

Chapter 6

Crisis Public Relations for Government Communicators

Brooke Fisher Liu and Abbey Blake Levenshus

Contents

Financial crisis. Natural disaster. Sex scandal. Technology snafu. Abuse of power. Misuse of funds. Terrorist attack. Flu pandemic. Crisis can strike any organization, but the stakes are especially high for governments and their public relations personnel because the government is charged with ensuring public health and safety. Lives and livelihoods can be at risk when crises occur, and government communicators often find themselves on the frontlines of intense media and citizen scrutiny during and after a crisis. With all eyes on the government, government communicators can help reduce uncertainty, lower residents' risks, and provide critical lifesaving information. Of course, it is never that simple.

Crises are complex, often unpredictable and unique. However, that does not let government communicators off the hook for planning and strategically responding to crises. The moment a crisis starts is not the first time to think about which media contacts to prioritize and how to oversee a coordinated response. Communication takes place at every level and stage of a crisis. This chapter first defines crisis and offers examples of types of crises facing government public relations staff. It then offers a glimpse of the current state of government crisis communication, citizen preparedness, and the case for government crisis communication preparation. The chapter then walks government communicators through the three phases of a crisis: (1) precrisis, (2) response, and (3) recovery. Finally, the chapter addresses trends and future directions for government crisis communication.

While this chapter is not a step-by-step how-to guide, it does provide an overview of government crisis communication today and helpful tools such as a crisis communication plan checklist and resources to find more particular information. This chapter gives government communicators the tools to make the case for strategic crisis planning *before* the crisis hits, the case for a proactive, unified voice *during* the crisis, and the case for a detailed review and organizational learning *after* the storm has passed. Before discussing the crisis phases, we provide common terms used for managing crises.

Crisis Terms and Types

Disasters, emergencies, and crises. This chapter treats the terms *disasters, emergencies,* and *crises* as interchangeable. Traditionally *disasters and emergencies* refer to catastrophic events primarily caused by extreme weather conditions such as hurricanes and *crises* refer to human-caused catastrophic events such as terrorism. In practice, this distinction often is artificial. Consider Hurricane Katrina in 2005. The hurricane itself was *natural*, but human errors aggravated the hurricane's effects. For example, New Orleans did not have an adequate levee system to prevent flood surges. Also, nearly one-third of the Louisiana National Guard was deployed in Iraq and consequently not able to help with the recovery.[1] Therefore, in this chapter we will use the terms *crisis* and *crises* to refer to all catastrophic events government communicators are responsible for managing.

To best manage crises, government communicators must identify an emerging crisis as early as possible. The five common characteristics of all crises help government communicators accomplish this goal: (1) crises involve the destruction of property, injury, loss of life, and/or reputation damage; (2) crises adversely affect a large number of people; (3) crises have identifiable beginnings and endings; (4) crises are relatively sudden; and (5) crises receive extensive media coverage and public attention.[2] These characteristics can help government communicators determine when an issue or risk becomes a crisis and thus requires activation of a crisis communication plan. An issue is a "contestable point, a difference of opinion regarding fact, value, or policy, the resolution of which has consequences for the organization's strategic plan and future success or failure."[3] An issue becomes a crisis when "an event that creates an issue, keeps it alive, or gives it strength."[4] A risk is a weakness that could develop into an issue or crisis, such as being located in a region prone to severe weather or diseases or having a service delivery process that is prone to breakdowns (e.g., airport passenger screening).[5] A quick test to determine when an issue or risk becomes a crisis is that key stakeholders such as citizens, media, and governmental partners perceive that a crisis is occurring. Therefore, in order to determine when an issue or risk becomes a crisis, government communicators must engage in constant issue monitoring and crisis preparation, which we discuss later.

Common crisis types. While each crisis is unique, crises can be categorized by type. Categories help communicators think through the types of crises their organizations are most likely to face. Thinking through crisis types can also help avoid, plan for, and respond to crises.

Government or public affairs crises mostly fall under three categories: systemic, adversarial, and image.[6] *Systemic crises* impact the overall organization's operations. For example, the World Health Organization declared the H1N1 influenza virus a global pandemic in June 2009, setting the stage for a potential systemic crisis for the U.S. government if it could not secure enough vaccinations for at-risk Americans. Systemic crises often occur outside the control of government and many times are difficult to predict.

Adversarial crises involve opposition to an organization. External opponents contest or attack some aspect of an organization (e.g., message, decision, position, or vote). For example, several European nations have accused the World Health Organization (WHO) of exaggerating the threat that H1N1 flu posed in order to benefit pharmaceutical companies. The WHO immediately began defending itself against these attacks. If not handled properly and quickly, the WHO could have experienced an adversarial crisis.

Image/reputation crises can raise doubts about the ethics, judgment, or credibility of an organization, often including its leaders. Some experts call these situations crises of public perception.[7] For example, if the public perceives that the WHO artificially incited fear over the H1N1 virus, the WHO could also find itself in the middle of an image crisis. Public perception, image, or reputation crises focus negative attention on an organization and can arise from negative media stories, blog posts, or even malicious rumors (spread online or offline). Whether these rumors or stories are true, false, or somewhere in between, they can have debilitating consequences for governments and their leaders.

Of course, crises are complex and can fall under more than one category at once or during the lifecycle of the crisis. For example, H1N1 may have started as a systemic crisis, but if a state health department had failed to appropriately administer vaccines to at-risk groups, the systemic crisis may have evolved into an image crisis for that state's health department and government leaders.

Other crisis communication experts point to various other crisis types common to governments. These include terrorist attacks (domestic or foreign), natural disasters, economic crises, and transportation crises. Evidence shows that most organizations will experience some sort of crisis. Having a general understanding of the different types of crises helps government communicators anticipate and plan for the types of crises that may affect their organizations. We now make the case for why government organizations should focus on crisis management. Subsequently, we discuss communicators' roles in preparing for, responding to, and recovering from crises. The chapter concludes with remarks about the future of government crisis management.

Why Focus on Crisis Management?

The current challenges and opportunities facing government public relations staff during a crisis are greater than ever before. Government communicators today face heightened citizen and media scrutiny. A survey of 976 communicators found that government communicators were more likely than corporate communicators to negatively evaluate media coverage of their organizations.[8] In addition to making crises more complex, technology has also given government crises a global audience. While traditional print and broadcast news media sources still demand communicators' time and attention, new technologies are also playing an increased role in crises. E-mail, blogs, websites, text messaging, and technologies like Twitter and Facebook are propelling rumors and information (whether true or not) farther, more quickly, and more persistently than in previous years. New media allow organizations' stakeholders to be more involved and communicative in the wake of a crisis.

While the challenges facing governments during crises may be growing, so are the opportunities that crises present governments and their communicators. New media are empowering organizations to bypass traditional media in order to tell their own side of the story and communicate directly with stakeholders during a crisis. Excellent crisis communications can help avert a crisis, hasten the end to a crisis, and help an organization recover more quickly and learn more from a crisis.

Some communicators may argue that because communicators can never fully anticipate a crisis, there is no point in planning for one. While communicators may not be able to foresee every aspect of a crisis, they can often predict the types of crises their organizations will face. For example, a local health department can predict that it might be impacted by high rates of H1N1 infection. A state transportation agency can imagine a transportation-related disaster like a metrorail crash or mudslides across a highway. The federal Department of Homeland Security can prepare for a potential terrorist attack.

In addition to thinking through the type of crisis, organization leaders can map out the building blocks of crisis response and management. Crisis management "seeks to prevent or lessen the negative outcomes of a crisis and thereby protect the organization, stakeholders, and industry from harm."[9] Thus, government communicators' idealistic goal is to prevent crises from occurring, while recognizing that it is inevitable that crises will occur. Realistically, then, government communicators can do the following:

- Identify and mitigate any risks and/or issues that could become crises
- Increase citizens' resiliency by helping them prepare for crises
- Establish a clear chain of command by assigning responsibilities for crisis planning, response, and recovery before crises occur
- Identify information dissemination strategies and processes before crises occur
- Build relationships with key partners before crises occur
- Develop clear benchmarks for evaluating crisis responses to ensure organizational learning

To meet these objectives, government communicators typically take an all-hazards approach to crisis management by identifying common preparation, response, and recovery protocols for all crisis types. This approach streamlines resources while recognizing that not all governments experience the same crises. To effectively manage crises, government communicators engage in planning, response, and recovery efforts. The benefits of excellent crisis public relations are most visible during the crisis response phase when there are high levels of stakeholder scrutiny. Nevertheless, excellent crisis managers spend more time planning for crises rather than responding to crises. In addition, these excellent crisis mangers drive postcrisis recovery efforts, emphasizing renewal and lessons learned. Finally, excellent crisis managers keep in mind key communication challenges especially prevalent in the government sector for all three crisis phrases: limited budgets for communication, high demand for information from citizens and mass media, speaking with one voice while coordinating intergovernmental crisis responses, and legal frameworks that limit how and when information can be disseminated.

Strategic crisis management provides many benefits to organizations. Having basics in place before a disaster (and adrenaline) strikes saves time when each minute is critical. Studies have shown that lack of crisis management planning can extend and worsen a crisis and its aftermath.[10] Some organizations reported that experiencing a crisis provided increased motivation and learning opportunities for the importance of being prepared for a crisis.[11]

Due to the increased media and public scrutiny and heightened need to communicate during a crisis, public relations practitioners can play a lead role in successfully mitigating and recovering from a crisis. Only 59 percent of government communicators reported having a seat at the management table in a recent national survey.[12] Only 36 percent of government communicators reported having a management title. For those communicators and public relations personnel looking to increase their role's recognized value within an organization, crises can spotlight the critical need for a strong communication and public relations function.[13]

Proper planning that either limits or successfully navigates a crisis can demonstrate to management the public relations function's excellence. On the contrary, missing or mishandling a crisis can quickly destroy the good works and good reputation of any government official, agency, department, representative, or body. One only needs to think about the many otherwise-respected and trusted persons who have not survived a crisis.

It can be challenging to convince the powers that be (or in some cases the principal) that crisis planning is worth the resources and time. Government communicators should come to the conversation armed with examples of the many types of crises that can affect and have affected similar organizations. Avoid examples of sex scandals and abuses of power that leaders or politicians might think could never happen to them. Stick with less personal, fathomable examples. For example, if you are trying to convince your local city manager to invest in a crisis management team, plan, and training, research weather-related or financial crises that have hit similar cities in the last year. Make a list and show how excellent planning helped some cities navigate these difficult situations and how poorly prepared government staff may have bungled their response efforts. The good news is that government organizations, particularly emergency management departments and agencies, tend to be better prepared for crises than private organizations are. The next section explores that preparation and planning in more detail.

Preparing for Crises

As stated previously, government public relations staff must constantly scan their environments in order to identify and monitor issues that could pose threats to their organization. As discussed earlier, crisis management is more than handling a crisis that has already erupted. Crisis management should also include strategic precrisis work. This precrisis work has three main goals.[14] The first goal is to lower the likelihood and frequency of crises. The second goal is to contain or limit harm from a crisis. The final goal is to help the organization learn from a crisis. This section provides an overview of crisis preparation activities. For a detailed example of a crisis preparation approach, see FEMA's Emergency Management Guide for Business and Industry (http://www.fema.gov/business/guide/index.shtm).

Environmental scanning and issues management. As discussed earlier, issues can turn into crises that demand immediate and intense attention. Environmental scanning can help reduce the likelihood of crises by identifying risks and issues and detecting the warning signs that a crisis is possible or imminent. Environmental scanning can be as simple as conducting Google searches of blogs and media reports. It is important to also conduct environmental scanning within your organization. Scanning internal feedback and correspondence from employees and related government entities can catch internal issues before they leak out into the media and public forums. Once an issue is discovered, government public relations staff can develop a strategy to manage that issue and hopefully successfully resolve or prevent it from escalating. For example, a mayor's staff may follow local blogs and notice a slight increase in postings criticizing increased crime in the area and faulting a lack of police presence. At this point, the mayor's public relations director may work with the mayor's staff and the police chief to address the situation in a coordinated fashion by communicating what police and the mayor are doing to address the situation. By being proactive and engaging bloggers and key community members in the effort, the mayor's office can demonstrate its commitment to the community and its safety. Without the early scanning, the mayor's office may have first heard about community complaints when they hit mass media sources or when community members organize in some way against the mayor's office. In addition to carefully and consistently managing issues, government public relations staff can help prevent and prepare for crises by managing relationships with key stakeholders.

Relationship management. Research indicates that prior reputations affect how people assign responsibility for a crisis.[15] If people have already developed negative feelings about your government organization prior to a crisis, chances are they will find your organization more responsible for a crisis than if they had positive feelings about you before the crisis. However, government communicators who focus on engaging their stakeholders before a crisis should not rely on a "halo effect" from a positive reputation to protect their organization from reputational damage during and after a crisis.[16] Government entities will likely still lose some reputational capital if held responsible for a crisis. That makes it even more important to develop and maintain strong relationships with stakeholders in order to bank more reputational capital should some be lost during a crisis.

There are many other good reasons to engage with your publics. Strong relationships and two-way communication channels with publics can also help alert government public relations staff to potential conflicts before they become full-blown crises. By having two-way communication channels in place to both send and receive messages and feedback from publics, government communicators can also communicate more quickly with affected and interested residents should a crisis occur.

Crisis management team. In addition to a crisis management plan, best practice recommends that organizations establish crisis management teams (CMTs). When establishing a CMT, it is important to include cross-functional specialists who can think across various roles and responsibilities. Teams should have diverse representation that matches the diversity of the publics that the government entity communicates with. It is a good idea to include alternative members who can join the team if the crisis keeps other members from being able to participate. A unified command structure can streamline a crisis response across different departments, agencies, or levels of government.

CMTs take different forms. You might have traditional teams that meet in person. Virtual teams may never be in the same place and coordinate using newer technologies like Skype, or virtual online meeting software. Partially distributed teams involve two or more teams located in geographically different places that also come together to form a single virtual team. For example a cyber attack might pose a crisis that needs the crisis response from two country's governments that might form a partially distributed CMT to address a technology crisis that spans geographical borders.

Crisis management teams should include members of an organization's core functions. In addition to communication functions like public relations, marketing, and media relations, other common functions represented include leadership (e.g., chief of staff, secretary, executive director), legal, IT, security, operations, and finance and budgeting. The team's membership should reflect the nature or type of crisis for which you are planning or to which you are responding. For example, if you are determining team members for a state-level health-related crisis, you would want to include a member of the state's department of health. This state health department may not, however, need a representative on a team dealing with an abuse-of-power scandal.

Fill the team with diverse voices and opinions that reflect the diversity of your audiences. These members will bring different perspectives and concerns to the planning table. Diversity can improve precrisis messaging (described later), which will benefit diverse audiences. A recent study found that citizens are more likely to feel prepared to respond to a crisis if they can access information that contains messages sensitive to them and their needs from sources similar to them.[17]

CMTs have many responsibilities. Teams are tasked with responding to crises and overseeing the decision-making process throughout the response and recovery. This includes collecting information about the crisis and determining its cause. It also involves monitoring publics' needs and responses to the crisis and disseminating important information to the prioritized stakeholders. All of those responsibilities relate to a crisis that is already taking place, but one of the team's most common and important tasks is designing, testing, and modifying a crisis management plan (see Table 6.1). In an ideal world, that planning would take place prior to a crisis.

Crisis management plan. The most commonly recommended strategy for precrisis management includes developing and maintaining crisis management plans (CMPs). CMPs can serve several purposes for the government. Most importantly, CMPs can reduce risk and help government entities respond to a crisis more quickly, efficiently, and with fewer mistakes and oversights. In doing so, CMPs can improve the organization's ability to recover from a crisis. CMPs can fulfill the government's moral and ethical responsibility to its employees and the people it represents. CMPs can oversee compliance with legal and regulatory requirements. They can also reduce the overall negative legal and public relations exposure for the government during a crisis. By planning well for a crisis and putting plans in place to mitigate any risk or crisis, the government communicates concern and responsibility to the people it serves.

Crisis management plans can include several components. The plan should include a risk assessment conducted by the crisis management team (or in some cases an outside consultant). The plan should also include a list of the crisis management

Table 6.1   Creating the Crisis Management Plan

Crisis Management Plan Components
• Risk assessment/inventory
• List of crisis management team(s) members and contact information
• List of key stakeholders and their contact information (e.g., employees, other government entities, resident groups)
• Designated emergency operations center/crisis command center (and back-up locations)
• Crisis communication plan (including media and stakeholder contact information, official spokespeople authorized to speak with media, predrafted templates, dark sites, etc.)
• Authority/authorization structure outlining streamlined decision-making process
• Business resumption plan (e.g., when to reinstate officially sponsored social events)
• Training dates and locations
• Trigger dates to review and refresh plan and components (e.g., risk assessment)

Note: For more information, see W. Timothy Coombs, *Ongoing Crisis Communication: Planning, Managing, and Responding*, 3rd Edition (Thousand Oaks, CA: Sage, 2012), chapters 5 and 6. [18]

team members and their contact information. In some cases, plans might include sample teams designed based on probable or possible crisis type. Some crisis management plans set up an emergency operations center or a crisis command center. This technique might help when various government agencies or levels need to coordinate response efforts. In some cases, a business resumption plan also can help provide guidance and structure for returning to normal governance.

Crisis communication plan. A crisis management plan should also contain a *crisis communication plan* that identifies key stakeholders (e.g., media, employees, and other government agency representatives) and their contact information for crisis communicators to use during a crisis. These stakeholders will vary depending on crisis type. In addition to media contact information, the plan can also include predrafted templates for news releases, messages from leadership and the organization, and other written materials that can be filled in with crisis-specific information. When public relations staff members prepare these materials in advance, they will have more time in a crisis to add in details as they arise and get quicker approval from the necessary players (legal, other departments, etc.).

Given the heightened need to work with the media and communicate during a crisis, a crisis communication plan should also spell out who in the organization is authorized to speak to the media. Deciding on official spokespeople to work with the media and represent the government's voice is particularly important. The plan should also focus on spokesperson training so that the appointed employees can practice addressing official media and working with other communicators who are coordinating messages across various media (websites, blogs, Twitter, Facebook, mobile phone text messaging, etc.). Mock press conferences and interviews can help spotlight gaps in training and knowledge before they show up in primetime. Other training options are discussed later. As a warning, organizations should not rely on spokespeople alone to get through to media during a crisis. One recent study found that traditional media were not using quotes from organizational representatives and spokespeople but instead relying on other sources.[19]

A crisis communication plan might also include developing a "dark site." Dark sites are websites or web pages that organizations have developed and created but are offline until a crisis strikes and the organization can bring the site online. These sites can be external or internal (meant for employees or other stakeholders with access). Research has demonstrated the importance of having a strong web presence during a crisis and has offered best practices for using the Internet during a crisis:[20]

- Make available online all of the organization's media relations materials (press conference transcripts, statements, news releases, etc.).
- Use specifics and direct quotes (that media can pull) from leadership in order to tell your side of the story.
- Harness the interactive features of the Internet to engage publics in the online content about the crisis.
- Provide different pages or sites designed to meet information needs and interests of particular stakeholders.
- Include hyperlinks and information about various government and nongovernment entities related to the crisis.

A recent study of public health agencies' press releases about avian flu resulted in several additional suggestions for future precrisis messaging and crisis responses:[21]

- Inform the public about the government's ability to effectively handle the situation in order to inspire public confidence in government recommendations and reduce hysteria.
- Build and establish communication channels to all publics—not just Internet-accessible ones.
- Localize a threat so that audiences understand its implications and what they should do to lessen their risks.
- Use consistent terminology to frame a threat (e.g., bird flu, avian flu, pandemic flu).

Of course, plans are only helpful if they are flexible enough to adjust to a particular crisis and are updated on a regular basis (e.g., annually). Crisis management team members must also be trained and prepared to carry out the plan.

Crisis training. Considering that 80 percent of crisis managers learn on the job, training could go a long way to helping crisis managers learn when mistakes are not in real time generating real consequences.[22] Once a CMP is in place, the crisis management team and other employees should be trained to execute the plan. Training engages employees in the crisis preparation process and helps demonstrate the possibility of crises and their potential consequences. Engaging employees in crisis training also gives them the opportunity to share feedback about the plan. By making crisis preparation more top-of-mind, employees may be more likely to identify and communicate issues and risks to organizational leaders before they turn into crises. Several training options exist (see Table 6.2).

Regardless of the types and combinations of training that an organization chooses, government communicators can help facilitate a posttraining debriefing. Debriefing allows training participants to analyze strengths and weaknesses of the plan and the response. Communicators then recommend additional training and changes to the plan.

Training should be ongoing so that the team and the plan are current and ready. Therefore, a crisis management plan should include a calendar with training and rehearsal or simulation dates to test the plan and update it accordingly. Training dates can also trigger an update of the risk assessment included in the plan in order to make sure it is current with the government's operating environment. Too much training on too much content in one sitting can impede learning. Break up the training into manageable chunks with application opportunities to reinforce learning.

Responding to Crises

The crisis response phase typically is the shortest of the three crisis phases, but also the most intense given high levels of media and citizen attention. Communicators' initial crisis responses are critical because these responses set the tone for the media coverage and thus public understanding of what occurred and why. Also, when an organization is the first to release accurate crisis information, citizens assign higher levels of credibility to that organization.[23] To help craft crisis response messages, communicators can consider how media are most likely to frame a crisis. For all crises, media are most interested in assigning responsibility. Media also frequently focus on crisis severity, economic consequences, who is responding to the crisis, conflict among those responding, emerging heroes, victims, and making comparisons to previous crises (see Table 6.3).[24] Knowing how media are most likely to frame a crisis helps communicators proactively counter these frames in their crisis messaging.

Table 6.2 Training Examples

Training Option	Description	Advantages	Disadvantages
Orientation/ seminar	Facilitated session walking through CMP, roles, and responsibilities, with key personnel either individually or in groups (e.g., spokesperson training, all-employee training)	Involves less planning and complexity than other options; flexible structure adapted to organization culture and needs; can be done online or face to face	May be difficult to hold attention; hands-off approach may not identify gaps in plan/approach
Tabletop exercise	Using CMP, key personnel talk through a step-by-step response to a fictitious emergency situation	Less planning and cost to organization than simulation; identifies gaps/issues with CMP; can be conducted online or offline; can be facilitated by internal or external facilitator	Without time constraints and pressure of actual (or simulated) crisis, response may be unrealistic and gaps in CMP overlooked
Drill/ rehearsal	Organization members practice some or all of the CMP (e.g., evacuate a building, conduct mock press conference)	Continuing drills can hone particular parts of a plan and keep them fresh in participants' minds; could be easier, less complex than a full simulation	Could become routine, disconnected from larger complexities of crisis situations
Simulation	Simulated crisis tests organization's CMP and team in real time, often with complexities and complicating factors added throughout exercise	Provides functional, hands-on training; time constraints help prepare for more realistic, high-stress environment; can be used to test coordination with additional organizations	Higher planning cost and complexity

Note: For more information, see W. Timothy Coombs, *Ongoing Crisis Communication: Planning, Managing, and Responding, 3rd Edition* (Thousand Oaks, CA: Sage, 2012), chapter 5 and FEMA National Preparedness Directorate's online training resources, available at http://training.fema.gov

Table 6.3   How Media Frame Crises

Frame	Description	Example
Anniversary/ Memorial	Portrays crisis planning, response, and/or recovery by discussing an anniversary of a major crisis or referencing a major crisis	Referring to the September 11, 2001 terrorist attack when discussing other large-scale terrorist actions
Collaboration	Portrays crisis planning, response, and/or recovery by emphasizing coordination among governmental and nongovernmental groups	Discussing how well national governments work with pharmaceutical companies to meet world demand for flu vaccines during a pandemic
Crisis severity	Portrays crisis planning, response, and/or recovery by emphasizing potential or actual damage caused by a crisis	Citing public opinion poll indicating that only 12% of citizens believe a government agency handled a crisis well
Conflict	Portrays crisis planning, response, and/or recovery by emphasizing disputes or tension between those identified as responsible for a crisis	Reporting that local government is blaming federal government for not providing enough resources to plan for a crisis
Economic consequences	Portrays crisis planning, response, and/or recovery by emphasizing outcomes related to the economy (positive or negative)	Claiming more than $100 billion lost from export ban after product-recall crisis
Emerging heroes	Portrays crisis planning, response, and/or recovery by emphasizing specific individuals and/or organizations who managed a crisis well	Reporting on government executive who secured large amount of funding to help citizens better recover from a crisis
Victims	Portrays crisis planning, response, and/or recovery by focusing on stories about individuals or communities negatively affected by a crisis	Drawing attention to unemployed mother living in temporary housing three years after a weather-related crisis destroyed her home

When setting message strategy, communicators' primary goals are to (1) resolve the crisis and (2) mitigate any reputational and relational damage caused. To best resolve the crisis, communicators work with the crisis management team to protect stakeholders from harm. They do this by providing instructing and adapting information.[25] *Instructing information* notifies citizens about what actions they should take to protect themselves from any physical threats associated with crises (e.g., where to seek shelter and disease prevention behaviors). Some crises, such as scandals, do not require instructing information, but for crises where physical threats are likely, communicators must inform citizens on how to protect themselves. *Adapting information* is required for all crisis types. Through adapting information, organizations (1) express concern for citizens affected by the crisis and (2) inform citizens how organizations will prevent similar crises in the future. For example, government communicators could acknowledge that a fiscal mismanagement crisis wasted taxpayers' money and report how the system will be changed to prevent mismanagement in the future. Research confirms that organizations' postcrisis relationships are stronger when they express concern during crises.[26]

After government communicators provide instructing information (when necessary) and adapting information, they attempt to mitigate any reputational and relationship damage. *Reputational damage* is how crises negatively impact stakeholders' opinions of organizations and individuals responding to crises. *Relational damage* is how crises negatively impact stakeholders' long-term relationships with organizations or individuals responding to crises. In order to mitigate reputational and relational damage, communicators should focus on being transparent and consistent in their crisis messaging.

Transparency means that communicators should be as honest as possible about why the crisis occurred and how the organization is responding. Transparency recognizes that sometimes legal constraints such as classified information and ongoing investigations prevent communicators from knowing or publicly revealing all known facts about crises. Taking these potential constraints into consideration, communicators should provide all possible verified information shortly after crises occur. Being transparent during crises is especially critical given that citizens and media are skeptical of government communication during routine times. This skepticism intensifies during a crisis, making the potential fallout more severe for communication that is perceived as not fully honest. Part of transparency is acknowledging your role in a crisis. A study of governments' responses to hurricanes Katrina and Rita found that government leaders were more interested in pointing fingers at one another and avoiding blame than admitting their own shortfalls in the responses to the hurricanes.[27] Admitting mistakes and working with other government bodies to unify and coordinate responses would be more effective.

In addition to transparency, an open, empathetic communication style can nurture public trust and acceptance of government messages, particularly when government officials are trying to persuade publics to take positive action or reduce harmful actions.[28] Government communicators and their scientific experts face a suspicious, cynical audience that has grown weary of political infighting and a perceived lack of scientific reasoning in decision making. Audiences now have access to multiple sources of information and no longer have to rely only on government information. In this challenging environment, it is important that governments work to communicate trust and credibility by communicating empathy, caring, competence, expertise, honesty, openness, and dedication and commitment.[29]

Consistency requires that crisis spokespeople communicate with one voice using the same message points. This does not necessarily mean that there should be only one spokesperson, which often is not possible in the changing media land-scape (as discussed at the end of this chapter). Communicating with transparency and consistency helps mitigate reputational and relational damage caused by cri-ses, going a long way toward improving trust in government communication and facilitating postcrisis learning and renewal. Keeping these baseline requirements in mind, we now discuss how communicators select the most appropriate crisis response strategies.

The first step to determine which crisis response strategies are most appropriate is to consider the crisis type, crisis history, and prior reputation.[30] We already discussed the different crisis types that government communicators frequently face. Categorizing the crisis type helps organizations determine their level of responsibil-ity for a crisis, which determines which strategies are viable options. Crisis history is whether the organization has experienced similar crises in the past. If the answer is yes, stakeholders will be less forgiving and the threat to long-term stakeholder rela-tionships is higher. The selected response strategies must reflect this reality. Prior reputation is how key stakeholders view organizations before crises occur. If orga-nizations have negative prior reputations, long-term reputational damage is more likely. The selected response strategies must also reflect this reality. While there is no specific roadmap directly linking crisis type, history, and prior reputation to the best response options, considering these factors helps government communicators predict which strategies will be most effective. For example, if an organization is responsible for a preventable crisis, such as a hiring scandal, then employing denial will not be effective from a communication perspective (though it may be effective from a legal perspective).

There are four broad categories of crisis response strategies: deny, diminish, rebuild, and reinforce (see Table 6.4). The *deny* category includes four strategies: attack the accuser, denial, scapegoat, and ignore.[31] Deny strategies are most appropriate for responding to rumors and unwarranted challenges. Government communicators use an *attack the accuser* approach to confront a person or group that claims a crisis is occurring, but the communicators do not think a crisis is occurring. For example, a government executive makes an off-color remark and a communicator states that a person or group is overstating the remark's severity and implications. Government communicators use denial to state that a crisis does not exist. For example, media claim a depression is occurring, but the government does not think the economy is in such a poor state. Government communicators use

Table 6.4 Crisis Response Strategies

Category	Strategy	Description	Example
Deny	Attack the accuser	Confront a person/group that claims a crisis is occurring when communicators do not think a crisis is occurring	A government executive makes an off-color remark and a communicator states that a person or group is overstating the remark's severity and implications
	Denial	State that a crisis does not exist	Media claim a depression is occurring, but the government does not think the economy is in such poor state
	Scapegoating	State that someone else is responsible for a crisis	Local government executive claims that national government is primarily responsible for a poor hurricane response
	Ignoring	Implicitly state that a crisis does not exist by entirely disregarding the crisis	Making no comment about a sex scandal
Diminish	Excusing	Minimizing organization's responsibility for a crisis	Devastation from a tsunami was so extreme that the government could not immediately respond to all the citizens' needs
	Justification	Minimize perceived damage caused by a crisis	An agency disrupts hundreds of terrorist plots a year. Thus, it is regrettable though not surprising that some terrorist plots are near misses

Table 6.4   (Continued) Crisis Response Strategies

Category	Strategy	Description	Example
	Separation	Disconnect organization as a whole from specific employees responsible for a crisis	Rogue police officer is responsible for racial profiling rather than an entire police department
Rebuild	Compensation	Financially support crisis victims	Providing small businesses emergency loans after a severe weather incident
	Apology	Express regret for a crisis	Apologizing for not preventing a scandal from occurring
	Corrective action	Identify root causes of the crisis that will be changed to avoid similar crises in the future	Changing policies for hiring military contractors after these contractors mismanage a mission abroad
	Transcendence	Shift the focus away from the immediate crisis to a larger concern or issue	Focusing on combating terrorism globally rather than why a country failed to prevent a terrorist attack
Reinforce	Reminding	Highlight their employers' past good deeds	Useful programs and services that agencies regularly provide citizens
	Ingratiation	Praise stakeholders	Thanking media for helping disseminate important crisis recovery information to citizens such as donation opportunities

(Continued)

Table 6.4 (Continued) Crisis Response Strategies

Category	Strategy	Description	Example
	Victimage	State that organization is the victim, rather than the perpetrator, of a crisis	Government is the victim of a catastrophic storm rather than responsible for inadequate planning
	Endorsement	Identify third-party support for organization's crisis response	International partners that help respond to a large-scale crisis

scapegoating to state that someone else is responsible for a crisis. For example, a local government executive claims that a national government is primarily responsible for a poor hurricane response. Government communicators use *ignoring* to implicitly state that a crisis does not exist by entirely disregarding a crisis, for example, making no comment about a sex scandal. This strategy can be dangerous because it allows media and citizens to frame the crisis story, but in some cases it is better not to add fuel to the media fire by commenting.

Diminish strategies are most appropriate for two crisis situations: (1) accidental crises when there is no crisis history and no unfavorable prior reputation and (2) victim crises when there is a crisis history and/or unfavorable prior reputation. Diminish strategies include excusing, justification, and separation.[32] Government communicators use *excusing* by providing a crisis explanation that limits the organization's responsibility. For example, devastation from a tsunami was so extreme that the government could not immediately respond to all the citizens' needs. Government communicators use *justification* to minimize perceived damage caused by a crisis. For example, an agency disrupts hundreds of terrorist plots a year. Thus, it is regrettable though not surprising that some terrorist plots are near misses. Finally, government communicators use *separation* to disconnect their organizations as a whole from specific employees who are responsible for a crisis. For example, a rogue police officer is responsible for racial profiling rather than an entire police department. This strategy is risky because rarely is a single or handful of employees responsible for a crisis. Therefore, separation often comes across as disingenuous and ignoring crises' root causes such as ineffective policies.

Rebuilding strategies are most appropriate for preventable crises. Rebuilding strategies include compensation, apology, corrective action, and transcendence.[33]

Government communicators use *compensation* to financially support crisis victims. For example, governments may provide small businesses with emergency loans after a severe weather incident. Government communicators use *apology* to express regret for a crisis. For example, government leaders may apologize for not preventing a scandal from occurring. Government communicators use *corrective action* to identify crises' root causes that will be changed to avoid similar crises in the future. For example, communicators can announce changing policies for hiring military contractors after these contractors mismanage a mission abroad. Finally, government communicators use *transcendence* to shift the focus away from the immediate crisis to a larger concern or issue. For example, communicators can focus on combating terrorism globally rather than concentrating on why a single country failed to prevent a terrorist attack.

The last category, reinforce strategies, focuses purely on improving the organization's postcrisis image. Consequently, these strategies should only be used in combination with other strategies. When used alone, they imply that the organization is only interested in its image, rather than in stakeholders' well-being. Reinforce strategies include four strategies: reminding, ingratiation, victimage, and endorsement.[34] Government communicators use *reminding* to highlight their employers' past good deeds. For example, communicators can underscore useful programs and services that an agency regularly provides citizens. Government communicators use *ingratiation* to praise stakeholders. For example, communicators can thank media for helping disseminate important crisis recovery information to citizens such as donation opportunities. Government communicators use *victimage* to state that their employer is the victim rather than the perpetrator of a crisis. For example, a spokesperson may report that the government is the victim of a catastrophic storm rather than responsible for inadequate planning. Finally, government communicators use *endorsement* to identify third-party support for their crisis response. For example, communicators can acknowledge international partners that help respond to a large-scale crisis.

In sum, the crisis response phase is characterized by intense scrutiny from stakeholders such as employees, citizens, and media. During this phase, communicators should (1) focus on resolving the crisis and (2) mitigate any reputational and/or relational damage. Communicators ultimately aim to shift stakeholders' scrutiny away from the crisis event and toward organizational learning and renewal. We now discuss the recovery phase during which organizations learn from the crisis through rigorous reflection and evaluation. We then conclude with remarks about the future of government crisis management.

Recovering from a Crisis

How does a government communicator know when the organization has entered the postcrisis phase? One way to tell is that the situation is no longer requiring the full focus and attention of the organization's management and leadership. While some attention may still be needed, managers are able to catch their breath and focus on other business. Once an organization has emerged on the other side of a crisis, the temptation is not to look back and to try to get back to normal. Resumption of business as usual is certainly one aspect of the postcrisis phase. However, crisis managers are tasked with helping an organization do more than merely survive a crisis (though sometimes that is a feat in itself). They want to see an organization recover from a crisis. The recovery period, which can last for years in some cases, has three objectives: learn, improve risk and crisis management, and maintain organizational legitimacy. Government communicators can play a role in achieving all three objectives by fulfilling information commitments made during the crisis, providing follow-up information to key stakeholders, and helping evaluate the organization's crisis management.

Follow-up information and action. During a crisis, organizations often make information or communication commitments to stakeholders. For example, an education department might promise media a list of past school shootings. A local school district might promise a parent group an updated emergency evacuation plan to review. A state transportation department might commit to local representatives an interactive map of freeway overpasses needing repair. These commitments made in times of crisis may not be able to be completed while the organization's attention is focused on the current shooting, evacuation, or emergency freeway repair. The postcrisis recovery phase is when crisis management teams and crisis communicators must make sure that these promises for information and communication are fulfilled. If not, stakeholders will lose more trust in the government's ability to prevent and respond to future emergencies. Similarly, government communicators can also oversee the release to internal and external stakeholders of any information updates about investigations, recovery efforts, or corrective actions.

Evaluation. In order to improve an organization's crisis prevention, mitigation, and response, government communicators should evaluate how well the crisis management team and organizational leaders performed at every aspect of crisis management during an actual or simulated crisis. Evaluation includes determining what worked well in addition to what needed improving. The amount and formality of evaluation depends on the level of crisis and organizational resources. Surveys, focus groups, interviews, and content analyses of media coverage are common evaluation techniques.

In general, organizations are assessing and evaluating four areas: damage (e.g., human, financial, and environmental), reputation (e.g., attribution of blame), media (e.g., amount and tone of news stories, visuals, and editorials), and public relations outputs (e.g., press conferences, news releases, and website content). In order to evaluate these different areas, communicators need to tailor evaluation mechanisms to each stakeholder group. For example, employees might be asked in a confidential, open-ended survey to provide their role in the crisis response, their level of satisfaction with how they were notified about the crisis, specific strengths and weaknesses of crisis management, and suggestions for improving any aspect of the crisis management team, plan, or response.

A thorough evaluation can result in an overwhelming amount of information to analyze. Dividing this data into phases (e.g., preparation, response, and recovery) or systems (e.g., human, technical, infrastructure, and cultural) can help organize the process. Of course, delivering a fancy evaluation report is only useful if the lessons learned are then incorporated into and applied to the organization's crisis management preparation and crisis management plan.

Renewal. Some crisis managers focus on *renewal.* Renewal signifies a more optimistic approach to crisis response in which organizations and their management learn from the crisis and emerge stronger and better than they were before the crisis. Renewal is much easier to engage in if an organization has acted ethically and responsibly prior to a crisis and if it had strong relationships with its key stakeholders before the problems occurred.[35] An example of a government organization engaging in renewal would be a federal transportation agency that, in response to a shooting on a train, uses new media to engage and empower members of the public in determining policy changes about train passenger screening.

Future Directions

We conclude this chapter with observations about emerging trends that will impact the future direction of government crisis communication. It is impossible to entirely predict the future of any field, but we believe three primary trends are changing the direction of government crisis communication: (1) growth in the emergency management and public relations fields, (2) increasing emphasis on counterterrorism, and (3) wider variety of communication tools.

Both the emergency management and public relations fields displayed strong growth in the last decade, leading *U.S. News and World Report* to rate both as among the fifty best careers of 2010.[36] The same ranking predicted that both fields will have strong growth over at least the next decade. This growth indicates the increasing value executives place on professionally executed communication during routine and crisis times. With more value placed on communication, government communicators are more likely to direct strategy rather than just execute tactics before, during, and after crises. The growth in the emergency management and public relations fields also leads to increased opportunities for professional development. With more emergency management and public relations job opportunities, more universities and professional associations will seek to train communicators to excel in these fields.

The second primary trend we see is a continuing emphasis on counterterrorism. After the 9/11 terrorist attacks in the United States, governments around the globe allocated more resources for crisis mitigation and preparation. This trend continues today, with more resources allocated after each subsequent reported major terrorist attack—both for the ones that are not prevented such as the 2005 London train bombings and the ones that are, such as the 2010 U.S. airline explosion attempt. Though it would be preferable for governments to allocate resources without public reporting of attacks, it is encouraging that governments increasingly recognize the value of crisis management. On the downside, this trend toward resourcing counterterrorism often prioritizes factors unique to terrorism that do not necessarily transfer to an all-hazards crisis management approach. For example, planning for a terrorist attack emphasizes mitigating the crisis occurrence whereas planning for a severe weather event emphasizes preparing the public for a crisis. Therefore, we predict that government communicators will continue to have to negotiate obtaining resources for planning for all crisis types, not just terrorist attacks.

Finally, we predict that government communicators will continue to have an increasing number of social and digital media tools to help manage crises. Current dominant tools include blogs, Facebook, Flickr, Twitter, and YouTube. These dominant tools may change as new ones emerge, but the impact of all social and digital media will remain the same. First, these tools allow for quicker communication with stakeholders before, during, and after crises occur. In the past, government communicators relied almost entirely on journalists to disseminate crisis messages, but now communicators can easily disseminate messages directly to the public. Importantly, all of these tools can be used via cell phones from crisis scenes, allowing for more efficient communication. See Leila Sadeghi's Chapter 7 in this text for a more in-depth discussion of social media in government.

Second, these tools have the potential to significantly increase public involvement in crisis planning, response, and recovery. For example, less than 24 hours after the devastating 2010 earthquake in Haiti, aide organizations raised millions of dollars by promoting text-message donations via Facebook and Twitter. Similarly, during the 2009–2010 global pandemic flu outbreak, health agencies worldwide relied on new media to spread prevention messages. For example, the U.S. Centers for Disease Control and Prevention sponsored a YouTube video competition for citizen-produced public service announcements about flu prevention, and the winning video received more than 1.5 million downloads.[37]

Given the enormous benefits of these tools, governments will need to more rapidly incorporate them into their crisis management. Currently, many government organizations are not up to speed in using these tools despite the fact that citizens widely embrace social and digital media to learn about crises. For example, a recent survey of U.S. residents found that citizens do not believe local governments adequately incorporate cell phone technology into their emergency alert systems. [38] Thus, by far the most significant challenge crisis communicators will continue to face is more effectively incorporating social and digital media into their crisis management.

This chapter provided a general framework for government communicators to use when establishing a crisis management approach for their organizations. This chapter addressed common crisis terms and types. It laid the case for building a strong crisis management team and plan. The sections describing the three stages of a crisis (preparation, response, and recovery) offered government communicators a view of the life cycle of a crisis and communication's role in the process. While the future trends discussed here may change the particulars of crisis management, the need for an effective public relations function to prepare for, detect, respond to, and recover from a crisis will not change. If anything, these skills will become more important in an increasingly complicated and connected world. While some government communicators may experience daily crises and others might never face one, risks, threats, and crises provide both challenges and opportunities for governments and their public relations staff. Hopefully, this chapter will help minimize the challenges and maximize the opportunities.

Endnotes

[1] Brooke Fisher Liu, "Natural Disasters" in *Encyclopedia of Journalism* (Thousand Oaks, CA: Sage, 2009).

[2] Liu, "Natural Disasters."

[3] Robert L. Heath and Michael James Palenchar, eds., *Strategic Issues Management: Organizations and Public Policy Challenges*, 2nd ed. (Thousand Oaks, CA: Sage, 2007), 93.

[4] Heath and Palenchar, *Strategic Issues*, 278.

[5] W. Timothy Coombs, *Ongoing Crisis Communication: Planning, Managing, and Responding* (Thousand Oaks, CA: Sage, 2007).

[6] Brad Fitch, *Media Relations Handbook for Agencies, Associations, Nonprofits and Congress* (Alexandria, VA: TheCapitol.Net, 2004).

[7] Matthew W. Seeger, Timothy L. Sellnow, and Robert R. Ulmer. *Communication and Organizational Crisis* (Westport, CT: Praeger, 2003).

[8] Brooke Fisher Liu, J. Suzanne Horsley, and Abbey Blake Levenshus, "Government Communicators and Corporate Public Relations Practitioners: More Differences than Similarities in How They Communicate?" *Journal of Applied Communication Research*, 38, no. 2 (2010): 189–213.

[9] Coombs, *Ongoing Crisis Communication*, 5.

[10] David W. Guth, "Organizational Crisis Experience and Public Relations Roles," *Public Relations Review* 21, no. 2, (1995): 123–136.

[11] Seeger et al., *Communication and Organizational Crisis*.

[12] National Association of Government Communicators, "Trends and Salary Survey," accessed September 1, 2008: http://www.nagc.com/AboutNAGC/OrderSurvey.asap.

[13] National Association of Government Communicators, "Trends and Salary Survey,"

[14] Seeger et al., *Communication and Organizational Crisis*.

[15] W. Timothy Coombs and Sherry J. Holladay, "An Extended Examination of the Crisis Situations: A Fusion of the Relational Management and Symbolic Approaches," *Journal of Public Relations Research* 13, no. 4 (2001): 321–340.

[16] W. Timothy Coombs and Sherry J. Holladay, "Unpacking the Halo Effect: Reputation and Crisis Management," *Journal of Communication Management* 10, no. 2 (2006): 123–137.

[17] Robert L. Heath, Jaesub Lee, and Lan Ni, "Crisis and Risk Approaches to Emergency Management Planning and Communication: The Role of Similarity and Sensitivity," *Journal of Public Relations Research* 21, no. 2 (2009): 123–141.

[18] For more information, see Coombs, *Ongoing Crisis Communication*, chapters 5 and 6.

[19] Sherry J. Holladay, "Crisis Communication Strategies in the Media Coverage of Chemical Accidents," *Journal of Public Relations Research* 21, no. 2 (2009); 208–217.

[20] Maureen Taylor and Michael L. Kent, "Taxonomy of Mediated Crisis Responses," *Public Relations Review* 33, no. 2 (2007): 140–146.

[21] Elizabeth Johnson Avery and Sora Kim, "Anticipating or Precipitating Crisis? Health Agencies May Not Be Heeding Best Practice Advice in Avian Flu Press Releases," *Journal of Public Relations Research* 21, no. 2 (2009): 187–197.

[22] Coombs, *Ongoing Crisis Communication*.

[23] Laura M. Arpan and David R. Roskos-Ewoldsen, "Stealing Thunder: Analysis of the Effects of Proactive Disclosure of Crisis Information," *Public Relations Review* 31, no. 3 (2005): 425–433.

[24] Brooke Fisher Liu, "An Analysis of U.S. Government Media and Disaster Frames," *Journal of Communication Management* 13, no. 3 (2009): 268–283.

[25] Coombs, *Ongoing Crisis Communication*.

[26] Dwayne Hal Dean, "Consumer Reaction to Negative Publicity: Effects of Corporate Reputation, Response, and Responsibility for a Crisis Event," *Journal of Business Communication* 41, no. 2 (2004): 192–211.

[27] Amanda Hall Gallagher, Maria Fontenot, and Kris Boyle, "Communicating during Times of Crises: An Analysis of News Releases from the Federal Government before, during, and after Hurricanes Katrina and Rita," *Public Relations Review* 33 (2007): 217–219.

[28] Barbara Reynolds and Sandra Crouse Quinn, "Effective Communication during an Influenza Pandemic: The Value of Using a Crisis and Emergency Risk Communication Framework," *Health Promotion Practice* 9, 13S–17S, 2008.

[29] Reynolds and Quinn, "Effective Communication."

[30] Coombs, *Ongoing Crisis Communication*.

[31] Coombs, *Ongoing Crisis Communication*; Brooke Fisher Liu, "Effective Public Relations in Racially-Charged Crises: Not Black or White" in *The Handbook of Crisis Communication*, ed. W. Timothy Coombs and Sherry Holladay (New York: Wiley-Blackwell, 2010), chapter 16.

[32] Ibid; (Coombs; Liu).

[33] Ibid; (Coombs; Liu).

[34] Ibid; (Coombs; Liu).

[35] Seeger et al., *Communication and Organizational Crisis*.

[36] Liz Wolgem, "The 50 Best Careers of 2010," U.S. News & World Report, accessed January 20, 2010, http://www.usnews.com/money/careers/articles/2009/12/28/the-50-best-careers-of-2010.html.

[37] ABC News, "CDC Picks Winning Video in Flu PSA Contest," accessed January 28, 2010, http://blogs.abcnews.com/campuschatter/2009/09/cdc-picks-winning-video-in-flu-psa-contest.html.

[38] "Communication News, Emergency Communications Outdate," *Communication News* 45, no. 2 (2008): 7.

Chapter 7

Web 2.0

Leila Sadeghi

Contents

> We don't have a choice on whether we do social media, the question is how well we do it.
>
> **—E. Qualmann**[1]

Introduction

A global transformation is happening and it has all to do with Web 2.0. These technologies are revolutionizing how we communicate and share information, how we interact with products and services, and how we rate our experiences with just about anything. Companies around the world, regardless of their location, have recognized the value in using Web 2.0 to spread the word about their products and services as well as listen to feedback from their customers. For example, in a recent Domino's Pizza *Show Us Your Pizza* campaign, customers are asked to photograph the pizza that they ordered with a chance at winning $500 for the best photo. While the concept of Domino's pizza hasn't changed much, by integrating Web 2.0, customers are reintroduced to the brand and the product. Customers are encouraged to tell their story, to create content to sell the pizza. In another example, Old Spice recently launched a highly interactive campaign soliciting questions from anyone through multiple social media channels—like Facebook, Twitter, YouTube, and blogs—to ask the "Old Spice guy," Isaiah Mustafa, which would be answered in a short video clip posted on YouTube. The creative team behind the campaign worked for eleven straight hours to make over eighty-seven short and creative videos in response to people's questions. General questions and even some with political undertones were sent in. ABC's *Good Morning America* tweeted the question, "The president's lost some female support. How does the White House get those women voters back?" Isaiah Mustafa responded in a video clip that President Obama ought to open the State of the Union Address with "Hello Ladies ..." and end the address while commenting on and pointing to his sculpted abdominal muscles—quite an effort to regain female voters' support. This same process was repeated for other comments and questions posted by the public. Even after the campaign ended, the videos have been viewed more than 4 million times and counting and revenues increased by 107 percent in one month—a testament to the power and utilization of the Internet. Old Spice reinvented itself through the use of Web 2.0. What was once considered your father or grandfather's cologne is now pretty hip.

What do we mean when we refer to Web 2.0? Web 2.0 represents a collection of Internet-based tools that enhance communication through openness and interactive capabilities. Through the use of these tools, such as blogs and social media platforms like Facebook, people have the added capability of producing content and being engaged in two-way communication. One of the main concepts behind the birth of these tools is to empower individuals through open dialogue. Where instant two-way communication was once considered impossible, Web 2.0 technologies continue to evolve at a very rapid pace making peer-to-peer connectivity easier and faster. Consider that it took more than 50 years for radio and television to reach an audience of 50 million, and only 7 years for the Internet and iPod to reach the same number of users.[2] Facebook, the most popular social media platform, is documented as adding over 200 million users in one year, with a total of more than 500 million users.[3] Twitter, a social media platform with over 125 million users worldwide, is credited for adding on average of 10 million users per month since February of 2010.[4] While some social networking platforms have not yet attracted such a large number of users, one could argue that Web 2.0 is still relatively new and we can expect to be introduced to more innovative technologies.

Across government, the Web 2.0 movement has demonstrated powerful examples of how Internet-based tools can enhance digital democracy and diplomacy efforts. The Obama presidential campaign of 2008 provides concrete evidence as to the power of the Internet in raising funds and getting out the vote. The Obama administration understands the power of utilizing Internet-based tools to organize communities of citizens around common goals. As President Obama moved into his new role, the push to integrate new media did not fade. His administration introduced Gov 2.0—which refers to the government's use of Web 2.0— and many federal agencies adopted social media, and some even integrated weekly blogs, discussion forums, and public contests in their agency's websites. Many of these efforts have been well received—citizens are using them to gain new information, post questions and comments, and provide innovative ideas to address government's complex problems.

While there are quite a few successful examples of federal initiatives, state and local efforts have not kept pace. Using traditional methods of communication, namely newsletters, flyers, phone calls, town meetings, and word-of-mouth, many state and local governments are missing an entire niche audience through the use of Internet-based technologies. In a recent poll to assess the use of Web 2.0 in the public and private sectors, of those Americans surveyed aged 18 to 65, 77 percent preferred engaging with government online, and 43 percent said it will take government one to five years to catch up to the private sector.[5] Given that a majority of the public wants to engage with government online, what can government do to respond to the majority interest? The aim of this chapter is to advance our understanding of Web 2.0 capabilities, in particular how governments are exploring and utilizing these technologies.

Government Utilization of Web 2.0

Unlike traditional methods of interaction, the Internet enables government to conduct its business and engage citizens online. Governments need to recognize that a majority of citizens are online searching for content, checking their e-mail, reading product reviews, and engaging in other activities. It is estimated that the average user spends about seven hours per month on Facebook, surpassing time spent using Google, and representing an increase of 143 percent over the last year.[6] According to a recent Pew survey, 78 percent of Americans 18 years and older are using the Internet on a daily basis, with 67 percent using the Internet at some time to visit a local, state, or federal website.[7] These statistics demonstrate that Internet-based technologies are increasingly becoming go-to sources for information. With

Web 2.0, governments are provided with a new set of possibilities to reach the public without investing an abundance of resources, including the ability to:

- Generate innovative solutions to public policies
- Rank policies, programs, and services as determined by citizens' needs
- Collaborate and generate innovation across levels of government and with citizens to reduce duplicative work, and to improve efficiency and effectiveness of services
- Improve e-government services to simplify online transactions
- Improve governmental transparency by providing accessibility to data and online documents
- Recruit, hire, and retain the best and brightest for agency personnel

President Obama's 2009 Open Government Directive required federal agencies to submit plans for achieving transparency, openness, and collaboration with the public in an effort to drive smart policy and increase government effectiveness.[8] While a directive alone may not be enough to push innovation with Web 2.0, it did force agencies to reevaluate their communication and outreach strategies with the public. For example, the Department of State (DOS) has demonstrated how diplomacy can be married to modern technology. In January of 2010 when the Haiti earthquake struck, within hours the DOS set up the Text Haiti 90999 program, to secure $10 donations for relief efforts from individuals, which amounted to over $40 million for the Red Cross. Such an effort may not have been possible—or may have resulted in fewer donations—without the use of the Internet and digital technology. In addition to raising funds, the DOS is credited with taking a leap into Web 2.0 with strong support from Secretary of State Hilary Clinton, who feels the agency should keep pace with technology and the world. In a recent article entitled "Digital Diplomacy," Secretary of State Clinton is quoted acknowledging the power in the Internet to build relationships between citizens and government: "One of the ways of breaking through [to Americans 30 and under] is by having people who are doing the work of our government be human beings, be personalized, be relatable."[9] The DOS has adopted several Web 2.0 and mobile technologies including a popular blog called DipNote, Facebook and Twitter channels, multimedia sharing through Flickr and YouTube, and providing the capability of streaming foreign policy news directly to handheld devices like the BlackBerry and iPhone.

The DOS is not alone. Other federal agencies have effectively adopted Web 2.0 technologies. The nation's Library of Congress, for example, went 2.0 in 2008 launching a pilot project on Flickr.com (http://www.flickr.com/photos/library_of_congress), an interactive tool that allows anyone to upload, tag, and post comments to photos. Within 24 hours of the pilot launch, Flickr reported 1.1 million views by the public, with over 3 million views the following week.[10] Since then, the Library of Congress has added an additional 40,000 photos from various historical collections like the Great Depression and World War II. The intent of its effort was to add historical data to photos dating as far back as the 1800s by soliciting input from the public about photos in the archives through tagging (labeling) and commenting. Since launching its Flickr channel in 2008, the photos have been viewed over 10 million times, over 65,000 tags have been added, and 7,000 comments were left on the photos. The library recognizes that without having shared these photos with the public through Web 2.0 technologies, the agency may have never gathered such vital information. In another example, the Transportation Security Administration (TSA) launched a blog (http://blog.tsa.gov/) to facilitate public discussion around security screenings. When the TSA announced it would pilot checkpoint body scan imaging in various airports around the country, the public outcry over violations of privacy intensified. In an effort to educate the public about the capabilities of the new screening devices, the TSA began posting information and sharing internal policy documents to satisfy public concerns over how they will delete body scan images and how these technologies will facilitate increased safety and security. The blog has received an enormous amount of comments from those in favor of and opposed to screening. The TSA continues to respond to these concerns by providing transparency of information related to how the scanning images operate and the process for deletion of scanned images.

The Health and Human Services (HHS) agency also uses a blog (http://blog. pandemicflu.gov/) to provide the public with health-related information and to respond to citizen comments and questions. This was especially important to inform the public regarding the flu outbreak and vaccine availability. People were submitting questions related to the influenza outbreak and concerns regarding the substances found in the vaccines. Similar to the HHS, the Centers for Disease Control and Prevention (CDC) integrated several Web 2.0 applications including social networking (http://www.facebook.com/CDC) and YouTube (http://www.youtube.com/CDCstreamingHealth) in an effort to provide the public with timely information related to product recalls, and health and safety updates and alerts. The CDC uses these platforms to engage the public in two-way communication and to increase visibility and openness of information. While these are only a few cases of federal agencies using Web 2.0 technologies, there are many others like NASA, the Office of Citizen Services and Communications at the U.S. General Services Administration, the U.S. Army, the Department of Defense, and the Federal Bureau of Investigation.

State and local governments are behind the Web 2.0 curve in terms of utilizing some of these technologies to reach local citizens and foster input. Unlike the urgency demonstrated at the federal level to adopt new technologies, the local level lacks a systematic plan to implement Web 2.0. While a handful of towns and cities can be found on Facebook, much of the activity has been stagnant. According to the Fels Institute of Government, for example, "Local governments' reactions to this expansion have been mixed. Some have made these services a central part of their communications strategies with the public and press; many others are ambivalent or concerned that social media are a distraction that they may nonetheless be asked to do something clever with."[11]

Much of the resistance at this level can be attributed to a number of factors. For one, there is a lack of understanding in terms of what is really needed to maintain a Web 2.0 presence and how it can be done with relatively few resources and little time. The best examples of government implementation of Web 2.0 were developed with a strategy. The strategy includes identifying a core team of staff, drafting policies for internal and external utilization, identifying the right platforms that match identified outcomes, and managing information and communication. Policies for utilization often detail how staff should deal with negative comments, inaccuracy of information, and misrepresentation of news online.

The next section will explore several snapshots of state and local government utilization of Web 2.0. Two of the cases are selected from the winners of the National Center for Digital Government's 2009 and 2010 Best of the Web and Digital Government Achievement Awards, which were recognized for their outstanding efforts at the implementation and infrastructure level (http://www.centerdigitalgov.com/survey/88). For over a decade, the National Center for Digital Government has held a Best of the Web Awards event at the state and local levels for government innovation. The third case highlights Morris County in New Jersey for its unique effort to build a Web 2.0 presence across several platforms, complemented by short educational videos on how to use the platforms, which can be viewed by the public at any time. Their efforts have gained the attention of Govloop.com (the "Facebook for government"), Gov 2.0 on blogtalkradio.com, as well as other organizations and leaders from the "Web 2.0 in government" community.

Cases in Government

Several cases of local government using Web 2.0 have made headlines. Manor, Texas, for example, developed ManorLabs, an innovative think tank for citizens to review and comment on proposed solutions or submit ideas on how to improve the business of government (http://cityofmanor.org/wordpress/). Citizens can sign in to the website and select an area. Areas are broken down by function; for example, should citizens want to report a street problem, they can enter it in the Public Works area, or post an idea on how to make information technology easier for citizens. Citizens are recognized and rewarded for their online involvement. For example, citizens who share innovative ideas are awarded "Innobucks," which are essentially coupons that can be used in any number of small businesses locally, or they can spend a day riding with the police chief or shadowing the mayor.

In Morris County, New Jersey, a Web 2.0 strategy was launched that encompasses several platforms that provide multiple opportunities for government to engage the public (http://co.morris.nj.us/generalHTML/socialmedia.asp). Its strategy includes a Facebook and Twitter profile, online documents, a multimedia channel on YouTube that contains a library of videos and Flickr for photos, and the ability to subscribe to a number of web pages that are customizable and delivered online through Really Simple Syndication (RSS) feeds. A major component also includes a "Learning 2.0" program to educate the public about these tools. This section includes free education and training around Web 2.0 scheduled over 9 weeks. Participants can move from one topic to the next at their leisure and discover how to utilize these tools to their advantage.

In another example, the state of Utah has developed an intricate Web 2.0 strategy that incorporates a variety of ways for citizens to obtain information and participate in state and local government (http://www.utah.gov/). The website provides a 24-hour live chat service with an operator, the ability to view and track the use of taxpayer dollars, and enables the user to receive up-to-date traffic photos from webcams and traffic alerts throughout the state's roadways. They can also follow Utah on Twitter. The website provides several iPhone or iPad downloadable applications like practice driving exams, maps of the state's parks and recreation facilities, and crime reports. This level of openness through information and mechanisms to participate in government is increasingly embraced by both government and its citizens.

Potential Uses of Web 2.0 Platforms

There are a variety of tools and platforms on the Internet that are cost effective and easy to integrate. These tools cover several areas within Web 2.0 like blogging and microblogging, social networking and geosocial networking, wikis and mashups, and posting multimedia content. Table 7.1 represents a working definition of each of these tools, an example of a platform from the Internet, and how the tool can be used by government.

Several Web 2.0 tools have been designed to meet the needs of government more specifically. One of these tools is Poll Everywhere (http://www.pollevery-where.com), a mechanism that can be used to poll citizens on legislation. Poll Everywhere can be used by governments to solicit citizen input through online surveys. A link to the survey can be shared through several Web 2.0 platforms like Facebook and Twitter. For example, a public manager can create a poll asking questions related to service needs in the local community. A link to the poll can be shared through the traditional forms of communication and a municipal website, but also through several Web 2.0 platforms like Facebook and Twitter. This increases government's ability to ascertain citizen needs and opinions, as well as engage a broader range of constituents. The Apps.Gov site (https://www.apps.gov/cloud/advantage/main/start_page.do) is a one-stop storefront launched by the General Services Administration to lower costs and drive innovation in government agencies through the use of preapproved cloud services and applications. The site provides users with web-based applications for cloud computing in which on-demand access to a shared pool of computing resources (e.g., servers, networks,

Table 7.1 Examples of Web 2.0 Tools

Web 2.0 Tool	Example	Utilization by Government	Link
Social networking: Web-based services that provide users with the ability to connect, share, and create content.	Facebook	Governments can use Facebook to engage citizens, post events and news, and share photos and short videos.	Facebook.com
Microblogging: Much like blogging, microblogging provides the same service although with more limited character space to post content.	Twitter	With a 140-character limit, governments can use Twitter to post short and relevant messages such as a reminder to attend a town meeting, or to participate in a free event, or take an online poll. Short messaging can be very effective for engaging citizens and requires minimal time and effort.	Twitter.com
Blogs: Blogs are online journals that can be edited and posted for people to view and comment on.	Blogger	Blogs can be used across government and by elected officials to provide depth and a more personal connection. For example, a town manager could write a weekly blog summarizing the town's activities and responding to citizen comments and questions.	Blogger.com
Geosocial networking: Social networking that combines geographic locations with content relevant to the location.	Foursquare	Foursquare can be used to match a geographic location with content through mobile phone technology. Users can check in to specific locations and view content virtually. For example, the town manager's blog can be linked to the town hall on a map. Therefore, anytime you check into town hall through your mobile phone, you are immediately provided with the manager's blog. In another example, a town can link coupons and discounts with small businesses to attract more people.	Foursquare. com

Mashups: Mashups are web pages or data integration applications that combine data from two or more functions or sources. Mashups can be used for a variety of purposes such as matching local news (or any data source) with a map. Mashups can be used for other purposes such as to integrate news from multiple sources on one web page.	Mapping Mashup	Chicago.everyblock.com is a mashup website dedicated to those living in or interested in Chicago. The website identifies local news about Chicago neighborhoods, restaurants, and small businesses, and matches them to an interactive map of Chicago. Users are able to scroll over the marked nodes on the map and read a recent story about that particular location. This tool can be used for any state or municipality looking to bolster economic activity, tourism, or simply to present information and news.	http://chicago.everyblock.com/
Wikis: Wikis are collections of web pages that provide users with the ability to contribute or modify content. They are essentially open applications.	Intellipedia	Intellipedia is a wiki established by a consortium of the U.S. intelligence community that is used for internal employee purposes. Employees with proper clearance, classified at three levels (Top Secret, Secret, and Sensitive but Unclassified), can use the wiki to share information, news, and other high-level data from over 16 agencies.	Wikipedia.com
Multimedia sharing: Websites that provide users with the ability to create and share multimedia content.	YouTube	YouTube is a video sharing website where users can upload and share videos. For example, the state of California has a channel on YouTube that provides the public with video clips of the various departments and agencies within the state. The public can view these videos, post comments, and share them through other Web 2.0 technologies like Facebook and Twitter.	Youtube.com

and applications) is made available. Agencies can use this "next generation of IT in which data and applications will be housed centrally and accessible anywhere and anytime by various devices" to work across sectors in an effort to exchange information and find solutions to problems.[12]

Creative Commons (http://creativecommons.org) is a nonprofit organization on the web dedicated to providing security through free licensing of open information. One of the reasons governments are often resistant to providing open access to information is largely due to copyrighting issues associated with public use. Creative Commons offers free and easy licensing for any user to post and share photos, videos, documents, and more. For example, the White House website (http://www.whitehouse.gov) uses Creative Commons to license intellectual property made available on the web by the public. Therefore, when the public wants to post content on the White House website, it must agree to the license that its content may be shared, distributed, or copied by anyone so long as it is attributed to the author, but does not imply that it is owned by the author.[13] The Nixle website (http://www.nixle.com) promotes geographically based public safety alerts and advisories delivered via Short Message Service (SMS) text messaging services to community residents. Since Nixle launched its site in 2010, over 4000 public safety and municipal agencies have used the service because it is free and easy to use, it is provided as a secure service, and any information relayed through the system can be delivered to geographically targeted citizens as an SMS text message via e-mail or through web access. For example, the Modesto Police Department uses Nixle as its primary site for automated public safety messages. Citizens have the opportunity to follow police department alerts and messages as full stories through a Nixle interface, or as abbreviated messages through their Twitter page.

Barriers to Adoption
The "Old" vs. the "New"

Generally, today's governments are hierarchically structured, oriented to command and control, and bureaucratic in nature. This combination is not the best recipe for embracing and adopting new and emerging technologies that can provide process efficiency. Despite the promising new opportunities that Web 2.0 offers, many governments are reluctant to use them, partly due to how they are organized and maintained, but also due to antiquated technology and computers. Another barrier has to do with fear of technology and the age of the typical government employee. Governments across levels are embracing a new generation of employees. Technologically savvy and open to collaboration and creativity, this "Net generation"—typically under 35 years old—embraces newer and faster ways to share and exchange information and work collaboratively across boundaries to solve government problems. On the other hand, a majority of government employees are baby-boomers (43 to 63 years of age) with less training in technology and hold a greater influence over processes within the workplace that can include the use of traditional methods of communication. The younger government worker has grown up with Smartphones, iPods and iPads, BlackBerries, laptops, and Web 2.0 technologies. As the baby boomers retire and phase out of government, it is likely that this new generation of workers will influence change within internal organization structures and in how they collaborate with the public.[14]

Usability and Maintenance

A second underlying cause for the resistance to Web 2.0 integration has much to do with usability and maintenance. Many in government fear the possibility of receiving negative comments from citizens, or the fear of posting information that may be erroneous and live on the Internet indefinitely. Others have trouble determining what to post, how much to post, and how often to post it without losing the followership of the public. This problem is endemic to all sectors as the power in Web 2.0 is about crafting messages that are attractive in order to lead people to continue to want to listen and engage in responses. Going hand in hand with determining the type of content to post is how to deal with privacy and security of information exchanged over the Internet. By utilizing a Creative Commons licensing umbrella with Nixle to publish content, for example, governments can avoid issues related to security of information and how that information can be shared and replicated.

A third main barrier has to do with response time. Many working in government, while realizing the vast potential in using Web 2.0, also assume that citizens expect them to function at a 24/7 level of availability to respond to comments and to fix reported problems. For example, a town manager from New Jersey recently talked about his first experience in receiving a SeeClickFix.com e-mail from a citizen reporting a problem. He had little idea as to how to respond to the reported problem using the Internet platform; however, he felt compelled to act on the problem quickly and report the outcome back to the citizen. In another example, at a social media event for government in 2009, a public manager reported that at one time she would receive e-mails that would prompt her to pay attention and feel compelled to respond quickly, and that now with the rapid-fire style of Web 2.0, the feeling to listen and respond quickly is even greater. While these are concerns that deserve attention, Web 2.0 is often misunderstood and dealt with as if it is more of a problem than a medium to a solution. When governments are in the initial stages of adopting Web 2.0 technologies, they should plan on choosing the right platform that meets their needs for engagement, develop a clear and simple plan that details who is expected to monitor citizen comments, questions, and concerns, and how these should be triaged and routed to the proper department or person (much of this can be programmed into the system to eliminate duplicative effort), and what to post and how often to post it.

Strategies for Web 2.0 Implementation

Steps to Consider in the Early Stages

Any organization—whether public or private—understands that the participation and input of citizens is a vital component of the community's future. Whether a public organization realizes the potential in utilizing Web 2.0 and social media platforms, at some point, taking the initiative to "go where the people are" is essential to keeping pace with what the public expects and the overall growth and movement within the field of public administration. By increasing participation with Web 2.0 platforms, local government can run public outreach campaigns to gain feedback from citizens on a variety of fronts, for example, land use planning or community growth planning. The following strategies can greatly assist local governments in developing a comprehensive communication strategy that incorporates Web 2.0.

The first step in the strategy process is to develop a list of the traditional methods of communication that are already being used by the municipality—this can include newsletters, a municipal website, listservs and e-mail, informational meetings, and even phone calls—and the frequency at which they are being utilized. For example, a public manager may distribute a monthly e-newsletter, or they may send weekly announcements. The purpose of this step is to gain a comprehensive view of how the public receives information and interacts with its local government. At this stage, it is important to understand that Web 2.0 platforms will not supplant the current communication strategy, but rather supplement it. Therefore, it is important to maintain current strategies for communication and add Web 2.0 strategies.

Once the communication strategy is mapped, the next few steps involve selecting several social media outlets, such as blogs, multimedia sharing, microblogging, and social networking, among others, that would enhance the communication strategy. For example, a public manager who wants to write a weekly summary to the public can easily do this with a blog that can be integrated into the website. Blogs are a less formal approach to sharing information and the town manager can use this outlet to be more personable and less formal with the community. Blogs can be posted to the website and shared across multiple social media platforms. There are many websites that provide free blogging accounts; see Table 7.1 for an example.

Step two in the strategy process involves identifying social networking websites to create community or municipal profiles. Social networking is another efficient and effective method to communicate and share information with the community. Facebook and Twitter are the most widely used social networking platforms and are ripe for government utilization. At the local level, municipalities are beginning to go "social" by creating town profiles, and increasing their audience through "fans" and "followers." These profiles are free and fairly easy to create, and provide the account holder with multiple setting options for privacy and usability. It is important to designate account settings so that all posts are open to the public for comment. The township can make routine updates to its social networking profiles about community events, meeting dates, school and health information, and to post links to online polling surveys (see the Poll Everywhere description above), blogs, and other important information posted to the website. This strategy increases both the number of followers as well as creating a loop back to the website.

Other Web 2.0 platforms for municipal consideration include Nixle (http:// www.nixle.com) and SeeClickFix (http://www.seeclickfix.com)—both of which are designed for notification purposes. Nixle provides the township with a method of delivering public safety messages via SMS text or e-mail to subscribed users (see previous section, "Potential Uses of Web 2.0 Platforms," for a more detailed description of this website). SeeClickFix provides municipalities with a stream- lined process for responding to reported problems such as potholes, fallen trees, cracks in paving, and other reported infrastructure needs throughout the commu- nity. Citizens, through their Smartphones (BlackBerries, iPhones, Androids, etc.), can capture a photo of the issue and upload it directly to the website, which gets routed to the appropriate department for action and generates a tracking number back to the citizen. This method is highly efficient because the reported problem is routed to the appropriate division for action, rather than through the central administration.

The third step in the selection process is to create Really Simple Syndication (RSS) feeds across several of the website pages. RSS feeds enable the public to subscribe, through URL links, to those web pages whose content they want to receive. For example, a user may want to receive only updates to the website home page. By placing an RSS feed on the home page, the township is providing people with the opportunity of receiving new content when it is posted to that particular page. Creating RSS feeds is not a daunting task, and multiple websites provide free and easy steps. In addition to RSS feeds, consideration should also be given to free multimedia sharing websites such as Flickr and YouTube. Through these platforms, the township can share video recordings and photos of community events and meetings. Photos and videos can be uploaded relatively quickly and shared across all social media platforms.

The final step involves linking the social media profiles together so that once an update is made on one platform, it will replicate across all platforms. Facebook and Twitter can be easily linked together to update simultaneously. Another option is to use a platform such as HootSuite (http://hootsuite.com) to manage updates across all social media platforms from one point of access. HootSuite also provides an efficient way for multiple users to access the social media platforms to make updates, in addition to tracking metrics. The final step also includes downloading social media icons that are chosen (such as the Facebook "f" or the Twitter "t") to the website home page. Any of the social media platforms that are implemented provide users with these steps.

Implementing Internal and External Policies for Use

Now that the Web 2.0 platforms have been selected, and prior to launching profiles across these platforms, policies for internal and external utilization should be considered. In terms of internal policies, consideration should be given to resource allocation, an approval process for any social media profile for all executive departments, and general guidelines to increase citizen participation across all communication media. First, an organization, including its executive departments, should decide the number of staff that will be designated as responsible for posting updates, responding to citizens' comments, and determining when a comment is out of scope with the acceptable policy for external users. In line with this determination, all social media profiles created by individual executive departments should be approved by the mayor's communication or public affairs director or the town manager. If neither of these positions is available, then the mayor can act as the approver.

Next, an internal policy for how staff maintain and update these profiles should be considered. For example, should posts be made in the mornings and afternoons? Should the information in the posts derive from press releases? How quickly should staff respond to comments and questions? These are just a few of the questions that can be addressed early on in the process. One of the fascinating aspects of social media has all to do with openness and freedom of thought. People share information with one another, comment on one another's blogs, photos, and videos, and reshare content among personal networks. Public managers should be comfortable with the public commenting on their posts. These comments may not always be positive and can in fact be criticizing at times. The policy should include information relevant to how staff members should conduct themselves online in conversations with citizens.

Finally, an external policy should be carefully crafted and posted to any social media profiles and the website. Typically, municipalities include a policy that details the purpose of the site as a vehicle for communication between the municipality and members of the public. Furthermore, the policy should also cite the type of content and information that shall not be allowed by the public, such as comments that include profane language, that support or foster discrimination, sexual content, or illegal activity, or comments that support a particular brand or political campaign. With a detailed policy such as this, staff members who are responsible for monitoring the comments posted to social media profiles will be able to readily identify the types of comments that are allowed and those that can be removed. Although it is very important to design and implement policies for use, it is important to note that removing offensive comments is not the norm. Most citizens will engage in a positive and constructive manner.

Conclusion

Despite the availability of a broad spectrum of Web 2.0 applications and the positive results associated with applying these tools in the private sector, government is slow to jump on the technological bandwagon. However, this is an emerging area of discussion, likely to lead many public administrators to question how Web 2.0 tools can be applied to public agencies, and how it can impact their relationship with the public. As government breaks new ground in this area, there are likely to be many unknowns and much uncertainty, as well as technical, security, and privacy concerns that can have a significant impact on whether government will actually utilize new media. One way to address these concerns, and foster the utilization of technology in future government leaders, is through professional development opportunities. For example, colleges and universities could offer online certificate programs in Web 2.0 and social media management, or they could infuse new technology courses in public administration and political science curriculum. Another way is to promote participation in professional organizations and associations focused on government utilization of Web 2.0 and other technologies such as Govloop, the Sunlight Foundation, and the National Association of Government Webmasters. Another possibility is the addition of sections or chapters to existing public administration associations that focus on Web 2.0 and social media implementation like the American Political Science Association, the National Association of Schools of Public Affairs and Administration, and the American Society for Public Administration.

Endnotes

1. E. Qualmann, "Socialnomics," July 30, 2009, accessed September 15, 2010, http://www.youtube.com/watch?v=sIFYPQjYhv8.
2. Qualmann, "Socialnomics."
3. M. Zuckerberg, "500 Million Stories," July 21, 2010, accessed September 20, 2010, http://blog.facebook.com/blog.php?post=409753352130.
4. Qualmann, "Socialnomics."
5. B. Ballenstedt, "Agencies Fall Short on Web 2.0," June 28, 2010, accessed September 20, 2010, http://www.govexec.com/dailyfed/0610/062810ww.htm#gov20.
6. Nielsen Wire, "Facebook Users Average 7 Hrs a Month in January as Digital Universe Expands," February 16, 2010, accessed September 20, 2010, http://blog.nielsen.com/nielsenwire/online_mobile/facebook-users-average-7-hrs-a-month-in-january-as-digital-universe-expands/; "People hanging out more on Facebook than Google," September 10, 2010, accessed March 16, 2011, http://news.cnet.com/8301-1023_3-20016046-93.html
7. Pew Internet, "Pew Internet & American Life Project Tracking Surveys," March 2000–May 2010, accessed September 22, 2010, http://www.pewinternet.org/Trend-Data/Online-Activites-Total.aspx.
8. P. Orszag, "Memorandum for the Heads of Executive Departments and Agencies: Open Government Directive," December 8, 2009, accessed September 18, 2010, http://www.whitehouse.gov/omb/assets/memoranda_2010/m10-06.pdf.
9. J. Lichtenstein, "Digital Diplomacy," *New York Times Magazine*, July 18, 2010, 29.

10. M. Springer, "For the Common Good: The Library of Congress Flickr Pilot Project," October, 2008, accessed September 22, 2010, http://www.loc.gov/rr/print/flickr_report_final_summary.pdf.
11. C. Kingsley, "Making the Most of Social Media: 7 Lessons from Successful Cities," March 9, 2010, accessed September 22, 2010, https://www.fels.upenn.edu/sites/www.fels.upenn.edu/files/PP3_SocialMedia.pdf.
12. V. Kundra, "Streaming at 1:00: In the Cloud." September 9, 2009, accessed September 14, 2010, http://www.whitehouse.gov/blog/Streaming-at-100-In-the-Cloud/; S. Walling, "Apps.gov Gives Cloud Computing a Slice of the $75 Billion IT Pie," September 15, 2009, accessed September 22, 2010, http://www.readwriteweb.com/enterprise/2009/09/appsgov-gives-cloud-computing.php.
13. Creative Commons, "Case Studies: Whitehouse.gov, " last modified November 19, 2010, accessed September 24, 2010, http://wiki.creativecommons.org/Case_Studies/Whitehouse.gov.
14. W. Boddie et al., "The Future Workforce: Here They Come." *The Public Manager* (spring 2008): 21–24.

MANAGING GOVERNMENT PUBLIC RELATIONS

Chapter 8

Strategic Communication Planning

Diana Knott Martinelli

Contents

In any organization, association, corporation, or group of people bound together to meet goals and objectives, it is necessary to create some kind of plan to achieve them. However, unlike corporate communications personnel, whose work must strategically support outcomes associated with the company's bottom line, many government communicators may be so busy reacting to what they *must* do, they may not take the time to proactively think through and plan their public affairs work.

This chapter builds upon Mordecai Lee's chapter, in which the purposes of government public relations were outlined. It will show how government communicators at all levels can incorporate all three major government public relations purposes: the mandatory (media relations, public reporting, and citizen responsiveness), the pragmatic (customer and client responsiveness and outreach activities), and the political (increasing public support), as desired, into one master document. Such planning helps government employees identify and specify their priorities to support the vision, mission, and goals of the larger agency or department. In doing so, it helps ensure that activities beyond the communicator's reactive "must-do's" are achieved throughout the year to help move the unit forward. In addition, it can help the smaller unit become more visible and valuable to administrators at the top.

Limited Agency Precedents

Strategic communications have been used in formal government communication campaigns for more than a century. Well-known examples include the Committee on Public Information's efforts in World War I and the Office of War Information's activities in World War II; lesser-known examples include Gifford Pinchot's promotion of the new U.S. Forest Service and the U.S. Children's Bureau's efforts to reduce maternal and infant mortality in the early twentieth century. Our federal government originated the title of "public affairs" to differentiate it from the self-serving publicity prohibited by the 1913 Gillett Amendment,[2] and today our federal government has the world's largest cadre of public information and public affairs employees with more than 10,000.[3]

However, given this vast scope of federal—not to mention state and local—government communicators, concentrated strategic communication efforts seem relatively rare. In a recent interview, Doug Matthews, the director of communications for the relatively large city of Austin, Texas, reported that he only recently started to develop annual communication plans.[4] While strategic planning is an accepted part of doing business in government agencies, annual strategic *communication* plans often are not. This lies in stark contrast to the private sector's use of strategic communications in its own public affairs, defined as "the public relations practice that addresses public policy and the publics who influence such policy"[5] and "communication with government officials and other actors in the public policy area."[6] In fact, such corporate activities have been recognized as a professional area of concentration since at least 1954, when the Public Affairs Council, a professional association of corporate public affairs officers, was developed. [7]

The *other* public affairs professionals—the government-employed ones—likewise have a professional group, which many reading this book may be familiar with or, as a professional interested in development, may well belong to: the National Association of Government Communicators. Although its roots stem from the same era, theirs was not a proactive formation, but a defensive one concerned with trying to save their jobs after a revival of Gillette Amendment sentiment in Congress and a cry to reduce government employees after World War II.[8] Perhaps this uneasy history is one reason why government communicators may be more comfortable working primarily within the familiar landscape of media relations and public meetings and less with more visible, strategic objectives to move their units forward.

However, since the late 1990s, there seems to be a growing recognition of the importance of both marketing and public relations by some government administrators.[9] While there are lots of definitions for public relations, the modern practice can be defined as a *management function that involves building and maintaining positive relationships between an organization and the publics on whom it depends through strategic two-way symmetrical communication.*[10] Symmetrical communication means that a dialogue is fostered between the unit and its constituents, both internal and external, to help the unit understand these publics' concerns, wants, and needs. This is foreign to the traditional model of public information, which has been classified as one-way communication, concerned only with disseminating information and not with the message recipients' understanding or feedback.[11] Such information is critical if the unit is to be more responsive and useful to the constituents it serves and if it is to practice good issues management.

Issues management by its nature is a strategic planning process. Far different from issue communications, it involves active environmental scanning, that is media monitoring, legislative monitoring, and active listening across constituent groups to help seize opportunities and thwart crises before they occur. According to the Issue Management Council, a professional membership organization for people whose work is managing issues, it is "the process used to align organizational activities and stakeholder expectations."[12] Therefore, regular scanning activities should be included in any communication unit's strategic communication plan.

The man credited with first defining and propounding issues management, Howard Chase, recognized its applicability in both corporate and public realms. He said it was a "procedure for more effective participation in the corporate and public policy process ... and can be seen as a vital tool in the total executive management decision making process."[13] In today's environment of increasing scrutiny toward and continued low trust in government,[14] it's more important than ever that active environmental scanning should be systematically planned for and carried out.

In addition to active issues management, government communicators may want to apply marketing principles in their communications efforts to engage more citizens in new or existing government services. In fact, marketing today has a more relationship-centered focus, which aligns it closely with public relations functions. Modern marketing goes beyond the traditional field's four P's of *product, price, placement*, and *promotion* to incorporate more broadly *customer needs and wants*; a recognition of the total *costs* of offering particular products or services to customers, citizens, or society; *convenience* options for accessing or purchasing these products or services; and *communication* with customers, not just one-way publicity or promotion.

During the past decade, there has been a growing recognition of the importance of modern marketing and public relations functions within government agencies. For example, a 2001 white paper report solicited by the Department of Energy reads, in part, that such activities can help "lead to the improvement of public affairs practice within the Department" and "facilitate discussion about the nature of public affairs between public affairs personnel and ... management."[15] Another example is evidenced by marketing specialist John Cagle, who wrote: "It is obvious that the success of [the Federal Highway Administration] in meeting its vision hinges on the agency's ability to 'create exchanges that satisfy individual and organizational objectives.' That means FHWA must know and meet the needs of its customers (including the general public) and its partners."[16]

Yet despite this growing recognition of the value of marketing and public relations techniques within government communications, there appear to be few strategic models that have been made publicly available for widespread emulation and surprisingly little scholarly research conducted in this area. However, one recent study used a sample of nearly 1,000 government and corporate public relations practitioners to determine how closely related public relations is within these two communication domains.[17] While the study found that both government and corporate fields showed potential for growth in the education of communication managers, the government communicators reported higher pressure to meet their public's information needs.

This pressure could stem from a number of factors, including increasing accountability and transparency expectations, lower levels of public trust and budget and staff constraints that typically prohibit the sophisticated public relations activities often pursued by industry. Therefore, it is recognized that any government communication plan must first and foremost be practical and realistic in terms of resources and expectations.

The identified need for communicator education coupled with today's accountability pressures are exacerbated by the scope of the public affairs profession and communication's role within it. For example, one thing is clear in the work this author has done over the course of more than 12 years of communication consulting with government agencies: There is wide variance in the relationships between communications staff and top-level administrators. Just as effective public relations must stem from the top—the *dominant coalition*—in any organization to be truly effective, so must it have the buy-in of top-level administrators within a government agency. If not, your communications planning process and efforts are likely to fail. A unit within a large Midwest state's Department of Transportation provides an example of this necessity.

After working with the unit to develop a strategic plan, the unit became a national model for other states and made good progress for 2 years on its strategic communication activities. Agency administrators were regularly apprised of the unit's progress and were pleased with the results. However, when a new administration took over, the leadership did not buy into the plan, likely because it was developed under the old leadership. The new administrators also did not see the value of public relations beyond its traditional, tactical media relations function, and thus did not understand the strategic, long-term benefits of the unit's resources being spent to develop and sustain positive relationships with its constituents. As a result, the communications personnel were frustrated, and although their strategic planning process remained, their plans became far more limited and short term.

Research First

So how does one begin the strategic planning process? First, the communicator should discuss the benefits of strategic planning to help the larger unit achieve its goals and get administrative buy-in to begin the process. Then the communicator or communications team needs to revisit the larger unit's vision, mission, and how communications contributes to and supports them. Depending on the size and culture of your agency or unit, you may or may not be familiar with this larger vision.

Often, visions—what the organization aspires to become—are disseminated only internally, if they have been articulated at all, or may have been filed away without having been regularly communicated to employees. Even if a vision has not been crafted for your agency or organization, it behooves you to have the conversation about vision with your top administrators. Their vision for the agency is important to understand, for all supporting actions should be consistent with this long-term aspiration. When administrators understand that your unit will help contribute to the agency's overall vision, mission, and specific goals in a systematic, real way, the progress and activities become recognized and valued as more than "must-do" work.

Agency Goals

Once the vision and mission are specified on paper, the plan should identify the larger agency's overall goals for the upcoming year and any specific public relations problems or opportunities to be addressed. Often it's helpful to think about overarching organizational goals as involving one of these three main aims:

- Reputation management
- Relationship management
- Task management

Reputation is just that—enhancing or repairing an agency's reputation with its publics. It may mean being perceived as more responsive, more modern, more efficient, more trustworthy, or something else. Relationship management goals might include fostering more dialogue with constituents, including media representatives, or building more buy-in from employees for new processes, procedures, or the agency's vision. Task management goals involve very specific actions, such as more voters, more attendees at public meetings, more compliance with regulations or safety programs, and the like. When thinking about your goals and your agency or department's goals for the coming year, these management categories can be useful ways to think about your communication work.

More research to define the unit's current situation should be conducted to better understand the specific problems, opportunities, or goals the agency faces or desires. The basic journalistic questions of who, what, when, where, how, and why will help you get a grasp of the problem, opportunity, or goal. For example, for whom is this issue a problem or opportunity? Who will be affected by this goal? What is the essence of the problem, opportunity, or goal? And so on.

To better understand the situation in which you will be planning to operate, your research should include a *situation analysis* of the unit's strengths, weaknesses, opportunities, and threats or challenges (SWOT/Cs) regarding this communication problem, opportunity, or goal. It also can be helpful to think about the situation from the perspective of the political, economic, societal, and technological environments (PEST) in which you are operating.

Target Constituents

Identifying the affected or desired audiences within your strategic plan is essential as well. Each affected or targeted audience should be defined: Who are they demographically in terms of age, income, educational level, size, and makeup of household? What about psychographically, meaning what do they value and what kinds of lifestyles, interests, and sensibilities do they share? Where are they geographically? What do they currently know and think about your organization or unit? Are they participating in your programs, services, and meetings? Are they offering feedback? Who and where are the people who can influence them? For example, are they trusting of government officials, church leaders, community organizers, social service leaders, educators? Whom do they respect and trust? Identifying such "influentials" can be helpful when you plan community meetings, for example, or when you profile certain service users for promotional purposes.

Because most government entities do not have the resources to conduct formal opinion polls, obtaining informal, anecdotal information from meetings, e-mail feedback, letters to the editor, and media coverage can help provide intelligence regarding your current standing in the community. We know from academic agenda-setting and framing studies that media often influence people in terms of the importance people assign issues in society and how—from what perspectives—they come to think of them. Therefore, media coverage, public feedback, and Internet chatter, which can be uncovered through simple Google searches, can provide a lot of intelligence for your agency.

If you have the funds and an important problem (such as some sort of controversy), opportunity (such as new developments and tax bases), or goal (such as an increase in public health service usage), you may want to solicit help from your local college or pay a local firm to conduct a formal opinion poll. However, for less critical information, you can gain information more easily through informal and relatively inexpensive means, such as intercept or other convenience polls, focus groups, or interviews. For most government entities, the information already available through your agency or unit in terms of numbers and types of calls, web hits, information regularly disseminated, media coverage, e-mails, and other such information is enough to help get a sense of any problem issues and to help identify meaningful objectives to work toward in the coming year.

Setting Objectives

Once you've identified the audiences you want to reach to help address the problems, seize the opportunities, or meet the goals of your division or your larger agency, and you have some understanding of what your key constituents already likely know, think, and are doing, you can set realistic, measurable, and deadline-oriented objectives that specify what you want these constituents to know, think, or do as a result of your communication activities.

An example of internal performance objectives set by a federal Department of Energy national laboratory included the following:[18]

- "Enhance the responsiveness ... of Laboratory communications with internal and external stakeholders[.]"
  - Specific activities to be measured could include inquiry and response documentation through a database to allow tracking of internal and external concerns, and the development and posting of standard agency FAQs on particular issues.
- "Create opportunities for stakeholder involvement and participation in Laboratory decision-making processes[.]"
  - Specific activities included development of a Community Advisory Council.
- "Achieve a better understanding between internal and external stakeholders."
  - Specific measurement activities included development of a community speakers' bureau.

Note that each of the specific activities should have a deadline, which might be a specific month or quarter by which each activity should be completed.

Key Messages

After preliminary information has been gathered regarding goals, audiences, and objectives, key messages should be identified. These messages should help the unit achieve its audience knowledge and reputation, attitude and relationship, and behavior and task management objectives; however, to be received and remembered, the messages must appeal to the audience's self-interest. In other words, what's the benefit to the audience of paying attention to this message? In marketing terms, we often call this the *unique selling proposition* (USP). Highlight the benefit or USP in the key messages to your audiences and repeat those messages regularly and through multiple media.

If your communication plan involves more than standard strategic activities—an important new information campaign, for example—perhaps a new slogan or tagline should be developed to reinforce the campaign message on the website, in brochures, on letterhead, in presentations, in public service announcements, and so on. Even if your annual communication plan does not include a large-scale, special endeavor of this kind, a slogan or tag line that is reflective of your vision and mission might be something to consider developing if one does not exist.

Other Strategies

Communication strategies you will likely want to incorporate into your annual communication plan include *interpersonal communication* and *interactivity*. Interpersonal communication is known to be the most persuasive form of communication, and it can be used in such activities as speakers' bureaus, open houses, speeches, or presentations to schools or local civic organizations. Mediated interpersonal communication or interactivity might include an e-mail link on the unit's website or a toll-free telephone number (but *only* if there are resources to properly monitor and respond to the messages), or even someone who "tweets" on Twitter to provide emergency or important updates, for example, to those who are interested in the unit and its activities. These strategies can help you more effectively tell your story, develop relationships, enhance reputation, and persuade people to act.

Repetition and *consistency* of your key messages are needed to cut through the cacophony and distractions of modern life. In your strategic communication plan, you can plan for this repetition and consistency by including your key messages in as many of your communication media to reach specific audiences as possible. This includes being consistent in the use of colors and agency logo and any tag lines or slogans on letterhead, websites, presentations, banners and signage, newsletters, public service announcements, brochures, fact sheets, and so on.

If there are *influentials* or *opinion leaders* who can speak on behalf of your unit or agency to carry public service messages or provide testimonials, this can help gain people's attention and help sway attitudes regarding your unit or its mission.

Likewise, testimonials from or spokespersons who are like your key constituents can be influential and persuasive through a communication concept known as *homophily*, whereby people are more open, receptive to, and persuaded by messages that come from people similar to themselves. In addition, messages that include both *emotional and logical appeals* can be effective, with the emotional appeals gaining attention and making messages more memorable, and the logical appeals attracting more educated and analytical audiences.

It is also helpful to keep in mind that in terms of task management goals, the more you are asking people to do in terms of action, the more logical appeals must be included in your messages. Typically, to get people to act, you must take them first through the knowledge/awareness stage, to attitude formation regarding the issue, and then—over time—people may take action. However, spurring behavior is always the hardest part of any communication campaign, and behavior change takes time and message repetition.

Communication Tactics

Finally, the communication plan must be formalized and specific tasks or tactics must be outlined to support the identified strategies, objectives, and goals. These are the actual messages to be distributed and the tools or media by which messages are disseminated. (For example, a tactic would be the actual scheduled and developed presentation to meet the objective "to schedule at least one external presentation per quarter to a local civic or school group" to fulfill the organization's reputation goal to "become more visible in the community.")

The development or updating of such communication tools or tactics, including any brochures, websites, and standard news releases during particular times of the year or around scheduled events, must be included in the plan. Each communication tool or tactic developed should include a specific call to action, which tells people what they can do to act on the message. For example, a web or e-mail address or phone number can be given, so people can learn more or register for a service or ask questions. These actions can then be tracked to help you assess response and results. Of course, personnel must be assigned to each task and tactic, as are budgets.

Timetable

It is helpful to create a Gantt-like chart in Excel or some other spreadsheet software to see at once the year-long communication plan's scheduled tasks/tactics and their respective personnel assignments. This helps the unit ensure regular communication across the year and that the workload is distributed throughout the year as well. Such a consistent "drip" campaign achieves the repetition of key messages and extends the presence of the unit's message throughout the year, which increases the chances that it will be seen, heard, and remembered.

An Inclusive Process

It is apparent that unit employees must be included in the process of developing an annual communication plan. With top-level support, the activities take on added importance, but it is critical that employees who participate in message dissemination, be it outreach activities or telephone or e-mail correspondence, understand the importance in moving the unit and agency toward its vision and goals and their own important role in the process. One disgruntled employee who, for example, believes that such activities only increase workloads, can derail the unit's efforts to enhance reputation, relationships, and to persuade people toward some action. Therefore, internal communication and realistic objectives are a must.

Ongoing Evaluation

In addition, communication plans should be dynamic documents that are evaluated on an ongoing basis and adapted accordingly to meet objectives and goals. Remember, too, that change takes time; patience should be practiced in terms of plan outcomes, and a new plan with revisited goals and objectives should be developed and shared among staff and management each year, even if it merely continues and builds upon the previous year's document.

With a formal plan in place, you can be sure your unit is moving forward toward its goals and those of the larger agency or department and is not simply reacting each day to its immediate demands. Such planning also can help create a renewed sense of unity and mission within an organization and can help you reconnect it to the community, which will likely grow in its appreciation of your service role.

A sample communication outline, with a few specific examples to help illustrate the steps, is included in the next section of this chapter. A more detailed outline that can be used as a worksheet is included on the book's accompanying CD. (A complete communication plan developed by the author for a state government unit and shared nationwide as part of a research project is also referenced within the endnotes if you would like access to a more complete strategic communication overview and plan.[19]) Of course, your plan will reflect your unit's own priorities and goals and those of your larger agency or department.

Strategic Communication Plan Outline

    I. Larger Agency/Department
      A. Vision
      B. Mission
      C. Goals

II. Unit
   A. Identify any PR Problems, Opportunities, Goals
      a. Mandatory/Pragmatic/Political
      b. Reputation/Relationship/Task Management
   B. Develop Background/Situation Analysis
      a. Strengths, Weaknesses, Opportunities, Challenges
      b. Political, Economic, Societal, Technological Environments
   C. Other Research to determine what people know, feel and do
      a. Media Monitoring
         i. Coverage content analysis
            a. Tone toward organization (positive, negative, neutral)
            b. Key/repeated messages
      b. Boundary Spanning
         i. Internal listening
         ii. External constituent listening
            a. Correspondence/calls/complaints
      c. New, primary research, formal and informal
         i. Polls, surveys, focus groups, interviews
III. Specify Objectives (specific, measurable, deadline oriented)
   A. What do you want people to know by when?
      • *Example:* Make people aware of new electronic service registration by June 30, 2011.
   B. How do you want people to feel by when?
      • *Example*: Make people feel they still receive personal attention through the new electronic service options; make people feel the new electronic service options are more efficient by October 31, 2011.
   C. What do you want people to do by when?
      • Example: Increase electronic service registration numbers by 30% by October 31, 2011.
   D. How will these objectives be measured?
      • *Example*: Media placements of news releases about new service and potential audience reached (media impressions) will be tracked for each placement; website hits of pages that discuss new service will be tracked.
      • *Example*: Constituent feedback and questions regarding new service will be tracked; media coverage content will be analyzed for key, positive messages about the new service.
      • *Example*: Electronic service registration numbers will be tracked and compared to traditional service registration numbers.
IV. Target Constituents/Audiences
   A. Demographic description
   B. Psychographic description
   C. Geographic description

   V. Key Messages Identified
      A. Benefits/USP to Target Audience
         • *Example:* Faster, secure registration that results in more efficiency and faster service for you and cost savings that can be put toward the service program; electronic service registration frees up 800 number for those without Internet access.
  VI. Strategies to Achieve Objectives
      A. Interpersonal/Outreach
         a. Sample Tactic:
            i. Seek out at least one opportunity per quarter to speak to a community group or organization.
      B. Mediated Interpersonal
         a. Sample Tactics:
            i. Regularly monitor, respond to, and track e-mail feedback on the unit website.
            ii. Post one new feature story per quarter that highlights electronic public service activity and personnel.
      C. Media Relations
         a. Sample Tactics:
            i. News release announcing new service to come by January 2011
            ii. Invitation to local reporter to log on and use new electronic registration service by March 2011
            iii. News release announcing new features on electronic registration service by June 30, 2011
      D. Opinion Leaders/Influentials/Spokespersons
         a. Testimonials
            i. Sample Tactic:
               1. Place testimonial on the front page of the unit website by May 31, 2011.
               2. Include a quotation from service user in each news release.
         b. Endorsements
            i. Individuals
            ii. Other groups/units
      E. Message Creation
         a. Emotional appeals
         b. Logical appeals
         c. Nonverbal/Design
         d. Tag lines/Slogans
      F. Message Repetition
 VII. Timetable
      A. Gantt chart or spreadsheet created for the year

VIII. Budget
- A. Research
  - a. Monitoring/Evaluation
- B. Message Creation/Production
  - a. Outside vendors
- C. Other planned tactics/tasks
- D. Employee time
  - a. Regular time
  - b. Travel expenses
  - c. Other

Acknowledgment

The author thanks West Virginia University P. I. Reed School of Journalism graduate student Jeff Yeager for his help in developing this chapter.

Endnotes

[1] Larissa A. Grunig, "Implications of Gender and Culture for Government Public Affairs," in *Government and Public Affairs*, ed. D. Vercic, J. Whites, and D. Moss (Bled, Solvenia: Pristop Communications, 1998), quoted in Elizabeth L. Toth, "Building Public Affairs Theory," in *Public Relations Theory II*, ed. Carl Botan and Vincent Hazelton (New York: Routledge, 2009).

[2] B. Baker, "Public Relations in Government," in *The Handbook of Strategic Public Relations and Integrated Communications*, ed. C. Caywood (New York: McGraw-Hill), quoted in Elizabeth L. Toth, "Building Public Affairs Theory," in *Public Relations Theory II*, ed. Carl Botan and Vincent Hazelton (New York: Routledge, 2009).

[3] Personal interview by Jeff Yeager, February 12, 2010.

[4] John Paluszek, "Editorial Note: Defining Terms," in *Practical Public Affairs in an Era of Change: A Communications Guide for Business, Government and College*, ed. L. B. Dennis (Lanham, MD: University Press of America, 1995), quoted in Elizabeth L. Toth, "Building Public Affairs Theory," in *Public Relations Theory II*, ed. Carl Botan and Vincent Hazelton (New York: Routledge, 2009).

[5] James Grunig, "Communication, Public Relations, and Effective Organizations: An Overview of the Book," in *Excellence in Public Relations and Communication Management*, ed. James Grunig (Hillsdale, NJ: Lawrence Erlbaum Associates, 1992), quoted in Elizabeth L. Toth, "Building Public Affairs Theory," in *Public Relations Theory II*, ed. Carl Botan and Vincent Hazelton (New York: Routledge, 2009).

[6] Public Affairs Council, "Who We Are," accessed February 7, 2010, http://pac.org/about.

[7] National Association of Government Communicators, "History of NAGC," accessed February 8, 2010, http://www.nagc.com/AboutNAGC/HistoryNAGC.asp.

[8] For example, in 1990, the National Transportation Research Board called on State Departments of Transportation to promote and market their research activities. See Susan C. Jakubiak, Richard R. Mudge, and Robert Hur, NCHRP Report 329, "Using Market Research to Improve Management of Transportation Systems."

[9] Adapted from a definition from Patricia Swann, *Cases in Public Relations Management* (New York: McGraw-Hill, 2007).

[10] Dennis L. Wilcox, Glen T. Cameron, Philip H. Ault, and Warren K. Agee, *Public Relations Strategies and Tactics*, 7th ed. (Boston, MA: Pearson Education, Inc., 2003).

[11] Issue Management Council, "Welcome," accessed February 6, 2010, http://www.issuemanagement.org/.

[12] Tony Jaques, "Howard Chase: The Man Who Invented Issue Management," *Journal of Communication Management* 12, no. 4 (2009): 337.

[13] According to the 2010 Edelman Trust Barometer, only 46 percent of US respondents indicated they trusted the government to do what is right. The good news is that this percentage is up 16 percent over the 2009 results. Edelman, "2010 Edelman Trust Barometer: An Annual Global Opinion Leaders Study," accessed February 8, 2010, http:www.edelman.com/trust/2010.

[14] James Grunig and Larissa Grunig, "Guidelines for Formative and Evaluative Research in Public Affairs: A Report for the Department of Energy Office of Science," March 2001, accessed February 9, 2010, http://www.instituteforpr.org/files/uploads/2001_PA_Research.pdf. p. 1.

[15] Cagle, J. I., "Marketing: Helping to Develop the Transportation System for the 21st Century," Public Roads, 62, no. 3 (1999), accessed March 23, 2011. http://www.fhwa.dot.gov/publications/publicroads/98novdec/marketing.cfm

[16] Brooke Fisher Liu, Suzanne Horsley, and Abbey B. Levenshus, "Government Communicators and Corporate Public Relations Practitioners: More Differences than Similarities in How They Communicate?" *Journal of Applied Communication Research*, 38, no. 2 (2010): 189–213.

[17] James Grunig and Larissa Grunig, "Guidelines for Formative and Evaluative Research in Public Affairs: A Report for the Department of Energy Office of Science," March 2001, accessed February 9, 2010, http://www.instituteforpr.org/files/uploads/2001_PA_Research.pdf. p. 32.

[18] Diana Knott and David Martinelli, "Communication Strategies for State Transportation Research Programs," *Transportation Research Record* 1924 (2005): 52–53.

Chapter 9

Ethics in Government Public Relations

Shannon A. Bowen

Contents

If you are working as a public relations practitioner in government, you have probably already realized the myriad ethical challenges and loyalties you will face. This chapter seeks to provide you with both the means of analysis needed for complex ethical dilemmas and the ways to articulate your rationale to others in those sorts of situations. You will learn why it is important to do that.

The ethical challenges faced by those who work in government public relations are perhaps more complex than those found in any other arena. The sheer magnitude of ethical challenges involved in government public relations belies their import—hundreds or thousands of people can be impacted by the consequences of each decision made. The ramifications of your decisions are enormous, and the responsibility to think through those decisions is weighty. Whether you are a public relations practitioner working for an elected official, a government agency, a nonprofit membership association or a nongovernmental organization (NGO), or any of the involved firms such as research and lobbying, you will face ethical challenges regularly. Using a real-world example, one of those challenges might look like the following case.

Case Example: Do Statistics Ever Lie?

Imagine that you are a research analyst at a Capitol Hill political polling firm who is working on the reelection campaign of an incumbent congressman. In analyzing the newest polls and focus groups from the congressman's district, you find his support rapidly slipping among a key constituency, probably due to some controversial statements he recently made to the press. His election is tight this time, so in your strategic report you focus on the slipping support among the key constituency, and on the critical issues your research revealed they care about most. You focus on how the congressman can regain support with those key voters, providing statistics to back up views on the issues that his constituents do care about. Analysis and report complete, you hand it off to your supervisor and head home to rest after a busy week.

On Monday, your supervisor calls you for a meeting about the report. She says that despite the congressman's slipping poll numbers, he has used your research firm for years and that she does not want to offend him by "reporting all of these negative data." You believe that your report is accurate and balanced, genuinely reporting what surfaced in your research. She points out a few of the more critical comments from constituents that you have included in your report for emphasis and explanation of their views. She tells you that his patronage of the research firm is far too important to endanger, and asks you to rewrite the report. Surprised, you tell your supervisor, "The numbers are the numbers," and you are simply reporting what they said upon analysis. She concludes your meeting by handing you the report and saying, "Well, just find a way to make the numbers look better. We can't give him this!"

In this real-world scenario, what would you do? Would you change the numbers, concealing more critical information from the congressman that might actually endanger his reelection? Would you simply focus on the more appealing and agreeable statistics in your report? Would your first loyalty be to the research firm that employs you, to your congressman as a client, to your supervisor, to your own livelihood and income, or even to your reading of the statistics themselves? Because the congressman has paid for the data collection, does he need to see all of it, even the critical, or only the more supportive viewpoints? What is the most ethical way to maintain your client's political prospects? Would you worry about your future, your income, and maintaining your job at the research firm? How could you resolve such a complex dilemma ethically? We will revisit this scenario at the end of the chapter.

Commonality of Ethical Dilemmas

You might be surprised to find out how often this "cheerleader versus critic" debate is played out in the offices around Washington, DC, internationally, and in state and local capitals. It also happens in corporate boardrooms, public relations firms, lobbying agencies, and any place that the challenge of defining facts is associated with setting public policy. The author of this chapter has been involved in more than a few of these "cheerleader versus critic" debates, and advises you to expect them as a part of the job in government public relations. This chapter should provide you with an overview of both the ethical thinking and the methods for rigorous analyses of ethical dilemmas in government public relations and public affairs.

Public relations practitioners today report that they are being called upon to counsel the leaders of their organizations on ethical dilemmas.[1] About 65 percent of public relations practitioners in a recent worldwide study report directly to the highest-ranking person in their organizations or said that they have regular access to counseling that person.[2] They reported that there are reasons for being called to counsel a chief executive officer (CEO) including a crisis, an ethical dilemma, an issue high on the media agenda, the CEO's credibility within the organization, or just having a leadership role in the organization. In applying these results to government public relations, you can see that you will most likely be called upon to counsel on crisis in ethics, especially when there is media attention or conflict needing your help to resolve. That type of issue can arise with elected officials, government agencies, nonprofits, lobbying firms, and the many support services that the government hires to conduct research or public relations activities. In short, you cannot escape ethical dilemmas, and the best time to prepare yourself to conduct an ethical analysis is *before* you desperately need an answer.

Definitional Issues

Government public relations is the type of communication function that deals with the interaction of the citizenry with the government, with governmental regulators, and the legislative (elected and appointed) and regulatory arms of government. Corporate public affairs differs slightly in that it is the type of public relations that manages how an organization interacts with the government, its governmental regulators, and the legislative branch of government. Although these two functions are often discussed as synonyms, there are some differences to clarify. Government public relations helps to facilitate communication with constituencies and with governmental publics. Public affairs is normally a corporate function that helps the organization maintain ties with legislators and government regulatory agencies, and to engage in lobbying on behalf of its interests. These two functions often overlap, but despite the fine differences between the two, the approaches to ethics put forward in this chapter can be used by practitioners in both government public relations or in corporate public affairs. Both government public relations and corporate public affairs have to deal with strategic issues on matters of public policy, meaning how their organizations interact with government and constituents. Heath[3] contended, *"Public policy issues are those with the potential of maturing into governmental legislation or regulation (international, federal, state, or local)."* (Italics added)

Public policy issues are difficult to manage because of the competing interests involved. On matters of strategic public policy, one must ethically weigh the responsibilities of the communication professional to publics, organizations, and government entities. Ethical choices are made every day in government public relations. You might ask yourself which master is being served with a certain decision, the purpose behind the decision, the underlying goal of the action, or the ultimate value underlying the action in order to understand which decisions truly force an ethical choice. Although most decisions have overtones of ethics, some of your choices will highlight the divided loyalties inherent in government public relations more than others.

The author of this chapter has designed a number of ethical decision-making models for use in public relations.[4] Although those models are useful and applicable, it helps to simplify their constructs and apply them directly to government public relations for the purposes of this chapter. There are three primary approaches to ethics that it helps to study: materialism, consequentialism, and nonconsequentialism. Each will be discussed below and two are offered as an ethical decision-making framework that you can use in your day-to-day operations of government public relations. First, we will briefly review how you can identify and spot those ethical challenges before they become major crises through using the communication function called *issues management*.

Strategic Issues Management

Ethics and government public relations cross at the intersection of a function called issues management. The public policy issues faced by governments, legislators, regulatory agencies, and their counterparts at various levels of government across any national setting must be monitored and managed with vigilance. Dramatically and swiftly changing public opinion coupled with the interactive relationships of organizations, governments, and their publics and constituencies lead to a dynamic information environment that requires the public relations professional to engage in sophisticated issues management.[5]

Issues management begins with research to identify new and emerging issues. Any issue that can affect the future of your organization, government, legislative initiative, or public policy issue is considered worthy of identification, monitoring, and analysis. The means of identification of issues varies from visiting with the leaders of activist groups to using sophisticated analytical software that can monitor social media discussion. Multiple sources must be monitored on a consistent and regular basis, through the use of keywords, names, or terms and groups that could be associated with the issue. Once an issue is identified, the real work of conducting as much research as possible to understand the issue begins. After an issue is identified, issue monitoring begins, seeing how rapidly it gains traction and saturation among publics. For example, the phrase "wild horse shootings" might score many mentions on the blogs, Tweets, and discussion boards of animal rights groups, and thus be identified as an issue for the Bureau of Land Management (BLM) and the Department of Agriculture.

Perhaps the most crucial phase of issues management in an ethical sense is the issues identification and monitoring stage. If a government public relations practitioner fails to identify a rapidly emerging ethical issue, the chance is lessened of creating a strategic and ethical plan to manage the issue. Once an ethical dilemma enters the public policy arena, the organization has less autonomy or ability to define the issue and the associated ethical evaluation. Timely identification of potential ethical problems is of the utmost importance in responsible issues management.

At this stage, it is common to hire a research firm that can conduct original, statistical data collection so that the public relations practitioner can base policy advice on a sound understanding of public opinion surrounding the issue. Research is collected in a variety of ways including focus groups, statistical polls, informal interviews, analyzing media mentions, and also internal (or intraorganizational) forms of data collection such as financial projections of the cost of certain responses to the issue. Using the previous example, the Congressional Budget Office might be asked to provide estimates to the BLM of the costs for alternative means disposing of wild horses such as auctioning them to private buyers.

In the next phase of issues management, the public relations manager explores various decision alternatives or issue action options, and tries to determine the ethics, pros and cons, and costs or benefits of each option. In this phase, many issues management meetings are held with leaders in the organization who each weigh in and provide a clear perspective on the issue. Many approaches to ethics are normally brought to the table and discussed regarding which of the decision options is "the right thing to do." It is also wise to ask publics or constituents who care about this issue to provide their perspective and advice or ideas regarding the options that are being considered. Incorporating the values of publics or constituents at this phase of issues management is exceptionally important for both an ethical perspective and the perspective of successful communications. A collaborative amalgamation of decision options from several different perspectives often results in the best resolution for an issue. Ethics is the first priority when dealing with issues management in this chapter, but many organizations need to be reminded of how important ethical considerations are to their credibility and long-term reputation.

Once an option is chosen as the best for how to manage an issue, a strategy surrounding that option is created by the government public relations professional. He or she examines data to create messages that resound with publics and motivate them to support the issue action initiative. Lobbyists may be deployed or grassroots campaigns begun. In this phase of issues management, it is expected to have numerous public relations practitioners involved in disseminating the strategic message around the issue in order to inform, persuade, or change public opinion. The length of this active issue communication campaign will vary due to the severity of the issue, the results that need to be achieved with constituencies, the interests of the news media, and the budget of the organization. After an ongoing issue communication campaign, the issues manager will conduct evaluation research to measure how much change has occurred surrounding the issue in the minds of key constituencies and target publics. The campaign will be evaluated, and will either continue seeking more change on the issue, refining messages, and strategically retargeting, or the issue may be considered resolved.[6] In the latter case, the issues manager moves on to the next issue that has certainly emerged by this point.

This ongoing cycle of issues management allows professional communicators to identify and understand the challenges they face and to potentially resolve them in an ethical manner before they become crises. Governmental public relations professionals should constantly strive to include ethical analyses in their issues management, to identify ethical issues, and to use the decision-making frameworks of ethics discussed in this chapter in their issue analysis and strategy. Doing so can result in more ethical issue responses, more transparency, and more honesty in government. Using the following ethical analyses in issues management should allow government relations professionals to have an active role in creating more ethical, responsive, and responsible organizations. Before turning to the ethical approaches, a brief case will be introduced that we can use as an example in discussing the approaches. The case will be revisited to illustrate the practical application of each approach to ethics introduced in the following text.

Ethics Case: Governmental and Public Policy Surrounding the Issue of Horse Roundups for Slaughter

Ethical issues in government public relations often arise around a conflict of values between constituents or publics, organizations, and one or more areas of government. A current example is an interest group or activist issue in the United States centering on protecting horses being sold for human consumption. Both domestic and wild horses have been sold to slaughterhouses in the United States, Canada, and Mexico and the meat shipped to Europe and Asia for human consumption. Animal rights and humane organizations have created initiatives and grassroots movements to lobby their elected officials and representatives to stop horse slaughter.

The values of these groups hold horses among a class of animals as workers and friends or pets rather than a source of human food, citing the long history of horse labor during the settling of the western United States as one example. Congress people in the U.S. House of Representatives introduced legislation on behalf of these animal rights activists to end horse slaughter for human consumption within America, and the U.S. Senate also has many cosponsors in favor of that bill, S727. Members of the House and Senate directly cited the active issue lobbying initiatives of the New York Racing Association, a thoroughbred group, and Fans of Barbaro, an activist group founded around the famous race horse. However, the meatpacking industry and cattlemen's associations vehemently oppose this legislation because slaughterhouses provide a convenient way to dispose of unwanted horses while making a profit. They see their freedom as being abridged by the government, and they value their freedom to decide what to do with horses above other considerations. The moral conflict surrounding this issue is fierce and leads groups to be in direct opposition. To further complicate matters, the Bureau of Land Management (BLM) and the Department of Agriculture routinely sponsor horse roundups in which the captured animals are sold to slaughterhouses for human consumption.

The lobbying efforts of the Western ranchers and the political appointees from those states support the Department of Agriculture and the Bureau of Land Management in these activities. However, the sentiment of large numbers of animal lovers and animal rights activists is on the side of the issue for treating horses with dignity. The government clearly has a stake in this issue, as do the meatpackers and cattlemen and the animal rights advocacy groups.

The Debate. The core ethical issue in this debate is a difference over the assessment and the value of equine life, as well as over the history and role of horses in U.S. society. The ranchers are using a utilitarian approach, arguing that the cattle that they feed on grasslands are provided in the public interest to feed the American market for beef. They argue that the cost of killing the wild horses or slaughtering unwanted domestic horses is outweighed by the good created by using the land to support their cattle. Many ethicists would agree that the ranchers are not using the correct yardstick in judging what is in the public interest. The animal rights activists argue that the practice of consuming horses is morally abhorrent, and that the creature should be treated with the respect and dignity due to a workmate or friend. They cite retired military horses, police horses, racehorses, carriage horses, and animals who assist children with Down's syndrome as examples of noble creatures whose intrinsic value should ensure them a worthwhile existence without the painful and horrifying end of a slaughterhouse.

Questions for further insight. Is the reputation of one or more organizations at stake? Where should the U.S. government stand on this issue? Which ethical paradigm should be employed to create the most enduring, rational, principled, and morally responsible decision in resolving this contentious issue? These issues will be addressed as we use each ethical approach to analyze the case.

The Three Ethical Approaches

Materialism

Materialist perspectives on ethics tell us that the decision maker should seek to satisfy his or her own needs first in a competitive arena. Materialism differs from that which is thought to be patently unethical because it is based on competitive positioning. The philosophy of selfishness has found little resonance within ethics scholarship, and needs a little study to be understood because of its basal instinct premise. If selfishness is the ethical motive upon which to act, those who act selfishly act in their own best interest and therefore satisfy the materialist requirement of the ethical. Obviously, there are many moral flaws with that approach, but it is a very common one today for people who operate in either government or business to make self-interested decisions. Scholars morally contend that self-interest alone is not enough to make a decision ethical, and that there must be further analysis.

Despite the commonality of a self-interested materialism approach in the modern world, it is a descriptive ethic rather than a normative ideal to which we should aspire. A more moderate approach to materialism is the objectivist philosophy of those who base their decisions on competition. In game theory terms, zero-sum games are those in which there is one winner and one loser in a scenario. The objectivist philosophy applies that zero-sum approach in the marketplace of ideas, in which the winner takes all and the loser gets nothing. This type of philosophy argues that it is ethical because if everyone looks out for him- or herself equally, suiting one's self-interest competitively should allow the best arguments and perspectives to compete successfully.

For practical application, the horse case offers many examples of materialism. The ranchers in western states find that wild horses grazing on their lands in competition with cattle cuts into their profit from cattle herds; therefore, it is in their self-interest to rid the land of wild horses. Elected officials from these states are lobbied by these ranchers, and often receive campaign contributions from them, so a materialistic analysis shows that it is in their self-interest to support the wild horse roundups. Activist groups who work on behalf of wild horses are normally not major donors to the campaigns of these legislators; therefore legislators' interests lie with the cattle industry. The Department of Agriculture and the Bureau of Land Management were given their charges by these legislators, and their self-interest lies in carrying out directives effectively so that their reviews (for raises and promotions, etc.) will show that they contribute to its organizational goals. Applying materialism in this case example is simple because that is the paradigm in use. However, most ethicists would agree that a materialist paradigm–induced case leads to immoral actions that gratify only selfishness rather than serving ethical principles or the public interest and greater good.

Although this philosophy is again very common in today's world of business and government public relations, it is less than ideal because it assumes a level playing field and cannot contend with the issues of different informational or resource-based advantages creating disequilibrium in what should have been a level playing field. Those advantages, disadvantages, and differing levels of media access and interest in order to inform and sway public opinion are incredibly difficult to quantify, much less to accurately include in an ethical analysis. Materialism turns out to be more descriptive of what happens in actual practice than a normative paradigm that is helpful in determining the ethical, because rather than helping to lend astute means of analysis it tends to degenerate into selfish materialism. Therefore, we need to turn to a more normative (best practices) mode of ethical decision making in order to have guidance and true help in navigating the complex waters of government public relations. Consequentialism and nonconsequentialism, or both, offer normative paradigms of ethical decision making to help us arrive at the *norm* or best case scenario in a situation. Normative ethical approaches require a mindset that strives for the ideal and are, no doubt, more difficult to implement than conducting analyses by gut instinct, intuition, or seat-of-the-pants decision making. However, the strength and rigor of the analysis brought by each will lend your public relations practice a new level of insight and defensibility.

Consequentialism: Utilitarianism

Consequentialism as a normative paradigm of ethical decision making tells the decision maker to look to the potential consequences for a decision in order to determine what is ethical. Most of the useful consequentialist paradigms fall into the utilitarian school of thought, based on the utility of a decision as predicted by its consequences. There are a few ways to define what kinds of consequences are best. Before we jump into the utilitarian calculus, let us consider for a moment the idea of maximizing certain consequences and minimizing other consequences. That idea is what we call the *utility* of a decision—essentially, what the decision does. The utility of a decision can be held to the maximins (pronounced "maxi mins") principle: the best decision will maximize good outcomes and minimize bad outcomes. What is the utility of your most recent decision in government public relations? In other words, think about the consequences of your decision and what that decision does, predicting potential outcomes and looking for the maximins principle. There is a long history of moral philosophy behind the maximins principle that we call the *utilitarian calculus.* The utilitarian calculus predicts what the potential outcomes of different decision options might be, and applies different measures of good, or different "yardsticks," for determining what is ethical. Here is a brief summary of the main approaches.

Hedonistic utilitarianism considers maximizing pleasure and minimizing pain as that which is ethical. *Eudaimonistic utilitarianism* defines the ethical as that which produces the greatest happiness, or applies the maximins principle to happiness. In that approach, the decision that maximizes happiness and minimizes unhappiness is the ethical course of action.

Finally, *ideal utilitarianism* does not confine the maximins principle to one concept, but seeks its application over all of the concepts that are considered intrinsically valuable. Those principles could be knowledge, honor, kindness, honesty, friendship, and so on. Defining the good is a challenge in any form of ethics, but in the utilitarian framework you have no doubt heard it phrased as "the greatest good for the greatest number of people." That idea does have resonance with those who work in government public relations because it gets to the heart of the matter of managing our responsibilities in accordance with the public interest.

In the world of government public relations, we are likely to face a situation in which ideal utilitarianism could be applied to maintaining relationships with publics and constituents. The maximins principle would then be applied to examine the different decision options that would help maintain the most positive relationship outcomes with publics and constituents, and would minimize the negative outcomes with those publics. There is likely to be a dominant consideration in utilitarianism that overrides some of the other considerations you might have to take into your calculus. Although utilitarianism does not ensure an ethical outcome, its overall use is thought to produce more good than harm, as the theory arose out of the need of the British government to consider the best interests of the citizens it governed. The utility of the decisions made in a utilitarianism framework should benefit the public interest, as is often a dominant consideration in government public relations.

Strengths and Weaknesses of Utilitarianism

Ideal utilitarianism provides a powerful means through which we can analyze the ethics of our decisions and government public relations. The idea of conducting public relations in the interest of the greatest good for the greatest number of people is a morally worthy one, and there is little doubt that viewing the consequences of our decisions upon publics is a responsible part of government communications. As with any moral theory, the approach is bound to a certain set of assumptions about predicting outcomes, and it comes with strengths and weaknesses that the user of the paradigm must always bear in mind. There are a few challenges to be faced by anyone using a utilitarian analysis:

■ You must accurately predict potential future consequences of your decisions.
■ You must know all of the options or decision alternatives that are possible.
■ You must know how various publics will react to the decision and consider all of those viewpoints.
■ You must try successfully to anticipate unintended consequences.
■ You must keep in mind that the rule of the majority should never edge out the valid concerns of the minority.
■ You must minimize harm.
■ You must not "sacrifice" a smaller public in the interest of a larger public in a way that creates harm or significant negative outcomes for the minority (they might have a valid point!).

With these weaknesses in mind, it is important to employ the utilitarian weighing of outcomes in as rational and objective a manner as possible, so as not to preference or bias the outcome of your decision. If you can maximize the good outcomes and minimize the bad outcomes, then your decision is an ethical one. The most beneficial course of action is the one that maximizes the utility of the decision or the ethically right course of action. Utilitarianism is a sound, relatively easy course of analysis to take in order to measure the impact of potential courses of action; it can be based on a hard number and you can weigh the final outcomes of the calculations to decide the best option.

Weighing the positive and negative potential outcomes of decisions should be a relatively easy task to master because it is a basic stage of moral development. It comes as second nature to us to conduct the cost-benefit analysis involved in utilitarianism, and this approach pairs well with weighing the costs and benefits of the various issue options in strategic issues management. Utilitarianism requires a more disciplined, thorough, and well-researched version of the innate utilitarian calculus that one applies in a cost-benefit analysis. However, knowing which decision options to weigh is an important part of creating the greatest good for the greatest beneficial outcome for the greatest number of publics. After all, government public relations must be conducted in accordance with the public interest. The public interest lends itself to siding with the majority in a number of cases, but creative research can help integrate the interests of many groups, including small but vocal minority factions.

Knowing and accurately predicting the future in both consequences and repercussions is difficult, even with the aid of the most sophisticated research. This is one area in which research, both informal and formal, can certainly help the public relations practitioner understand the values, needs, and priorities of different publics. In doing so, judging potential reactions of publics can be easier. However, there is always the potential of misunderstandings or for negative information in the media to take the predicted consequences awry. Opposing sides of an issue may point to different evaluations of what the good to be maximized is or should be. In seeking to weigh the good against the bad, utilitarianism will often look for rules or systems that should be dominant considerations in the analysis. Those norms are established in a manner that society can support, so the utilitarian sees this system as one that is commonly accepted and can speed or ease the utilitarian's detailed analysis.[7]

Conducting research should also help the political public relations practitioner be familiar with the potential options (also called *decision alternatives*) that could be used to resolve an issue. The adroit use of research both inside and outside of the government organization can create a number of decision alternatives, and then these alternatives could be examined in detail for their potential consequences before any decision is made. Further, a good use of informal research and collaboration with constituent publics is to create collaborative options in which those groups weigh in on decisions and add their collective thoughts. In that manner, new decision options can sometimes be created that have an advantage over one-sided thinking, in that they are collaborative, integrated, and come up with new viewpoints to be considered.

Another weakness of utilitarian theory is that it does not lend itself well to matters that are difficult to reduce to numbers.[8] For instance: What is the value of a person's life? Is it better to further the living prospects of five people than it is to significantly help one person? Or, is the same amount of human labor worth more money in one country versus another? Is it best to require vaccinations for everyone in a society in support of the greater good, knowing that some people will have an allergic reaction? Quantifying human value and moral principle becomes extremely complicated, especially in matters of life and death, freedom and security, and public interest. For this reason, applying utilitarianism in concert with a nonconsequentialist theory that looks at moral principle, as discussed in the next section, strengthens the overall analysis.

Finally, in weighing the decision options available in utilitarianism, the majority always wins. In that manner, utilitarianism can be used to justify or create unjust decisions. It is important to remember that majority rule can be stifling and create hegemony against the minority. One way to guard against this particular pitfall is to make sure you have heard and included alternate viewpoints, even those of the smaller groups who wish to have a say in the issue. Finding collaborative ways to integrate the ideas and interests of multiple publics will indeed create a greater good for the greater number. Utilitarianism has the potential weakness of reducing people to group samples that allow decisions to be made on small or shifting numbers rather than moral principle. As long as you, as the public relations practitioner who seeks common ground among the publics, work to guard against disenfranchising the ideas and values of smaller publics, utilitarianism can be used to create ethical decisions.

Implementing Utilitarianism

Cognizant of the above strengths and weaknesses of utilitarianism, the government public relations practitioner could perform a utilitarian analysis on almost any situation concerning government and public policy. The approach lends itself well to public relations because it considers the consequences of our actions on the strategic constituencies involved or related to a decision. The steps involved in conducting a utilitarian analysis are presented in Figure 9.1.

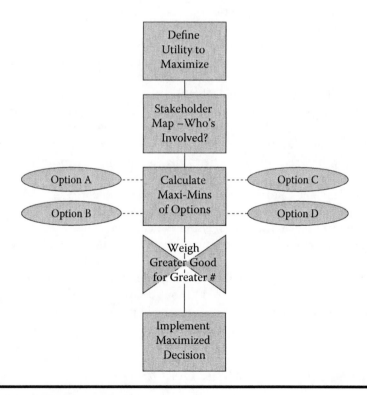

Figure 9.1   Utilitarian analysis.

Applying a Utilitarian Analysis to the Horse Case

As a worker in government public relations, your charge is clearly to work on behalf of the public interest, as with other governmental functions. That means that you would use an ideal utilitarian approach to resolving the case. Referring to Figure 9.1 might help as you consider how to analyze the case. The utility to be maximized is clearly to create a wild horse policy for the Department of Agriculture and the BLM that works in the public interest and maximizes the support for those agencies among the citizens they represent. You want to minimize reputational damage to your organization, including bad press, attacks from bloggers and activist groups, and grassroots lobbying against your organization because utilitarianism seeks to minimize the potential for these negative outcomes. The stakeholder map to develop would use research to identify and understand who is involved in the decision and how many members there are of each public: cattlemen, ranchers, animal rights activists, humane activists, horse enthusiasts, slaughterhouses, course shelters, auctioneers, horse transportation companies, the horse racing and showing industries, potential adopters of wild horses, state legislators in involved states, voters, American citizens, and so on.

At this point, you formulate options for resolving the issue: those options should maximize benefit or positive outcomes and minimize harm or negative outcomes. Working in the public interest would mean that the largest public to be served is American citizens, who might not be concerned about the issue at this point, but if it were a major news story, would certainly be concerned. Research shows that the majority of the American public believes that selling horses to slaughter for human consumption is morally offensive or even barbaric. You should formulate other options that are feasible, taking into account the viewpoints of your majority public. You might meet with animal welfare experts to ask for their suggestions on how to resolve the wild horse issue effectively. The options that you create (options A, B, C, and D on the figure) should serve the public interest, so they should include no-slaughter solutions such as relocating the wild horses to adoption shelters or animal welfare sanctuaries. If you are to create the greatest good for the greatest number of members of your citizenry public, you must choose the option that can be supported by the greatest number of citizens. Moving the horses without slaughter satisfies the majority of the public, minimizes the harm created to the meatpacking industry (a small public), and minimizes potential harm to your organization through negative publicity. Your decision creates the greatest good for the greatest number, and it can therefore be implemented and discussed as an ethical choice.

Nonconsequentialist Analysis: Deontology

Based on the title of this section, you are probably wondering how one can make an ethical decision without the consequences in mind. Let me assure you that the consequences do come into play in this type of moral analysis, but consequences are only one factor among many and are not the overriding outcome that will determine the ethical nature of the decision. The *decision factor* or the most important consideration in this perspective is a duty to moral principle. Nonconsequentialist reasoning is named that as a contrast to the consequentialist-based perspective of utilitarianism. Even the most committed nonconsequentialists, such as Immanuel Kant, offered: "There can be no will without an end in view."[9]

Nonconsequentialist reasoning is otherwise known as *deontology* because it is based on a duty to uphold moral principle (the word deontology comes from the Latin term for duty). Discovering the underlying moral principle behind a decision and supported by it is the ultimate goal of deontology. This analytical framework is a bit more complicated than most others, and requires the understanding of a few basic concepts before we can proceed. The first of those concepts is *rationality*. In the Enlightenment-based philosophy of deontology, rigorous rational analysis of all decision alternatives available from each of the various perspectives of any public involved should be conducted. Decisions in deontology need to be made from a rational perspective so that they cannot be compromised or influenced by bias, selfishness, fear of retribution, or something similar that would taint the analysis. In the government public relations world, it is easy to imagine that the loyalty to the candidates, an employer, or a political party might provide temptation to privilege certain outcomes of a decision. That temptation should be avoided through the use of an objective and rational perspective in which you attempt to maintain as much detachment and objectivity from the decision and its outcomes as you can. The philosopher Kant said that rationality is what makes all humans equal, and what gives each person the ability to engage in upholding moral principle. You might think of that approach as maintaining professional distance, but it also implies a rational and more balanced type of decision analysis than you would engage in without making the effort to be objective. Further, that objectivity allows you to see the meritorious viewpoints of various constituencies or publics involved in a decision. Perhaps a better decision or improved legislation can ultimately result from such inclusion.

The second concept that needs to be ensured before endeavoring to discover the underlying moral principle behind a decision is *autonomy*. Autonomy refers to the idea of how independent you are to make moral decisions. Similar to the concept of rational objectivity discussed above, examining the decision makers' autonomy in a given situation seeks to ensure the decision against bias, prejudice, or other factors that may influence it or add an element of capriciousness that should be avoided. Moral autonomy asks the following questions: Do you have the means necessary to make a moral decision? Do you have the independence that is necessary to engage in objective, rational analytics? Do you have the authority and voice in your organization to be able to diplomatically differ with others on your assessment of the situation and to be heard? Autonomy is a moral construct that differs from actual authority. *Authority*, as the codified power and structure in an organization, is earned or assigned. *Moral autonomy* is free to anyone who is able to engage in a rational thought process. However, that thought process must not be impeded by fear, or an inability to have any say or influence on the decision. If one lacks the autonomy to have any say or influence in an ethical analysis, you cannot be a morally responsible agent. Rationality and autonomy really go hand in hand because to result in a truly ethical conclusion, one must be able to engage in moral analysis without being compelled in any particular direction. One example of where that process might go awry could be when a junior-level public relations specialist feels threatened in raising the question of whether a particular course of action is ethical. She or he might feel constrained in a meeting, afraid of losing a newly acquired position or income, or might even be the recipient of overt indications from a superior such as, "Just write what you are told to, and let us worry about the ethics." In such an example, the moral autonomy of the lower-level public relations specialist is compromised, and he or she no longer has the ability to make the ethical determination about an issue.

Government public relations practitioners should seek to avoid creating or working in the type of environment in which any group member is afraid to question assumptions, voice objections, or raise a point for ethical analysis whenever he or she feels it is warranted, no matter what level in the organization the person occupies. Having moral autonomy is vitally necessary to be able to conduct a rational analysis, free of fear of repercussions and free of bias based on personal desire, self-interest, greed, or quid-pro-quo deals.

Basing decisions on a rational motive analysis and being morally autonomous are two necessary steps in using a deontological approach. If those requirements are met, the government public relations practitioner can move forward to analyzing ethical dilemmas. One of the weaknesses of deontology is that it requires rigorous study and thorough application of its tests, and that in turn requires the time necessary to do so. Of course, one must also realize that an ethical dilemma exists in order to conduct a deontological analysis, and that is often the first problem when issues are not defined as ethical problems. As a government public relations professional, you must be on the alert for ethical issues, conflicts of interests, and the myriad other ethical challenges to be faced. If your honest and frank self-assessment reveals that you are a rational decision maker and reasonably morally autonomous, you are ready to apply the next test in Kant's theory, which is named the *categorical imperative*. It is termed *categorical* because everyone who is rational is obligated to act morally, and *imperative* because its main concepts must be considered for a decision to be deemed ethical.

Implementing Deontology: The Categorical Imperative

In the categorical imperative, there are three tests: dignity and respect, intention, and duty. A potential action must pass all three of these tests affirmatively in order to be ethically sound. In the first test, Kant asked us to pose the following question, adapted here for public relations: "Does the option I am considering maintain the dignity and respect of all publics involved in the issue?" If the answer is affirmative, and the publics would feel respected by the decision and not have their dignity stripped, then the decision is ethical and one can proceed to the next test. If the answer is confused or negative, it is not ethical to strip the publics of dignity or respect based on the desires of an organization, government, or representative. The ethical theory Kant used underlying this test is that having human dignity and being respected is based on an innate moral good that is not to be abridged. In violating human dignity or respect, a decision becomes patently unethical. For example, a government imprisoning those who speak out against it is unethical because it violates those objectors' rights to dignity and respect. Reasonable people can disagree respectfully and maintain the dignity of an opposing party. To disrespect or abridge that ability strips a public of the moral autonomy to create its own rational assessment of a situation, which is so vital in nonconsequentialist ethics.

One deontologist, a philosopher named John Rawls, attempted to make this step of the categorical imperative test easier by designing what he called the "veil of ignorance."[10] To use the veil of ignorance, imagine that you do not know your place in society, your race, class, gender, or ethnicity, or your relation to the issue at hand. By imagining that you do not have any of these factors, you can detach yourself from the outcome of the decision and create a more fair and respectful resolution to the issue because you could ultimately find yourself on the opposite side of the issue. The veil of ignorance is simply a method through which one can think of the decision from any number of various perspectives, without showing a preference for personal desires or attitudes. Therefore, it is a useful tool to help maintain the dignity and respect of the many publics and constituencies you must handle in government public relations. If your decision does maintain the dignity and respect of involved publics, you should move on to the second step of the categorical imperative.

In the second step, the question should be posed, "What is the intention underlying this action?" This question is Kant's most stringent test of morality. Answering this question requires bare-bones honesty, self-reflection, and integrity. Deontological theory holds that only decisions made from a basis of goodwill or pure moral intention are ethical. That means, for instance, giving funds to a senator to build a new dam in her state in exchange for her vote on an issue you are concerned about is unethical. Funding the new dam because the new dam is needed and your intention is to appropriate the funds in the most ethical manner possible is the ethical decision. The result is the same—the new dam gets funding—but the intention behind the latter decision is ethical because it is based on good intention rather than a *quid-pro-quo* exchange. In the world of governmental public relations, intentions must be checked on a regular basis, especially when politically motivated decisions involve an ethical issue. Only the intention to do the right thing is ethical. Other intentions that serve a biased self-interest or create games

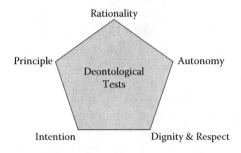

Rationality

Principle

Deontological
Tests

Autonomy

Intention

Dignity & Respect

Figure 9.2   Deontological analysis.

for reasons other than the rightness of doing so are deemed unethical. Kant called goodwill or good intention the ultimate norm of morality because it is his strongest test. If the option that you are considering, after thorough analysis, is based on goodwill and only an intent to do the right thing, you can move to the final test of the categorical imperative.

The third test of the categorical imperative is to ask if the decision upholds a duty to universal moral principles. That means, could you obligate everyone else who faces a similar situation to do the same thing you are about to do? Is the decision reversible—in other words, is the decision still ethical if you were on the receiving end? If you had to walk a mile in the shoes of the other involved publics, would you still see the logic, rationality, dignity and respect, and good intention behind the decision? These concepts are represented in Figure 9.2.

The universal moral norms that Kant discussed simply mean that any person or constituency, in various positions, could examine the option and be evaluated as ethical. So, publics, regulated industries, or competing political opponents would assess the moral nature of the decision as one that upholds a larger duty. Kant wrote this test in order to help us find the underlying moral principle on which most people can agree. Most universal moral norms include intrinsically good concepts such as the right not to be murdered, honesty, dignity, industriousness, liberty, and knowledge. This test does not obligate everyone involved in the decision to agree with the decision, only to acknowledge that the decision upholds a moral principle. For example, many publics might disagree with the form of protests used by opponents of the fur industry; however, they should not disagree with the right of those protesters to draw a moral conclusion that leads them to protest.

Applying the three decision tests of deontology to the various options you are considering for resolving your ethical issue should help you conduct a rigorous moral analysis. The ethics involved in deontology; rationality, autonomy, dignity and respect, goodwill, and pure intention are thought to produce the most rigorous ethical analysis offered in moral philosophy. If the action you are considering passes all of these tests, you are on morally defensible ground.

That does not mean that constituents or publics will agree with the action, but it does mean that it is analytical and morally defensible, making it an ethical decision.

Several research studies have found that most public relations professionals use a deontological approach to ethical reasoning in their issues management.[11] It is arguably the most comprehensive ethical paradigm provided by moral philosophy. In applying deontology, the government public relations professional can explain decisions to constituencies, legislators, governmental agencies, and the news media, and other publics. Deontology provides the most rigorous means of analysis, but the analysis is strengthened when used in conjunction with a utilitarian approach. By conducting both utilitarian and deontological analyses, the practitioner can be reasonably certain that no publics have been left unconsidered, no views disregarded, no costs or benefits overlooked, and that the strengths of deontology are maintained through dignity and respect, good intention, and upholding moral principle.

Applying Deontology to the Horse Case

You do not base your decision in the horse case on the consequences or potential outcomes, but rather on moral principle and Kant's decision test known as the categorical imperative. In your analysis of the case, you work to rationally and objectively understand the issues from the perspective of each of the involved publics listed in the case. You recognize that competing interests exist, but you do not privilege any one interest over the interest of another based on size of the public, financial concerns, campaign contributions, or other factors. Are you morally autonomous? The decision maker in this case must not be working in the interests of the ranchers or slaughterhouses, or in the interests of the animal rights activists, but must be beholden to rationality alone.

You seek to understand the underlying moral principle behind the case and determine the most important decision factor, that is, the highest-level or most important moral principle involved. Most rational beings, regardless of society or culture, agree with the moral principle that one should not murder wantonly or murder for profit. You recognize that the principle involves human life, but you also realize that animal cruelty or the eating of pets is a crime in most rational societies. So the underlying moral principle depends on the value of a horse and you recognize that your primary public, the citizenry served by your government, and most of the other involved publics consider the horse a pet or a workmate rather than a food source. You conclude that the principle of not murdering wantonly or murdering for profit should extend to the horse because a rational, objective person considers the practice offensive. Therefore, it violates moral principle for the government to round up horses for slaughter. The option to round up the horses still exists, but not if it leads to slaughter or human consumption, as that practice violates a higher-level moral principle.

If you applied Rawls's veil of ignorance to this scenario, you could be any one of the publics on the receiving end of your decision, including a wild horse or a rancher! Could you still understand the decision not to include slaughterhouses as an option for the wild horses? Most likely you would conclude that the decision is an ethical one.

You must question whether the dignity and respect of the involved publics are maintained. Removing the option for slaughter will work against the interests of the slaughter industry, but it still maintains their dignity and respect because you considered their point rationally and found an overriding moral principle that is more important than their ability to profit from wild horse slaughter. The dignity and respect of the horses themselves, the American citizenry, and the animal humane groups are all maintained, as is that of the ranchers because as long as their interests are included in the problem resolution, they are respected. You meet with both the ranchers and the leaders of the pro-horse groups to ask for input on how to manage the situation. Listening to their perspective maintains dignity and respect for those publics. Finally, you question your intention with the possible options on the table for resolving the horse issue. What maintains goodwill alone? What decision option is the morally praiseworthy thing to do? You arrived at a decision and implement policy in which auctioning the horses for slaughter is banned. The horses can be rounded up and removed from rancher property with the aid of the animal rights groups, who will provide adoptive homes for gentler horses and medical care for those in need. They will help you relocate the herds to animal preserves and national parks where they will be safe. There, the horses can become a unique part of the experience for tourists, as wild and free representatives of the rich legacy and history that is the American West.

Resolving the Statistics Case That Began the Chapter

What happened to the young research analyst at a polling firm in the beginning of this chapter? Do you think that she should change the research report? How could she weigh her superiors' demands against her moral duty to provide the best information possible? Which type of moral framework would you use to analyze a similar situation?

In actuality, the young research analyst did not have the intellectual tools that you now possess with which to apply a utilitarian analysis, much less a more complicated deontological framework. She was uneasy with her supervisor's request, and articulated the reasons that some of the more negative data should stay in the report. However, after her supervisor's second request based on a materialist paradigm, she softened some of the more critical points in the analysis because she lacked the autonomy to do otherwise. It felt unfair because the client needed knowledge of his weaknesses to make a real bid in the reelection campaign, but she did provide him with accurate data and satisfy the all too common materialist perspective of the firm. He ultimately won reelection. She kept that job only a short while longer—she decided to return to graduate school to earn a Ph.D. and study ethics in public relations.

Endnotes

1. Shannon A. Bowen, "What Communication Professionals Tell Us Regarding Dominant Coalition Access and Gaining Membership." *Journal of Applied Communication Research* 37, no. 4 (2009): 427–452.
2. Bowen, "What Communication Professionals Tell Us."
3. R. L. Heath, *Strategic Issues Management: Organizations and Public Policy Challenges* (Thousand Oaks, CA: Sage, 1997), 45.
4. Shannon A. Bowen, "Expansion of Ethics as the Tenth Generic Principle of Public Relations Excellence: A Kantian Theory and Model for Managing Ethical Issues." *Journal of Public Relations Research* 16, no. 1 (2004): 65–92; "Foundations in Moral Philosophy for Public Relations Ethics," in *Public Relations: From Theory to Practice*, ed. Tricia L. Hansen-Horn and Bonita Dostal Neff, 160-80. (Boston: Pearson A and B, 2008), 160–180; "The Nature of Good and Public Relations: What Should Be Its Normative Ethic?" in *The Sage Handbook of Public Relations*, ed. R. L. Heath (Thousand Oaks, CA: Sage, 2010): 569–583; "A Practical Model for Ethical Decision Making in Issues Management and Public Relations." *Journal of Public Relations Research* 17, no. 3 (2005): 191–216.
5. O. Lerbinger, *Corporate Public Affairs: Interacting with Interest Groups, Media, and Government* (Mahwah, NJ: Lawrence Erlbaum Associates, 2006).
6. R. A. Buchholz, W. D. Evans, and R. A. Wagley. *Management Responses to Public Issues: Concepts and Cases in Strategy Formulation*, 3rd ed. (Upper Saddle River, NJ: Prentice Hall, 1994), p. 41; and R. L. Heath, *Strategic Issues Management: Organizations and Public Policy Challenges* (Thousand Oaks, CA: Sage, 1997).
7. Richard T. De George, *Business Ethics*. 7th ed. Boston, MA: Prentice Hall, 2006.
8. De George, *Business Ethics*.
9. Immanuel Kant, *On the Old Saw: That May Be Right in Theory but It Won't Work in Practice*, trans. E. B. Ashton (Philadelphia: University of Pennsylvania Press, 1793/1974), 25.
10. John Rawls, *A Theory of Justice*. Cambridge, MA: Harvard University Press, 1971.
11. C. B. Pratt, S. H. Im, and S. N. Montague. "Investigating the Application of Deontology among U.S. Public Relations Practitioners." *Journal of Public Relations Research* 6, no. 4 (1994): 241–266; D. K. Wright, "Can Age Predict the Moral Values of Public Relations Practitioners?" *Public Relations Review* 11, no. 1 (1985): 51–60; D. K. Wright, "The Philosophy of Ethical Development in Public Relations." *IPRA Review* (April 1982): 22.

Chapter 10

Doing Right and Avoiding Wrong with the Law and Politicians

Kevin R. Kosar

Contents

Author's Note: The views expressed herein are those of the author and are not presented as those of the Congressional Research Service or the Library of Congress.

Many modern democratic governments have laws or political norms that differentiate between appropriate and inappropriate public relations activities. Yet, the line between appropriately persuasive communications and odious propaganda is often far from clear. Government public relations practitioners must be cognizant of the dangers of appearing to do wrong and setting off political and public consternation.

This chapter will help the public relations practitioner think about how to navigate the ambiguous border between appropriate and inappropriate activities. The approach described here aims to be applicable in modern nation-states generally, but it will be illustrated by use of examples from the U.S. federal government, as it exemplifies the diverse nature of the sorts of ambiguous prohibitions that practitioners can unwittingly cross.

Right and Wrong: What's the Difference?

Who wants to do wrong? Assuredly, everyone does wrong at one time or another and some individuals even take delight in bad behavior. However, nobody—except for the truly disturbed—wants to be caught doing wrong. It is a painful experience. Humans are social animals, and human groups tend to punish those who violate their norms. When caught, the wrongdoer often suffers tangible retribution, such as fines, and intangible punishments like shame and the loss of one's reputation.

For the government public relations practitioner, doing right and avoiding wrong is an existential imperative. The essence of his occupation is to provide useful information to large audiences, sometimes numbering in the tens of millions. The moment his audience views him or even his colleagues as untrustworthy, he loses the power inherent in his position. In high-profile instances, the opprobrium of an entire nation can pour upon him, washing him out of his job.

But how can he do right and avoid doing wrong? Right and wrong are not always black and white—one need not be a nihilist to recognize that. In different times and places, the same words can have fantastically different effects.

Unfortunately, there is no all-encompassing list of do's and don'ts that the government public relations practitioner can keep tacked on a corkboard by his or her desk. Learning any formal rules that may exist is critical, but that will not save him from slipups. This is because the perception of wrongdoing is not limited to those actions that are actually wrong. There is a much larger realm of behaviors that can provoke condemnation. Those who violate these unwritten rules often suffer blowback from politicians, the media, and the public for "the appearance of wrongdoing." Whether the action broke a rule often becomes secondary to the mere fact of audience outrage. Again, the efficacy of a government public relations practitioner is greatly dependent upon his audience's and colleagues' trust.

Figuring out what is good and bad is awfully complex. To increase his odds of staying in the right (or at least, out of the wrong), the government public relations practitioner may find it useful to learn think about the right and wrongdoing in terms of his institutional position. Specifically, he can consider how a proposed action would appear when placed within the five macrocontexts in which he, as a government public relations practitioner, operates: (1) his occupation, (2) his agency, (3) his country's laws, (4) his country's constitution, and (5) his nation's sense of the sacred.

To operationalize this, the practitioner would ask himself before executing a public relations activity, "How does action X look in the context of (1) my occupation, (2) my agency, and ...." If a proposed action squares with each of these contexts, he might feel comfortable going forward with it (an expanded set of actions is included in Table 10.1). Conversely, if the action does not comport with one or more of these contexts, he should think hard about the perils of proceeding.

The Five Institutional Macrocontexts

Occupation

While this chapter speaks generally of the government public relations practitioner, clearly there are many species of this professional. In the United States, there are agency liaisons, spokespersons, public information officers, communications directors, and more.

With the different titles often come different job descriptions, and to make matters even more confusing, there is no governmentwide position description for each of these job titles. The communications director for an elected official has a very different job than the communications director for the U.S. Army.

Accordingly, wherever one is employed, the government public relations practitioner must familiarize himself with his agency's policies and rules, and its past public outreach activities. Additionally, he should peruse media and talk to members of the public in order to get a sense of how people outside the agency perceive it. What do they think that it does? What do they think that it ought to do? If the government public relations practitioner can find time to consult with the legislators who control the purse strings for his agency, all the better.

In the United States, government public relations practitioners can be divided into two types—civil servants and political appointees. Civil servants are hired by agencies based upon their knowledge, skills, abilities, and experience. It is a merit-based process. In exchange for life tenure in his position, a civil servant is expected to serve the public good, and not shill for any particular politician. A political appointee, on the other hand, is chosen by a president or agency head (who also is

Table 10.1   Government Public Relations Institutional Checklist

To do right and avoid wrong, the government public relations practitioner should consider the following contexts before acting:

____Position

1. Are you a civil servant or political appointee?

2. How does the public perceive your role as a government communicator? For example, are you expected to serve the public or to serve the agency?

3. In your position, are you expected to speak frankly on agency-related matters? Or are you expected to be cautious about releasing information?

____Agency

1. Does the public expect your agency to engage in public relations activities?

2. In thinking about the perceptions of your agency and its communications, what activities has it engaged in historically? Has it changed its public relations work in recent years?

3. Does your agency's nature oblige it to communicate with the public? If the answer is yes, for what purpose(s)?

4. What are your agency's policies or rules concerning employee information and the public? For example, may an employee speak freely with reporters? Must an employee's communications with elected officials be reviewed by the agency's leadership beforehand?

____Legal

1. Do any statutes authorize or direct your agency to communicate with the public? If the answer is yes, for what purpose(s)?

2. Does your government have appropriation laws or other forms of legal authorities that affect the authority of government agencies to communicate with the public?

3. What laws affect the ability of your agency's employees to speak on agency-related matters?

____Constitutional

1. What basic ideas and principles does your nation's constitution hold?

2. How does your nation's constitution conceive the relationship of the public to the government?

____Sacred

1. What aspects (dates, events, ideas, items, persons, places) of your society's history are especially treasured by the public?

2. What are the narratives that are important to your nation, state, or municipality? (For example, a movement toward equality among races, an expansion of opportunity?)

---

nominated by a president), and the political appointee serves as an advocate for and an executor of the president's agenda. His time tends to be short—no more than a few years—as he has little job protection beyond the goodwill of the president.

Hence, the government public relations practitioner must be clear which he is—a servant of the public and the agency or a player on the president's team. The former is expected to deliver messages that are more substantive and less political and promotional; the latter is freer to sell a president and his programs.

Agency

The extent of activities that a government public relations practitioner may undertake is partially a product of the nature of the agency for which he works. Generally, the question is: What does my agency do, why, and for whom? More specific, the questions might include: Does it provide services to other government agencies or the general public? Is the agency's job to collect income taxes from the public or to deter certain behaviors that are individually and socially dangerous (e.g., using illicit drugs)?

Once these questions are answered, the government public relations practitioner may then consider what sort of communicative activities flow from the nature of his agency. So, for example, the U.S. Navy is an agency that staffs itself through voluntary service (rather than conscription). Accordingly, it spends millions of dollars each year running high-profile advertisements (e.g., during televised major sporting events) encouraging young men and women to enlist in the Navy. Few people object to these expenditures as they are understood to be necessary for the agency to do what it does—pay individuals to serve, fight wars, and defend the nation's interests.

Similarly, nobody complained when in 2009 the Department of Health and Human Services held a competition to see who among the public could submit a video that would most effectively encourage individuals to get flu vaccinations. (The rapping "Hip Hop Doc" took the $2,500 prize.)[1] Though a little unorthodox, the campaign was perfectly in keeping with the agency's legal duty to promote public health.

And even though there are serious questions as to its efficacy, the White House Office of National Drug Control Policy's (ONDCP) permanent media campaign against illegal drugs continues with little significant political criticism.[2] Whether advertisements are an effective deterrent to illegal drug use is not for the ONDCP to decide; that is the job of politicians. Its job is to promote drug-free living, and the agency does this with gusto.

Legal

Government agencies are born from laws, and laws both create and curb the agency's authority for action. Some agencies, for example, may collect taxes and fees; others may not. Every government public relations practitioner should have some familiarity with the statutes that encourage and limit his agency's work. Ideally, he also should become familiar with any adjudications on these laws, whether a court ruling or the official perspective of an enforcement agency. Not only is it the right thing to do, but it can give the practitioner a real sense of what is permissible and what is not, and keep him from putting his agency in legal jeopardy.

In the United States, the federal government has two sorts of statutory controls relevant to government public relations activities—two laws, and a provision that appears in annual federal appropriations laws.[3] One of the laws was enacted in 1913, and reads, "Appropriated funds may not be used to pay a publicity expert unless specifically appropriated for that purpose"[4]. Another law from 1919 forbids a government agency from encouraging the public to lobby on its behalf. An agency may not directly or indirectly to pay for any personal service, advertisement, telegram, telephone, letter, printed or written matter, or other device, intended or designed to influence in any manner a Member of Congress, a jurisdiction, or an official of any government, to favor, adopt, or oppose, by vote or otherwise, any legislation, law, ratification, policy, or appropriation, whether before or after the introduction of any bill, measure, or resolution proposing such legislation, law, ratification, policy, or appropriation[5].

In 2002, the latter law was amended to allow penalties of up to $100,000 for wrongdoing. Additionally, each year Congress passes laws to appropriate federal funds for spending by agencies, and frequently it includes this boilerplate language in these laws: "No part of any appropriation contained in this Act shall be used for publicity or propaganda purposes not authorized by the Congress." (Few laws, it should be noted, carry any language permitting publicity experts or publicity activities.)

At first glance, then, it would appear that the U.S. government does not do much public relations because of the tough statutory limitations—and that reading would be utterly incorrect. As with most laws, understanding what they mean in practice requires looking at the official interpretations of these laws. Both Congress and its auditing agency, the Government Accountability Office (GAO), can police these statutes, so too the Department of Justice (DOJ), which is the agency responsible for enforcing federal laws. Curiously, the sum total of the interpretations and applications of the aforementioned statutes is much more relaxed than the laws themselves. The GAO has issued the most thoroughly explicated interpretation. Illegal government public relations communications include those that:

- involve large-scale publicity campaigns to generate citizen contacts with Congress on behalf of an agency's position on pending legislation;
- involve "self-aggrandizement" of the agency, its personnel, or activities;

- are "purely partisan in nature," that is, is "designed to aid a political party or candidate"; or
- are "covert propaganda," that is, the communication does not reveal that government spent money to craft or spread the message.[6]

So, for example, if a government public relations practitioner drew up a press release touting his agency's successes of the past year, sent it to newspapers around the country, and offered to sit for interviews, that likely would be viewed as appropriate. If, however, this same practitioner were to mail this flyer to members of the public and urge them to call their Congressmen and demand more appropriations for his agency, it may well provoke ire and GAO, DOJ, and congressional investigations. And finally, if this government public relations practitioner paid a citizen to ghostwrite an op-ed condemning a bill before Congress, he might well find himself out of a job and facing government prosecution. To some degree, then, the restrictions discussed reflect elected officials' limited tolerance for government agencies attempting to influence the lawmaking process. Understanding why politicians feel this way requires an appreciation for the constitutional presuppositions that underpin the U.S. democratic republic.

Constitutional

A nation's constitution both reflects and affects the sentiments of its people. A constitution holds explicit and implicit ideas (or principles) about the relationship between the governors and the governed, and the general goals of the nation-state (e.g., liberty and equality).

In most modern nation-states, the general view is that political power flows from people, and elected officials and their bureaucratic servants are obliged to use this power in accordance with the public's sense of right. To this end, the public elects legislators and executive figures to represent the public. These elected officials are responsible for directing the governmental apparatus that gets things done. The public pays government employees' compensation, and it often feels that this makes it the boss of government.

This arrangement is tremendously complex. While the people do have beliefs and feelings about many matters, they most assuredly do not have well-formed opinions on the myriad issues that governments deal with daily. This is not a matter of stupidity; it is simply inherent to modern mass government. (Quick— who among this book's learned readership can explain, say, the top priorities of the International Monetary Fund, or the total value of U.S. agricultural subsidies in fiscal year 2010?) An elected official faces an ineradicable tension between serving as a delegate to do as the people demand and operating as a trustee who is to make decisions in the best interests of voters. Similarly, the public does recognize that government employees have jobs to do and have only a limited discretion to do them. Yet, the public often gripes about the things that government agencies do and condemns public servants for failing to serve the public's whim du jour.

Muddled as this arrangement may be, there is one general principle that is beyond dispute—the public will little tolerate either elected officials or government employees deceiving it. The entire governing arrangement is predicated on trust—it is a fiduciary relationship between the governed and their governors. Yes, the public will tolerate the government's efforts to honestly persuade it, but it will turn on anyone who appears to be trying to put one over on it. The government public relations practitioner must keep this in mind.

Beyond this, the government public relations specialist should be mindful of other principles contained within the constitution of his country. The U.S. Constitution explicates a vision of limited government with certain enumerated ends. It also establishes a federal system, one where public policy responsibilities are divided between the national government and subnational (state) governments. The federal government, for example, is entrusted in matters of war and peace. State and local governments, on the other hand, have the authority to operate schools and license gambling establishments. Limited government and federalism are but two of the many principles within the Constitution.

The government public relations practitioner would benefit from familiarizing himself with his country's basic constitutional ideas. This does not mean he must take a course in constitutional law or history. Rather, it means he ought to ponder how his public relations efforts fit or collide with the ideas in his country's constitutional ideas. These principles serve as both curbs and opportunities. Messages that are consonant with a nation's constitutional ideas likely will have greater resonance with the public; dissonant messages may have the opposite effect.

Sacred

Nearly every nation has a founding and developmental myth that tells how its people came to be and who they are. Here *myth* should not be read to mean *untrue story* or *fantasy*, like the "myth of the Loch Ness Monster." Rather, here a myth means the sociological process by which a people construct a narrative that defines their society and its ordering institutions.[7] In short: Who are we? How did we get here? Where are we going? Why do we do things as we do?

While Mother Nature may impel people to love their family, nations' founding and developmental myths play a critical role in developing the bond between a citizenry and its government. They bridge the gap between the particular (me) and the abstract whole (America), and thereby enable citizens to assume a national identity and to recognize certain rights, duties, and perspectives as a member of that nation. Founding and developmental myths socialize people to treat some aspects of their nation as sacred. Some aspects of these myths and stories are intangible, such as ideals (equality) and memories (a great battle), and others are tangible (the nation's flag, or the house where a revered citizen once lived). With the passing of time, founding myths and developmental stories are reinterpreted by societies. One age's heroes may be unknown to another.

Those individuals who have run political campaigns well understand the power of a narrative that taps into the nation's story. But to many government public relations practitioners, this all might sound a bit nebulous. Make no mistake—founding and developmental myths are very real, and they can have profound effects on how people perceive your actions and words. The government public relations practitioner who runs roughshod over something sacred likely will face outrage that borders on the irrational.

Examples of the Macrocontexts Applied in the U.S. Federal Context

Occupation

Every government agency has an interest in communicating with the media and public, and every agency wants to see that it is perceived positively. This holds true for political appointees and civil servants alike. Only a fool would want his agency to look bad. Bad press and hostile public opinion get picked up by elected officials—the folks who oversee agencies and provide an agency's operating budget.

"You gotta accentuate the positive" is an old slogan in the public relations world, and the public has remarkable patience for political appointees selling their bosses' policies. Appointees can give speeches extolling their bosses and their grand plans and nobody bats an eye. It is expected behavior. However, when civil servants join them in aggressive public relations activities, politicians, the media, and the public take exception.

Too bad the people in charge of public relations for the Social Security Administration (SSA) a few years back did not recognize this basic point. The SSA and its employees long have had a dowdy reputation. They collect payroll taxes, then use the money to pay retired workers a small pension. The SSA need not advertise its services much, and its communications tend to be about as exciting as an accountancy lecture—"Here is the current funding level of the Social Security Trust Fund; here are the expected levels of disbursements in 50 years, which is based on actuarial assumptions drawn from ..."

Critics long have raised honest questions about the long-term fiscal health of Social Security program as currently structured. Some have suggested that the program would benefit from adding a private investment account to it, a sort of Individual Retirement Account that could provide additional funds to retirees. (Federal employees have had this sort of arrangement for decades.) President George W. Bush was a strong advocate of adding private accounts to Social Security, and some of his SSA appointees decided to use the SSA and its employees to stoke public opinion in favor of improving the SSA.

The agency produced a "strategic communications plan" that urged SSA employees to disseminate the message that "Social Security's long-term financing problems are serious and need to be addressed soon." President Bush undertook a "60 stops in 60 days" tour of the country and took SSA civil servants with him.

The Congress largely was not amused. In a hearing, Senator Paul S. Sarbanes stated,

> I have great respect for Social Security employees. I think they're very much committed to their mission. ... But I think they've always understood that they're outside of or removed from politics, that politics ought not to come into play. Politics is done elsewhere and by other people, but not by career employees of the Social Security Administration. And I am deeply concerned about this effort now to depart from this traditionally neutral role with respect to the Social Security career employees in policy debates in an effort to make them part of a highly politicized public relations campaign. It's so contrary, not only to what has been the practice, the precedent, but it's so contrary to essentially the integrity of government. I mean, the government is not there to be used in any way possible by a particular political group to its advantage. I understand the temptation is there, but in the past, we've succeeded in forestalling that temptation.[8]

The SSA public relations campaign backfired. A lot of the media coverage focused on the controversy of using SSA and its civil servants to stump for a contentious policy change. The campaign did not boost the public's receptivity to adding private accounts to Social Security, and in the end the president's proposal went nowhere.[9]

How Can This Government Public Relations Challenge Be Solved?

Regardless of political party, there is widespread recognition that the Social Security program faces long-term financing challenges. There are a variety of ways to approach this policy problem, and some are better than others.[10] *How might an agency express its expertise-based views on reforms without being perceived as pushing an agenda?*

Agency

In the United States, the conception of government is that politicians decide what policy should be pursued, and then a government agency is supposed to execute that policy. The reality is messier than that, of course, as elected officials are constantly asking for the advice of agencies as to which policies work better. Nonetheless, those who face the voters consider themselves the policy deciders.

Too often, this simple notion has been breached, to ill effect. There is an old barb that the first casualty in war is the truth. Sadly, this barb has proven true innumerable times. The job of the Department of Defense (DOD) is to defend the nation from attacks, and to fight wars as directed. The DOD is free to inform the president and Congress about its views of any particular confrontation either before or during the fight. But it runs great political risks when it attempts to sell a war to the public.

Not long after the start of the Iraq War in March 2003, the DOD began propagating a story about the heroics of Private Jessica Lynch, who fiercely fought an ambush before being captured and abused. (It was barely half true.)[11] A year later, the DOD told another tall tale, claiming that former football star Patrick Tillman had died while fighting in Afghanistan. (In fact, he was killed by friendly fire.) These were feel-good stories for inflaming patriotism. These were just the tip of the oleaginous iceberg.[12]

During the run-up to the war, political appointees at the agency's public affairs office had undertaken a formidable and stealthy public relations effort. One part of it involved identifying high-ranking, retired military officers (RMOs) who they thought would be sympathetic to the DOD's sunny view of the war and its progress.[13] The DOD provided these RMOs with private briefings and junkets to Iraq and elsewhere to see how well things were going. The RMOs then made themselves available to television and print journalists who were looking for scoops on the war. Many of them performed exactly as the DOD had hoped—as "message force multipliers" for the agency, who told the public that the war was necessary and would be low cost.

Though it took a while, this agency campaign was sniffed out by reporters and retribution was swift and severe. The Congress investigated, as did the GAO and the DOD's inspector general. Although these activities were not found to be illegal, they elicited palpable disgust. Much of the public had been against the invasion of Iraq, and this public relations mischief fueled its anger further. Rather than just fight the war, the DOD had done as it so often had done before—entered the political fray over the wisdom of war making in the hopes of bolstering support for one side.

How Can This Government Public Relations Challenge Be Solved?

In most modern nation-states, military agencies report to elected officials, who usually have very divergent views on where and when to employ military force. When should a military agency weigh in on these debates? How can it communicate its views without being perceived as favoring certain elected officials over others?

Legal

Even though the United States' legal prohibitions on government public relations are pretty lax, some practitioners have nonetheless broken them. When the breaches are small, there is seldom an outcry. But brazen transgressions of the laws inevitably invite a punitive response.

In December 2003, President George W. Bush signed the Medicare Prescription Drug Improvement and Modernization Act of 2003. This law changed and expanded the nearly four-decade-old insurance program for senior citizens.

Shortly thereafter, a division of the U.S. Department of Health and Human Services (DHHS) began a $120 million multiyear campaign to promote the law. The alterations to the law were complex and difficult to understand, so it was critical that DHHS reach out to beneficiaries to educate them on how the program had changed. The agency plan included mailings, a website, and print and television advertisements.

The agency also hired a contractor to produce video news releases (VNRs), copies of which were distributed to local television news stations. The VNRs contained slickly produced, newscastlike interviews and reports that featured agency officials and persons pretending to be reporters.[14] Though informative, these VNRs were aggressively promotional, touting only the positive aspects of the revised Medicare law. And the VNRs did not include any disclosures that the faux news broadcasts were government media products.

Both the media and Congress quickly discovered this and a major outcry ensued. The VNRs were denounced as "propaganda," and when the GAO examined the situation, it agreed with them. It noted that some local news stations had run the VNRs, and that members of the public had no clue that what they were viewing was a government communication. For years, the GAO had been quite clear that agency communications must be labeled as such. But DHHS failed to heed this rule, and both it and the Bush administration saw their very expensive and very important outreach effort get swamped in accusations of wrongdoing.

How Can This Government Public Relations Challenge Be Solved?

When a government creates a new program, it is obliged to explain the program to the public, and especially to those persons who are eligible to participate in the program. *How does the Medicare promotional campaign example relate to the purported politics vs. administration dichotomy?*

Constitutional

Elected officials and government employees well recognize the power of television and online video to persuade the public. The ubiquity of video cameras has encouraged them to script and sculpt more and more of their public appearances. There is nothing objectionable about an official working up smooth answers to questions before they are asked. Governing is complicated, and even a slight misstatement might be misconstrued by the audience.

But, in their zeal to control their message and frame the debate, some government public relations figures frequently have gone too far in recent years. This has happened in at least a few of ways. First, press conferences often have become less than what they are supposed to be—an opportunity for government officials to provide information and take questions from reporters. Politicians' and agency heads' handlers sometimes have prescreened media and audience members to ensure that the questions asked are softballs or that the issues raised are those that the speakers wanted to discuss. Worse, some press conferences have been faked entirely. In October 2007, the deputy administrator for the Federal Emergency Management Agency (FEMA) held a press conference to address FEMA's efforts to control wildfires in California. His performance was flawless, and soon it was discovered why—his audience (which the cameras did not show) consisted of FEMA public affairs employees.[15] Despite the fact that the deputy administrator was providing good information that was useful to the media and reporters, he drew mocking condemnation. Not only had he offended members of the press by co-opting their constitutional role as public watchdogs, he had deceived his boss and the public by pretending to hold a press conference.

Second, government public relations practitioners also have gotten in trouble by taking agency information or datum and altering it to fit a political agenda. For example, political appointees working for the Office of Public Affairs of the National Aeronautics and Space Administration (NASA) were caught downplaying evidence of climate change.[16] Beyond the poisonous optic of the politicization of science, there was the fundamental problem of deception. The guilty parties did not want NASA's experts sharing their views honestly with the public. The withholding of facts and the censoring of expert testimony rubbed wrong a public that had the constitutional right to decide by voting or by sitting on juries.

Finally, there is the hullabaloo that embarrassed a recently elected president. In late August 2009, President Barack H. Obama's administration revealed that it was going to give a "welcome back to school" speech at a public high school in Virginia. This was not a novel bit of public relations. Previous presidents, including Ronald W. Reagan and George H. W. Bush, had given school speeches. It was far from radical stuff—the president would discuss the importance of schooling and encourage students to take responsibility for their studies and grades. His speech would be broadcast to schools nationwide, which were free to tune in or not.

Nonetheless, a small political firestorm erupted, and some parents threatened to boycott the speech by keeping their children home from school. In part, the backlash was simply politics—some members of the political far right sincerely disliked and distrusted the "liberal" president.

But the administration itself tripped a constitutional landmine through public relations overreach. Apparently it was not enough to have the president give the speech and broadcast it around the nation. The Department of Education went a step further and hired a contractor to produce curricular materials related to the speech, which would be distributed to the schools. This was a very bad decision. The U.S. Constitution does not give power over the schools to the federal government, and for over 50 years there have been vitriolic political disputes over "unconstitutional federal meddling" in the schools and their curricula.[17] Although the federal role in schooling has grown, about 90 percent of school funding still comes from taxes collected by states and localities. But it gets worse—the initial curricular materials urged students to "Write letters to themselves about what they can do to help the president." Somehow, somebody in the public affairs office missed this gaffe.

The picture was terrible, and critics pilloried the president for spending tax dollars to indoctrinate children and use them to promote his political agenda.[18] The administration reworked the offending curricular materials and spent a great deal of energy tamping down the flames. In the end, the speech came off well, but the president's image had taken a harsh and needless hit.

How Can This Government Public Relations Problem Be Solved?

Most governments have programs that provide benefits for children. Yet, children are children. *Where do we draw the line between promoting children's programs and using children as political props?*

Sacred

The modern American president is quite plainly a highly visible public figure. Much of what he does is make public appearances for the sake of advocating his policies and persuading both the people and legislators. Like other public officials, he has scores of employees who help him with public relations activities, and who oversee the acquisition and production of presidential trinkets and memorabilia—paper weights, photographs, and the like. (The president is not alone in this. The U.S. Congress has both Senate and House of Representatives gift shops that sell golf balls, shirts, and coffee mugs stamped with each chamber's emblem. Some federal agencies, such as NASA, also sell self-promotional souvenirs.)

By all accounts, Louis E. Caldera was a fine person to be appointed the director of the White House Military Office, which provides military support to the presidents. President Obama no doubt saw plenty in Caldera's résumé to inspire trust—Caldera had served as Secretary of the U.S. Army, as a California state legislator, and as the head of the University of New Mexico. Six months after he took his White House post, though, Caldera was engulfed in a public relations firestorm and lost his job. What went wrong? In short, Caldera approved a government public relations activity that violated the sacred.

In April 2009, Caldera's office approved a photo shoot using one of the presidential jet airplanes. This was not unprecedented, and it should have been no big deal. Take the plane up, have another plane or two follow it and snap some photographs—voila, the White House would have nice pictures to share with media and the public.

The day of the photo shoot, the Boeing 727 and two Air Force fighter jets took off bright and early in the morning and headed toward the Statue of Liberty, which would serve as a handsome backdrop in the photograph. The sky was blue, the sun was coming over the horizon; it was a perfect day. In order to get good pictures, the jets had to drop down to a mere 1,000 feet over the ground and swing over New Jersey and the southern tip of Manhattan. The public had not been notified of the flyover, and had it been, it no doubt would have objected strongly as the flight path led right over the site of the horrific 9/11 attacks that demolished the World Trade Center and World Financial Center buildings and killed 2,800 people.

And so there was a small public panic. People saw the fighter jets tailing the large plane at a height not much above the city's skyscrapers. Government, police, and 311 hotlines lit up, some buildings were evacuated, and New York City Mayor Mike Bloomberg was furious. "Why the [federal government] wanted to do a photo-op right around the site of the World Trade Center catastrophe defies imagination."[19]

A White House review of the matter revealed a series of bureaucratic slipups that led to the flyover being kept mostly secret from the public and some local officials.[20] Remarkably, one of Caldera's aides had told him that the flyover was not going to elicit local media attention. (Never mind that the city is the nation's media center.) Caldera himself reported that he had approved the flyover, but that he did not realize how low the planes would be flying.

Despite the fact that nobody was injured in the mini-panic, despite Caldera's decades of public service and proximity to the president, and although the incident was the result of honest errors, there had to be a bloodletting. The government's public relations effort had come off as grossly insensitive and a violation of a part of New York City that many American feel is sacred. (Anyone who has seen how tourists and others silently queue up to view the area is struck by their solemnity.) Two weeks after the flyover, Caldera resigned, noting that controversy had become a "distraction" to the president.[21]

How Can This Government Public Relations Problem Be Solved?

As the New York City jet flyover example illustrates, the public often responds harshly when a government agency offends the public's sense of the sacred. *When an agency makes this sort of mistake, what steps should it take to respond to the outcry?* Review the transcript of Press Secretary Robert Gibbs's response to tough questioning on the flyover.[22] *How well did he do?*

Conclusion: Thinking Institutionally

Doing government public relations is not for the faint of heart. No matter how conscientious a practitioner is, someone somewhere will grouse. This chapter aimed to help the government public relations practitioner do right and avoid doing wrong in a big way. The approach advocated here does require the practitioner to undertake substantive learning. For example, to understand a constitution's ideas, one needs to read a constitution or a good primer on it and its interpretation.

But the major thrust of this approach is to argue that a practitioner should think institutionally, to consider how his actions and messages fit within five macrocontexts that derive from his position as a government public relations practitioner. This institutional approach, assuredly, does not cover the whole of right and wrong conduct. But this chapter does show that a great deal of trouble can be avoided if government public relations practitioners simply pause to consider whether this particular public relations activity be construed as: (1) an abuse of my position, (2) inconsistent with my agency's duties, (3) illegal, (4) offensive to my country's constitution, or (5) an outrage upon the sacred.

Endnotes

1. "H1N1 Rap by Dr. Clarke," YouTube, accessed March 2, 2011, http://www.youtube.com/watch?v=_gwUdmPl0bU.
2. Mark Eddy, *War on Drugs: The National Youth Anti-Drug Media Campaign* (Washington, DC: Congressional Research Service, 2009).
3. Kevin R. Kosar, "The Law: The Executive Branch and Propaganda: The Limits of Legal Restrictions," *Presidential Studies Quarterly* 35 (2005): 784–797.
4. 5 U.S. Code 3107.
5. 18 U.S. Code 1919.
6. Government Accountability Office, "Lobbying and Related Matters," in *Principles of Federal Appropriations Law*, vol. 1 (Washington, DC: Government Accountability Office, 2004): 4-188-4-323, accessed March 2, 2011, http://www.gao.gov/special.pubs/d04261sp.pdf.
7. H. Mark Roelofs, *The Poverty of American Politics: A Theoretical Interpretation* (Philadelphia, Temple University Press, 1992), 17–22.
8. Democratic Policy Committee, *An Oversight Hearing on the Bush Administration's Plans to Privatize Social Security*, (January 28, 2005) 51, accessed March 2, 2011, http://dpc.senate.gov/hearings/hearing18/transcript.pdf.
9. Robert Pear, "Social Security Is Enlisted to Push Its Own Revision," *New York Times*, January 16, 2005, 1.
10. Social Security Administration, *Understanding the Benefits* (Washington, DC: Social Security Administration, 2010), accessed March 2, 2011, http://ssa.gov/pubs/10024.pdf. Government Accountability Office, *Social Security: Costs Associated with the Administration's Efforts to Promote Program Reforms*, GAO-07-621R (Washington, DC: Government Accountability Office, August 10, 2007), accessed March 2, 2011, http://www.gao.gov/new.items/d07621r.pdf.
11. John Kampfner, "The Truth About Jessica," *The Guardian*, May 15, 2003, accessed March 2, 2011, http://www.guardian.co.uk/world/2003/may/15/iraq.usa2.

12. Committee on Oversight and Government Reform, U.S. House of Representatives, *Misleading Information from the Battlefield: The Tillman and Lynch Episodes*, H. Rept 110-858, (September 16, 2008) accessed March 2, 2011, http://www.gpo.gov/fdsys/pkg/CRPT-110hrpt858/pdf/CRPT-110hrpt858.pdf

13. Government Accountability Office, *Department of Defense—Retired Military Officers as Media Analysts*, B-316443 (Washington, DC: Government Accountability Office, July 21, 2003), accessed March 2, 2011, http://www.gao.gov/decisions/appro/316443.pdf.

14. Kevin R. Kosar, *Medicare Advertising: Current Controversies*, RS21811 (Washington, DC: CRS); Government Accountability Office, *Department of Health and Human Services, Centers for Medicare & Medicaid Services—Video News Releases*, B-302710 (Washington, DC: Government Accountability Office, May 19, 2004), accessed March 2, 2011, http://www.gao.gov/decisions/appro/302710.pdf.

15. Al Kamen, "FEMA Meets the Press, Which Happens to Be … FEMA." *Washington Post*, October 26, 2007, A19.

16. National Aeronautics and Space Administration Office of Inspector General. *Investigative Summary Regarding Allegations That NASA Suppressed Climate Change Science and Denied Media Access to Dr. James E. Hansen, a NASA Scientist* (Washington, DC: National Aeronautics and Space Administration, June 2, 2008).

17. Kevin R. Kosar, *Failing Grades: The Federal Politics of Education Standards* (Boulder, CO: L. Rienner, 2005); Department of Education, *The Federal Role in Education*, accessed March 2, 2011, http://www2.ed.gov/about/overview/fed/role.html; and Kevin R. Kosar, "Higher Education Standards: We'd Love to But …," Annual Meeting of the American Political Science Association, August 27–31, 2003, Philadelphia, PA, accessed March 2, 2011, http://www.eric.ed.gov/ERICDocs/data/ericdocs2sql/content_storage_01/0000019b/80/1b/51/85.pdf.

18. Jake Tapper and Sunlen Miller, "WH, Dept of Education Revise Language on Students Outlining How They Can 'Help the President.'" ABC News online (September 2, 2009), accessed March 2, 2011, http://blogs.abcnews.com/politicalpunch/2009/09/obamas-back-to-school-message—scribbled-with-some-controversy.html.

19. A. G. Sulzberger and Matthew L. Wald, "White House Apologizes for Air Force Flyover," *New York Times* (April 27, 2009), accessed March 2, 2011, http://cityroom.blogs.nytimes.com/2009/04/27/air-force-one-backup-rattles-new-york-nerve/.

20. White House Counsel's Office, "Internal Review Concerning April 27, 2009 Air Force Flight," (May 5, 2009), accessed March 2, 2011, http://www.whitehouse.gov/assets/documents/Report_by_President.pdf.

21. Scott Wilson, "N.Y. Flyover Results in Resignation," *Washington Post*, (May 9, 2009), accessed March 2, 2011, http://www.washingtonpost.com/wp-dyn/content/article/2009/05/08/AR2009050803755.html.

22. White House, Office of the Press Secretary, "Press Briefing by Press Secretary Robert Gibbs," (April 28, 2009), accessed March 2, 2011, http://www.whitehouse.gov/the_press_office/Briefing-by-White-House-Press-Secretary-Robert-Gibbs-4-28-09.

Chapter 11

Internal Public Relations for Personal and Program Success

Anne Zahradnik

Contents

Planning and Managing Your Internal Public Relations

Having read the previous chapters, you have considered sound advice on planning, integrating, executing, and tracking your public relations (PR) program. It may seem as if we have already given you plenty to do. You have, however, one other important matter to attend to ... communications to establish, improve, and maintain relations with your internal stakeholders.

Remember the budget scenario at the very beginning of Chapter 2? Discussion of the line item for communication and outreach in the budget turned into a crisis communication situation. That scene is all too plausible because elected officials do not always understand or appreciate the important role of communications. Taxpayers (and the people they voted into office) often see communications as a frill rather than a necessity. They may misunderstand the role of public relations and see your function as working to mislead the public rather than inform. They do not understand the value obtained from the investment in time and funds, and may even see communications falling within the classic "waste, fraud, and abuse" trilogy.

Defending your job while you do your job can be uncomfortable and time consuming. It is, however, often a fact of life in the communications professions. Fortunately, as a public relations professional, you can adapt and apply the skills and tools you already know to ensure your internal stakeholders are not only aware of your actions but also understand and appreciate the results you produce. Do this part of your job well, and you will avoid the type of scene described at the beginning of the book. Do this part of your job well, and the rest of your job will be less stressful. It may even pay better.

The first hurdle you must overcome when planning and executing your internal communications is the same hurdle you must drag your clients over. You have to be convinced that internal public relations is more than a nice thing to do when you have spare time. You must believe it is a necessary, important part of your job that deserves to be a high priority. If you view internal communications as second-tier work you will get around to some day, you simply will not get around to it at all. If you don't plan, manage, and execute a high-quality internal communication program, at some point you'll pay the price personally and professionally.

Watson puts it bluntly when he says, "Without evidence of the effects of public relations communications, the decision to invest is based on belief. Decision-makers generally prefer measures and precedent to guesswork and assurance."[1] He goes on to explain that even a perception of a lack of accountability threatens investment in public relations. What type of investment is he talking about? Your salary for one. He was talking about the need for an ongoing PR evaluation component, but he could as easily have been discussing the need to communicate the results of that evaluation too. An earlier chapter explained how to plan for, track, and report PR accountability. That fixes one part of the problem. The other part of the problem has to do with perception. You may be doing wonderful work, but if people do not know about it or understand its value, you are not changing their perceptions of public relations. Evaluation and tracking efforts will go to waste if you do not effectively share the results of your findings. As funding at all levels of government gets tighter and tighter, the need to communicate in defense of your function is increasingly urgent.

There are many good reasons for making internal public relations a high priority. Avoiding budgeting controversies is one benefit of having an effective internal communications plan in place. You will also gain and maintain credibility for your department and for yourself, making raises and advancement more likely. And you will greatly improve your chances of having funding requests approved.

This chapter will cover specific tools and techniques for identifying your internal publics and their priorities; planning communications for your internal audiences; having your plans, projects, and budgets approved; reporting results to internal audiences; and gaining and maintaining credibility for yourself and your department. Plan and execute your internal communications well and you will not end up like the public relations professional at the beginning of the book. You will be more effective at your job and you will gain more personal satisfaction from your work.

How to Begin

Start by having a clear, concise explanation of PR in your head so you can quickly and clearly tell anyone and everyone who asks, "What do you do?"

The Public Relations Society of America (PRSA) National Assembly formally adopted a definition of public relations, which remains widely accepted and used today: "Public relations helps an organization and its publics adapt mutually to each other."[2] This rather ethereal definition is followed by a more specific list of public relations management functions. If you have staff, make sure everyone, from the receptionist on up, can understand and put this definition into their own words. They should be able to answer two primary questions: "What is it you do?" and "Why should the organization spend money doing that?" So the first step in improving your internal public relations is to come up with a polished answer to these questions yourself.

This can be surprisingly difficult. The nature of public relations work is such that your "typical" day is never typical. Most PR professionals have a diverse, frequently changing set of roles and responsibilities. Most of us enjoy the variety, but it does make it hard to come up with a clear, concise answer to "What do you do?" But remember, you must have a succinct, convincing description of what you do to answer the very important follow-up question, "Why should we spend money on that?"

Use Tables 11.1 and 11.2 to help organize your thinking, and to make sure you include all of the important tasks and roles. The PRSA's list of public relations functions are in the left-hand column. Consider each function carefully, comparing it to your weekly and monthly list of tasks and duties. Put a check in the box for functions you already do. Put a star next to functions you do not do yet, but would like to develop in order to increase your value to the organization. Jot down specific projects in the notes section as examples of that function.

This is also a good time to pull out your job description. Compare your responsibilities to the PRSA functions. Has your role experienced mission creep? Are you being kept busy with tangential projects and not paying enough attention to the core functions? Are there any gaps—places where you should be applying more resources? Review the possibilities carefully.

Table 11.1 Public Relations Society of America List of Professional Public Relations Functions

PRSA Function	Do?	Notes
1. Anticipating, analyzing, and interpreting public opinion, attitudes, and issues that might impact, for good or ill, the operations and plans of the organization.		
2. Counseling management at all levels in the organization with regard to policy decisions, courses of action and communication, taking into account their public ramifications and the organization's social or citizenship responsibilities.		
3. Researching, conducting, and evaluating, on a continuing basis, programs of action and communication to achieve the informed public understanding necessary to the success of an organization's aims. These may include marketing; financial; fund raising; employee, community, or government relations; and other programs.		
4. Planning and implementing the organization's efforts to influence or change public policy. Setting objectives, planning, budgeting, recruiting and training staff, developing facilities—in short, managing the resources needed to perform all of the above.		

Source: Adapted from Public Relations Society of America, http://www.prsa.org/AboutPRSA/PublicRelationsDefined/

If you have one or more staff members, taking time to sit down with them and review the PRSA functions together is also worthwhile. You may find redundancies or mismatches of responsibilities. The list can also serve as the basis for a discussion of staff members' own career development. Whether you review the list by yourself or with a coworker, giving the exercise thoughtful consideration will

Table 11.2   Connecting PR Functions to the Audiences Who Should Know about Them

1. Anticipating, analyzing, and interpreting public opinion, attitudes, and issues that might impact, for good or ill, the operations and plans of the organization.			
Who benefits from these activities?	*How often am I communicating those benefits to him/her? In what form? Am I being effective?*	*Who influences decisions and funding of such projects?*	*How often am I communicating with him/her? In what form? Am I being effective?*
2. Counseling management at all levels in the organization with regard to policy decisions, courses of action and communication, taking into account their public ramifications and the organization's social or citizenship responsibilities.			
Who benefits from these activities?	*How often am I communicating those benefits to him/her? In what form? Am I being effective?*	*Who influences decisions and funding of such projects?*	*How often am I communicating with him/her? In what form? Am I being effective?*
3. Researching, conducting, and evaluating, on a continuing basis, programs of action and communication to achieve the informed public understanding necessary to the success of an organization's aims. These may include marketing; financial; fund raising; employee, community, or government relations; and other programs.			
Who benefits from these activities?	*How often am I communicating those benefits to him/her? In what form? Am I being effective?*	*Who influences decisions and funding of such projects?*	*How often am I communicating with him/her? In what form? Am I being effective?*
4. Planning and implementing the organization's efforts to influence or change public policy. Setting objectives, planning, budgeting, recruiting and training staff, developing facilities—in short, managing the resources needed to perform all of the above.			
Who benefits from these activities?	*How often am I communicating those benefits to him/her? In what form? Am I being effective?*	*Who influences decisions and funding of such projects?*	*How often am I communicating with him/her? In what form? Am I being effective?*

Source: Adapted from Public Relations Society of America, http://www.prsa.org/AboutPRSA/PublicRelationsDefined/

organize and clarify your thinking about your roles and responsibilities. It also lays the foundation of your internal communication plan.

Now that you have thought through what you do, make a complete list of all of your internal audiences. It is very important to make a thorough list. You want to include everyone in the organization you interact with while performing those functions, anyone who cares (or should care) about the results of those functions, and anyone who influences or approves the funding of your job or activities.

As you make your list you will see it goes well beyond a layer or two of bosses. Your list should include people above, below, and on the same level as you in the organization. If appropriate to your position, it may include elected officials. And it should include everyone (elected, appointed, or civil servants) who may have a say in funding your projects, staffing, facility, and your position. Table 11.2 will help you make a thorough inventory of your internal audiences.

For each box in Table 11.2, list the appropriate people. Make notes about how, and how often, you communicate with them. Remember, this is not project-related communication, such as having them sign off on an invoice or approve a press release. This is communication *about* the function listed. It is about work that has been done—things such as results of a recent campaign, a report on a public opinion survey, a scrapbook of clippings, or other communication about the results of the work done in your department. What information are you sharing with your internal audiences to increase their understanding of your functions and your contributions to the organization?

Do you see any gaps or room for improvement in Table 11.2? See anyone you are not communicating with often enough or effectively enough? On the other hand, do you see any places where you are investing too much time and effort? Places where you are preaching to the choir? See someone who may be getting too many messages from you? That could be a problem if too-frequent communication means they start to treat your information like e-mail spam, deleting it without reading.

Keep notes as you brainstorm ways to fill in the gaps or reallocate resources. Ensure you are covering all necessary bases by communicating with sufficient, but not excessive, frequency and effectiveness to everyone who influences your job and department. If you currently are not communicating at all, or if your communication is spotty and infrequent, you have many opportunities for improvement. Happily, you know how to fix that situation. You will start by writing a plan.

Writing and Executing an Internal Communication Plan

The internal communication plan is for your use, or perhaps for use by your immediate staff, so it does not need to be as detailed as a budget-justifying plan. On the other hand, don't get too casual with this document. Be professional about it so that you maintain the importance of the internal PR functions as highly as the external PR functions.

Make the plan multidirectional to ensure you are not missing any audiences. Organizational communication textbooks describe communication happening in three directions. Adler describes the three primary directions for internal communication in terms of an organization flow chart. Downward communication is any information you send to people below you in the flow chart. Lateral or horizontal communication goes to your peers, those who may have very different job functions from yours, but who share the same level on the organization chart. Upward communication goes to your boss, her boss, and her boss's boss.[3]

While you don't want to neglect downward or horizontal communication, upward communication should be the primary emphasis of your internal PR communication. Adler goes on to describe four different types of upward communication: "What subordinates are doing. Unsolved work problems. Suggestions for improvement. And how subordinates feel about each other and the job."[4] Your plan will generally focus on the first type of communication, what subordinates are doing, but with a very important added component of *why* you are doing what you do. Simply passing along a copy of coverage from the local newscast is good, but not enough. Along with the video clip, you need to include a brief synopsis of the viewership, the context of the message, and the value this particular medium hit brings to the organization.

Remember, internal communications is not a sneaky or sly thing to do. You are simply covering all of your bases. Do not be shy because you think it is self-promotion. It is indeed self-promotion and that's O.K. Adler and Elmhorst explain the need for upward communication to ensure that your boss and others know what you are doing and why you are doing it.

> Upward communication is especially important for women. Females who engage in more interactions with their supervisors advance in the organizational hierarchy faster than those who do not spend as much time communicating upward. A probable explanation for this fact is that women are less connected to the kinds of informal networks [such as golf or clubs].[5]

A word of warning: do not get gossipy in your internal PR plan. It would be quite unwise to put into print anything that might be a personal or professional embarrassment if it were read by the general taxpaying public or by a member of your internal audiences. Although you do not intend this document for general circulation, write it as if it were going to be read by the world, because it just might be. Papers are accidentally left in photocopiers. Wrong documents are incorrectly attached to e-mails and sent to the world. Disgruntled ex-employees pass along electronic copies of documents to news reporters. Do not be the cause of your own crisis communication situation. Write a concise, but still professional, plan that would cause you no embarrassment whatsoever if it were widely circulated.

While writing your plan, keep in mind the widely circulated "8 Cs of communication" as a good framework for composing the objectives of your internal PR strategies and tactics. First, control the content of the message. The way to do that is to be first to communicate. If the PR person in a bind at the beginning of the book had been communicating with her various publics all along, there would not have been suspicion around the budget item. Everyone would have already known what she was doing and what the money was buying.

Consistency and continuity: You would not expect a single press release or backgrounder to effectively spread the word about a new program or policy. You know from experience that it takes repeated exposure for a message to be understood and retained. The same thing is true for your internal communication tactics. One annual report each year, no matter how well prepared, is not enough communication on the value of your function. Consistently and continually let your boss and the internal audiences you have identified know what is being done, and the effects those actions are having, to build a long-term effective communications bridge.

Context of message and customer benefits: One piece of advice has been handed down to communications professionals over the decades—WIFM (what's in it for me?). Every time you are communicating, be sure to keep the reader's implicit, primary goal in mind. On some level the reader will be thinking, what is in it for me? As you write your next activity report or summarize the results from the latest campaign, keep in mind that the reader should know what was in it for them after they've read your report. The city councilperson should learn that your educational campaign on the need for a new sewage treatment plant not only scored 400 inches of generally positive coverage in the local press, it also made life easier for the council members by educating key members of the public on the need for passing the funding.

Take your analysis a step further by explaining how communication on the topic means the voting public is better informed. Then explain how a better-informed public will make wiser choices when voting on the referendum. As a communications professional, this connection may seem obvious to you and spelling it out may seem patronizing. Of course, you should avoid a patronizing tone, but do not be shy. Be explicit about the connection between communications and consequences. The busy reader probably does not have the time, energy, or expertise to make those connections by himself. Connect the dots for him and make the most of every opportunity to reinforce the impression of competency and professionalism you work so hard to maintain.

Channels of communication and capability of audience: When planning external public relations you rarely rely on just one channel to get your message out. Your plans are generally multifaceted, making use of print and broadcast media, special events, press conferences, websites, and social networking media. You do that because you must to achieve the frequency of exposure you need to make your point. Think in the same terms with your internal audiences as well. Not everyone will make time to read your reports. Use multiple channels to get your message across. Do e-mail blasts. Prepare a multimedia presentation for the next meeting. Be sure to do personal selling by explaining the value of what you do in face-to-face encounters. Do not wait for a major media hit to share the results of your efforts. More frequent, smaller bites of communication will be more effective in the long term than one big report. To avoid charges of self-aggrandizement, couch the accomplishments in terms of benefit to the organization or agency. Use "we" rather than "I."

Credibility of the messenger: The communication tool must be credible for the message to be received and believed. In this case, the communication tool is you. The best way to gain and maintain credibility is to know what you are doing and do it well.

As a PR professional you need to keep your skills sharp and up to date on two fronts. Obviously, you must stay current and skillful at being a PR professional. The fact that you are reading this book is a positive sign in that regard. You care about how well you do your job. To keep up to date with industry developments, join professional organizations, take courses to keep up with changing technology, and interact with other professionals to learn from them. The Public Relations Society of America is a good place to start. It offers free web-based training for less-experienced practitioners and an ongoing series of topic-specific webinars. The accreditation process is rigorous and will be an impressive credential to add to your resume.

While you don't need to be a public health professional or civil engineer, you do need to know the basic concepts and vocabulary of whatever technical field your organization deals with. You should be able to ask intelligent questions while doing an interview for a media release. You should be able to follow the gist of the conversation when a new project is being discussed in a meeting.

Take time to study the technical aspects of your organization's area of expertise so the people you work with do not feel as if they are wasting their time when they talk to you. Set up meetings during slack times for backgrounder briefings. Take key people from different departments to lunch and ask them to tell you what they do. Ask them about the greatest challenges in their job and the greatest rewards. Ask them about how people in their section interact with the public. People are generally flattered by the attention, the sessions will help you move up the learning curve, and you will be establishing a relationship in advance of when you really need to catch someone during a crunch time to get information. Background sessions will also give you a reserve of information to draw on so you can ask more intelligent questions during interviews.

To help move people's perceptions away from the self-serving stigma attached to public relations, you simply cannot repeat the mission-based message too often. Remind them of this frequently. Include it as a special point in any written plans or proposals. Discuss it any time you meet with an internal audience member. Give it its own slide in your PowerPoint presentation.

You want to make and remake this point for two main reasons. First, it is to educate your internal audiences on a legitimate point in support of your professional actions. Second, it gives them ammunition they will need when they are asked about why they supported funding a communications position or communications projects. Do not assume your internal audiences (including the boss you report to directly!) can do this. In fact, it is safest to assume they cannot do it on their own right now and will require information and coaching from you on an ongoing basis.

There is another advantage to constantly thinking about and communicating about how your work supports the agency, department, or council mission. The need to communicate about the relationships among mission and plan and project means you also *must* think about the connection. And frankly, you should not be working on projects that do not support the organization's mission. This acts as a check on your decision-making process and as a quality improvement step for you in your work. If you can clearly communicate the mission connection for a project, then it is probably a good use of your limited resources. If you cannot clearly communicate it, then you should think long and hard about how the project can be changed, or if the project should be done at all.

Call to Action

Just as you evaluate the effectiveness of your external communication plans, so should you periodically stop and evaluate the effectiveness of your internal plan. Compare your progress against the objectives you set earlier. Does your boss now have a good idea of what you do? Are you more likely to be included earlier in the planning process of a new program because your coworkers have a high opinion of the contribution you will make? Do the elected officials you work with understand and appreciate the value of your function? If you are making good progress toward those goals, keep going. If your evaluation shows your progress is not as strong as you would like, then review your communications plan to see where it is lacking.

Keeping those general principles in mind and with a copy of Tables 11.1 and 11.2 in front of you, completing the plan outline should go fairly quickly. You have already done the thinking that goes into planning. Now you just need to put it down on paper for future reference.

Your internal communications plan is for your use, or for the use of your immediate staff. This plan is not designed to justify funding an expensive campaign. Therefore, you don't need to go into the detail you would present in a plan to others who are not communications professionals. It can be just a couple pages long. It is still vital that you put it into writing, because doing so helps formalize your commitment to this important part of your job.

While your internal communications plan is a streamlined version of a full-blown public relations plan, you still want to make sure you do all of the steps. The good news is that you already have a head start. The first step in planning is to define a problem, issue, or opportunity. The second step is to do a situation analysis. You essentially did those steps when you filled out Tables 11.1 and 11.2. You now know your situation—the gaps or weak spots you have in your current internal communications. You also know with whom you should be communicating. You are ready to jump right into the next step.

Next, you will set goals and objectives. Here I will repeat the word of warning I gave earlier. Since your goals and objectives are personal, they do not need to be spelled out in the minute detail you would provide in a plan for others in the organization. Most plans are a form of justifying the expenditures proposed in the plan. This plan is different. It has no role in convincing external audiences. It is about convincing *internal* audiences. Your goal should be to improve your own reputation, and the reputation of the public relations function, by increasing awareness and knowledge of the contribution you make in your organization. That is an ethical and proper workplace goal. But be careful how you word it in your plan. Write the goals and objectives for this plan in such a way that they will not cause you embarrassment if someone accidentally picks your draft out of the printer bin.

After setting your goals and objectives, list the strategies you think will help meet those objectives. Good strategies are actionable. What actions should you take to get to where you want to be? What specific things will you do to support your goals and objectives? Being specific is the key to implementation success.

Listing tactics will push you to become even more specific. Vague terms and descriptors such as "Meet more often with Bill," allow you to drift without making progress. How often is "more often?" A tactic along the lines of "fifteen-minute meeting every two weeks with Bill to present progress report on current projects" gives you benchmarks against which you can measure. You know whether or not you are giving Bill those progress reports every two weeks. If you are not meeting regularly, give careful thought to how you can.

Items to think about in the strategy and tactics stages of your plan include the same things you consider when developing an external communication plan. They include message frequency, message audience (see your Table 11.2 for this), message content, scheduling, and who will be responsible for imple-mentation. If you are a one-person department, you know who is responsible. If you have staff, however, clarify who needs to do what, and when. Assigning responsibilities to people helps reduce confusion, redundancy of effort, or drop-ping the ball.

Finally, consider how you will evaluate your internal communications. Numbers-driven accountability is a fact of life in professional public relations, and you should definitely give such measuring and tracking your attention in an exter-nal communication plan. This is one area, however, when you can cut yourself a little break in this plan. While you do not need to set measurable objectives in this circumstance, it will help you clarify your thinking if you have a clear idea of what success will look like. As your internal communications have their desired effect, what differences do you expect to see? Will project approvals go more smoothly? Will funding for your activities be less perilous? Will interactions with your peers be more harmonious?

Indulge yourself here. Apply WIFM (what's in it for me) to your own work and career. Be sure to check on this as you implement the plan. Six months and twelve months from now, stop and consider if the increased awareness and credibility you should get from this communication is helping to make your job go more smoothly. Put an item in your calendar to reconsider your internal communications plan in six months. When that time comes, close your office door, review to make sure you are doing the actions you planned, and do an honest assessment of the effects of those actions. Look for areas where you can do an even better job, revise your plan, and jump in for another six months. The internal plan review and self-assessment cycle does not need to be time consuming. But it will give you mileposts for progress in your own career development.

Your internal communication plan should only be three or four pages. Follow this outline to ensure you do not skip anything:

1. Table 11.1
2. Table 11.2
3. Goals (no more than three)
4. Objectives (keep it simple, with no more than three per objective)
5. Strategies
6. Tactics
7. Evaluation
8. Revision and second cycle of implementation

Properly done, your finished plan will logically flow from one step to the next. Your goals will address gaps and issues you find while filling out Tables 11.1 and 11.2. Your objectives are derived from and directly support your goals. Your strategies describe what tools you use to meet your objectives, and your tactics are the specific actions you will take to enact your strategies. Evaluation and revision close the loop, making sure you are putting your time to best use.

Having Your Plans, Projects, and Budgets Approved More Easily

The most effective way to gain faster, easier approval of plans and projects is to have built up a solid track record of success that is well communicated through your internal PR plan. If your internal plan has not been in place long enough to have that wonderful effect, there are still steps you can take to ease the approval process.

First, be sure any projects you propose are directly in line with your organization's mission. Do not assume your audience will make that connection for themselves. Spell it out, early in the proposal. Explain exactly how the project you are proposing will help the organization meet its goals. Connect the dots for your readers since they may lack the time, expertise, or ability to do it themselves. Conversely, this is also a good test of your idea. If you struggle to explain how your proposed project supports the organization's mission, you need to seriously rethink or even scrap your plan.

Second, once you have described how the proposed project supports the organization's mission, describe how it makes good business sense, particularly from an opportunity-cost point of view. These days, even public service organizations need to make sound business decisions. When someone decides whether to approve your project, one of the big considerations they will take into account is what else could be done with that money. To effectively generate support for your idea, you need to think about that in advance. What else could be done with that money and why should funds be spent on this idea rather than another? Be prepared to answer that question before you make your proposal.

That preparedness will have several positive effects. Having a ready answer to that question will, quite justifiably, make you appear more competent and capable. It will also give the listeners the impression that you have the organization's interests at heart. And once again, thinking through this answer in a disciplined way means you will have given more thorough consideration to the project. Your proposed activity will be stronger for having been subject to rigorous justification before you go public with it.

Effectively Managing Your Relationship with a PR Agency

If you are fortunate enough to have the budget to use outside PR counsel for some or most of your public relations planning and activities, you have the added responsibility of maintaining relations with the agency and acting as the go-between for the agency and your organization. The agency's work also represents you, so work with them effectively to help ensure your projects come in on time, on budget, and meet your communication objectives.

While managing the relationship with your agency takes time and effort, having access to an agency can greatly expand your role in your own organization. In the most basic way, having more heads and hands to do the work means you can produce more communications projects. Having agency expertise on tap may mean you produce more effective communications projects too.

The agency–client relationship runs the range. It can be adversarial or you may end up being good friends with agency staff members. Everyone who has worked at a PR, marketing, or media agency knows that at least occasionally, the client will blame the agency for something the client did wrong. Agency staff does not like it, but they tolerate it with a grim sort of gallows humor. You may have done this yourself in the heat of a meeting. It can be all too easy to blatantly or subtly shift the blame to the agency for everything from budget overruns to campaigns that did not meet their objectives.

Do not, however, be tempted to go to this well too often. A legitimate mistake by agency staff should definitely be addressed. You should remember, however, that if the agency was chosen based on your advice, every time you make agency staff look bad in a meeting or report, it is a reflection on your judgment. Or, what can be even worse, if your boss chose the agency, every time you make the agency look bad in a meeting or report you are making your boss's judgment look bad—not generally a great career move.

You will also find that if you cover for your agency when the occasional inevitable mistakes do occur, they will be more likely to cover for you when you make mistakes. Properly nurtured, the client–agency relationship can be mutually supportive, and you can develop excellent, cost-effective communications.

Below, two experienced communications professionals give advice on how to maximize your effectiveness and make the most of the relationship with hired public relations counsel.

Tracy Swartzendruber, Marketing Communications Program Manager, Eaton Corporation, Kalamazoo, Michigan has worked on both the client and the agency sides of the business. She offers this advice for public relations professionals:

> Make sure metrics are baked into everything you do. This is critical to measuring success and guiding future efforts and is essential to an organization that is data-driven. Even if your organization isn't data-driven yet, providing metrics on a program/project's success to a boss who hasn't looked at this in the past can make you look like a rock star.
>
> To that end, establish communication channel(s) and frequency early. How do you prefer to communicate with the agency? Is it conference call, face-to-face, e-mail? Do you want weekly status reports or is communication based upon program/project milestones? Make sure budget/estimate updates are an integral part of the communications. And, do you have access to everyone at the agency, including the creative director, digital guru, etc.? It's far more efficient and effective to be able to communicate directly with certain folks rather than go through your account manager. Oftentimes meaning gets lost in translation with the middleman.
>
> Be as transparent as possible with the business, program objectives, office politics, etc. If there is a potential landmine that could derail a program, or just something that may indirectly impact it, agency staff needs to know.
>
> Make sure your agency challenges you and vice versa. The agency is your sounding board, your creative resource and you to them. It should

be a dynamic, give-and-take relationship of thoughts and ideas. If a tactic is suggested that just doesn't make sense, speak up! Shut them down and redirect. It doesn't help anyone to implement something that isn't worthwhile.

When dealing with digital, project scope and wireframes are imperative to keeping costs down and launching on time. Don't let a programmer loose until everyone has agreed upon every aspect of the project, including design, architecture, user experience, etc. Document everything in Word or PowerPoint and review with your internal client(s) to obtain sign-off. Make sure they understand the consequences of changing scope or direction once programming has begun. Ensure the project can scale to meet any future needs anticipated. Now, release the programming hounds.[6]

Dick Hill, President of Atrax Marketing in Grand Rapids, Michigan, has decades of experience working with marketing clients. He offers this advice for getting the most out of your relationship with your public relations agency.

Successful agency–client relationships recognize two basic facts:

1. You know your organization better than the agency.

    The quality of the agency's work will be limited by the quality of the client's input. Give your agency an excellent verbal briefing. Then back it up with carefully selected written materials to help them quickly grasp the details. Later, this also means you must carefully proofread for accuracy any material that they write.

2. The agency knows more about PR than you do.

    You should listen carefully to the agency's advice and give it serious consideration. Don't reject something just because it wasn't your idea. The agency will draw on their broader experience and come up with plans that fit your situation. This also means your proofreading should be for accuracy only. Don't waste time haggling over style. If you chose the right agency, they know what they are doing.[7]

A good agency will give you frequent progress reports and will keep you well informed of communications results. You can pass this information along as part of your internal communications. You can also use the agency's format and approach for ideas on how to organize and present your own internal communication materials. Agency staffers are professionals at oral and written presentations. Ask their advice. Since your actions help them as well as you, they should be happy to help. Learn from them.

One Last Reminder: Why Internal Communication Is Important

Having made it to the end of this book, you may be feeling overwhelmed with the many directives and tasks the authors have put before you. If you follow the advice collectively given here, you will be performing at the highest level of your profession. Your work will be focused and effective and it should be meeting your organization goals. However, all of that time, effort, and high-quality work will be for naught if you do not include internal communications in your workday. Plan for, schedule time for, and complete the tasks in your internal communication plan as well as your external plan. You owe it to yourself, your career, your department, and your organization.

Endnotes

1. Tom Watson and Paul Noble, *Evaluating Public Relations: A Best Practices Guide to Public Relations Planning, Research, and Evaluation* (Sterling, VA: Kogan-Page Limited, 2005), p. 43.
2. Public Relations Society of America, "Public Relations Defined: PRSA's Widely Accepted Definition," accessed February 1, 2010, http://www.prsa.org/AboutPRSA/PublicRelationsDefined/.
3. Public Relations Society of America, "Public Relations Defined."
4. Robert Adler and Jeanne Marquardt Elmhorst, *Communicating at Work: Principles and Practices for Business and the Professions* (New York: McGraw-Hill, 2006), pp. 14–15.
5. Adler and Elmhorst, *Communicating at Work.* p. 15.
6. T. Swartzendruber (personal communication, January 10, 2010).
7. R. Hill (personal communication, January 11, 2010).

Chapter 12

Using Monitoring and Evaluation to Measure Public Affairs Effectiveness

Maureen Taylor

Contents

The previous chapters in this book provide details and case studies of how public relations strategies and tactics can help a public administrator be more effective in his or her communication with internal and external publics. Let us assume that every professional who reads this book follows through on the suggestions to create clear communication outreach to their stakeholders and the communities they serve. As you reflect on your communication outreach, you are pleased to see that your organization has an updated website, uses social media when appropriate, knows the line in ethical behavior, and you know how to gather information from the people inside and outside of your organization.

Now what? The next logical step in your development as an effective public administrator is to be able to prove that your increased and enhanced communication has been successful. You need to be able to show that the extra time, resources (financial and human), and energy you have devoted to enhanced interpersonal and mediated communication had an impact on improving the quality of life in your community. Sadly, the ability to prove impact is often the most difficult (and often neglected) step in proving public relations effectiveness. When called upon to explain the effectiveness of public relations efforts, many public affairs professionals, especially in local government, have a difficult time producing anything more than a clipping file of news stories appearing in the local media or anecdotes of small-scale successes. In a results-driven public sector, these tactics are no longer enough. This chapter takes the public administrator one step further in their ability to prove impact. It explains how to use monitoring and evaluation tools and methods to develop, refine, and prove public communication effectiveness.

This chapter will discuss best practices in creating easy-to-use, systematic, and useful monitoring and evaluation (M&E) indicators that help us measure the impact of your efforts. Monitoring and evaluation is becoming an increasingly common professional tool for measuring communication effectiveness, but it has not yet become widely used in the public sector. The chapter begins with a brief discussion of the philosophy behind M&E. It then moves to a concise and practical explanation of how public affairs professionals can take traditional social science methodologies, such as content analysis, to show measurable outcomes of their efforts. The chapter ends with specific examples and lessons learned of how public sector agencies (civilian as well as military) and nonprofit organizations have used this method to showcase their success, track crisis communication, and perhaps more importantly in a tough economy, argue for additional resources.

Why Monitor and Evaluate Your Communication Outreach?

Today, large and small organizations alike are being held accountable by stakeholders, the media, and the community. This is true for corporations, nonprofit organizations, the military, and local-, county-, and national-level government offices. Operational topics including budgets, expenditures, and hiring decisions are all subject to scrutiny. The tools and evaluation methods in this enhanced accountability process are known by many names. A common government concept for tracking accountability is called a *Performance Management Plan* (PMP). PMPs are used by U.S. federal government agencies as part of meeting the Government Performance and Results Act (GPRA) requirements.

According the Office of Management and Budget (OMB), the purposes of this Act are to:

1. improve the confidence of the American people in the capability of the Federal Government, by systematically holding Federal agencies accountable for achieving program results;
2. initiate program performance reform with a series of pilot projects in setting program goals, measuring program performance against those goals, and reporting publicly on their progress;
3. improve Federal program effectiveness and public accountability by promoting a new focus on results, service quality, and customer satisfaction;
4. help Federal managers improve service delivery, by requiring that they plan for meeting program objectives and by providing them with information about program results and service quality;
5. improve Congressional decision making by providing more objective information on achieving statutory objectives, and on the relative effectiveness and efficiency of Federal programs and spending; and
6. improve internal management of the Federal Government.[1]

Federal agencies such as the United States Agency for International Development (USAID) use the PMP process to guide their activities and provide evidence of results. Additionally, federal agencies ask their implementing partners to develop their own PMPs to help set out "strategic objectives" and "intermediate results" with corresponding results indicators. Many USAID missions devote resources to have in-house or external consultants train members and implementers in developing the PMPs. "Missions might also spend money to collect some data for them. But in many cases they rely on data collected by partners or from third-party sources (e.g., the host government, local [nongovernmental organizations] NGOs) and rely on mission staff to develop the plans and compile data and thus would not have a budget line item dedicated to PMPs."[2]

The philosophy behind M&E is quite simple: your efforts are intended to have an impact and you need a way to prove that your efforts have indeed had the impact you anticipated. You are not alone in your need for increased reporting. A number of government agencies have begun to develop useful performance monitoring systems. Government agencies and the military have developed various methods to provide information on topics such as program quality, program outcomes, and impact indicators. World Bank assistance projects require that both donors and recipients regularly monitor (usually on a quarterly or semiannual basis) a variety of process and outcome measures.

You might ask, how are a USAID or World Bank program's evaluation requirements relevant to my local or county office? The answer is simple: measuring effectiveness is now required by every governmental organization. Everyone needs to monitor and evaluate his or her impact. The terms *monitoring* and *evaluation* are often used together but they are not synonymous.

> Monitoring is different from evaluation in two ways: data are collected repeatedly, preferably on a schedule, and monitoring asks: is the activity/strategy progressing as planned? The monitoring function does not analyze causal relationships although a monitoring system may. Managers review the monitoring data with two questions in mind: how are things going? Is the expected amount of change occurring? It is an assumption that the change measured is because of the intervention as planned. This data added to the manager's knowledge of the environmental context and other competing explanations can lead to a pretty good informal "evaluation" of the results. Together these might be parts of a monitoring system, but monitoring alone means only the repeated collection and reporting of data.[3]

For the public administration professional, monitoring examines whether or not the intended outputs, outcomes, or impacts of a program or activity were actually achieved. When done well, monitoring can be invaluable to project implementers and managers to make midcourse corrections to maximize impact. When done poorly, even the most effective communication or operational efforts appear to be haphazard and arbitrary. Your goal should be to develop a systematic process for planning, implementing, and evaluating your public administration (PA) outreach. There is no cookie-cutter approach. Each organization will develop its own unique procedures reflecting:

> client characteristics, local conditions, and other factors beyond the control of program staff. At local, state, and national levels, performance monitoring systems are beginning to be used in budget formulation and resource allocation, employee motivation, performance contracting, improving government services, and improving communications between citizens and government.[4]

When Communication Efforts Should Be Evaluated

Effective management in any type of organization comes from regularly collecting information, analyzing the information, and then making changes to help improve a service or product. Governments are in the service business and their activities can be measured just like anything else. Having clear goals is one way to manage communication. The Management by Objective (MBO) trend, popularized by Peter Drucker (1954), suggested that personal and organizational goals need to be clearly articulated and measured. The mere act of sitting down and stating what you want to accomplish over the next three months, six months, or year provides a roadmap for actually accomplishing those tasks. Drucker as well as management experts in public administration have shown that individuals and organizations that identify goals and state how to measure the accomplishment of these goals are in a better position to be effective leaders.[5] Thus, public administrators need to be able to use a systematic method to plan and evaluate their communication.

This chapter will use a hypothetical recycling example to illustrate the different concepts and tools for M&E. Let us imagine that the town of Springfield wants to increase recycling. For the past year, the town has been placing posters around town, sending out news releases to the local media, mailing pamphlets to homes in the community, and reminding citizens about the location of the recycling centers on their water and tax bills. It has worked. Residents have been bringing their aluminum, glass, and paper to the three recycling centers around town. According to the sanitation office responsible for recycling, there have been approximately 1,000 tons of cardboard, 700 tons of newspaper, 200 tons of glass, 100 of mixed paper, 150 of plastic, 30 of steel, and 20 of aluminum brought into the recycling centers in town during the last year. Recycling is a viable way to deal with waste and the city is now ready to institute curbside recycling. Planning this effort requires that we identify in advance what it is that we want to accomplish. In public relations research, there are essentially three different points when it is best to collect information that helps organizations accomplish their public relations objectives:

1. Collect baseline information *before* you begin any new communication effort. The research conducted before a public relations effort is called *formative research*. Formative research is valuable because it identifies the beginning point, or baseline, from which you are starting. Baselines are also known as *benchmarks*. The value of collecting basic information during the formative or baseline stage is that it provides a mark of where you started. The amount of recycling materials noted above (1,000 tons of cardboard, 700 tons of newspaper, 200 tons of glass, 100 of mixed paper, 150 of plastic, 30 of steel, and 20 of aluminum) comprises *the baseline of recycling in Springfield*. The city is now ready to begin curbside recycling. Beginning January 1, all residents will have the opportunity for curbside recycling. The goal is to increase recycling in all areas (cardboard, newspaper, glass, mixed paper, plastic, steel, and aluminum) by 50 percent over the next year. To accomplish this worthwhile task, the residents need to have more information about recycling,

should develop positive attitudes about the value of recycling, and be willing to engage in recycling behaviors. M&E suggests that over the year, we take time out to evaluate the progress of the program.

2. Collect midpoint information *during* the communication effort. The research conducted at the midpoint of a public relations effort shows progress from the baseline. This monitoring process allows the organization to do a "reality check" on the viability of accomplishing the objectives. Monitoring at this point allows the public administration professional to reflect critically on the assumptions that guided the initial program. This is the time to reflect on strategy and tactics. Is the program too ambitious? Have new factors emerged that will influence the program? Have resources been shifted or have key personnel changed? The answers to these questions allow for midcourse changes to the program.

   Example: At the six-month point (June), the city needs to evaluate its efforts and track the levels of recycling. If the numbers are too low, then the city will need to do a better job publicizing the benefits and rules for recycling. Additional public relations tactics may need to be employed. For instance, are there any trends in recycling? Does one section of town recycle more than others? Is there confusion about what gets recycled and what does not? This midpoint is the time to take stock of what has worked well and what efforts have not been as successful as anticipated. But you are not done yet. After you have followed all of the steps of good planning, it is now time to see the impact of your efforts. To do this, you need to revisit your program goals one more time.

3. Collect information *at the end* of the communication effort. The data that are collected at the end of the public relations effort is called *summative research*. At the end of the recycling campaign, the town must measure how many tons of paper, aluminum, and glass have been recycled. Which neighborhoods were the most successful? Where were there problems?

   Example: The way to measure this summative figure is to subtract the baseline amount of recycling from the end amount. The end amount is compared to the baseline to see progress. It is important to measure outcomes on a regular basis to see if there need to be changes in communication outreach.

Which Communication Efforts Should Be Monitored and Evaluated?

City and county governments have to justify every administrative line and every penny spent on salaries. When it comes time to cut a budget, governments are slow to cut services to taxpayers. Instead, it is easier to look for ways to trim staff and operating expenses. The budget supporting the public affairs function may appear to be one of the easiest positions to eliminate. This is especially true when government leaders fail to understand that the role of public affairs or public information goes far beyond sending out news releases and scheduling events. Sadly, most people in government do not fully understand the public affairs function. Hopefully, the earlier chapters in this book have provided public administrators with a better appreciation of the great potential of the public affairs function. Yet, potential is not enough. The public affairs function needs to prove that it too contributes to the quality of service and quality of life of residents in the community. With appropriate M&E, you can make the case that the public affairs function should be one of the last positions considered for cuts.

The ability to measure public affairs outcomes is the first step in proving the value of the public affairs function. Remember that monitoring and evaluation are two different steps to help understand trends and provide evidence of impact. Knowing that you will have to be able to measure the impact after you have done it actually helps us plan an action.

There are two types of indicators that are useful in planning and then evaluating public affairs activities: *process indicators* and *outcome indicators*. "Evaluation, in other words, can be done by measuring both process and outcome indicators."[6] Each one is a valuable way to measure public affairs. When combined, they provide a well-rounded picture of the impact of public affairs efforts.

Process measures are things that you and your organization control. Process indicators are the *tactics* that you and your organization use in public relations. These are communication tools for informing and persuading. For instance, in M&E you can count a number of measures:

- News releases
- Flyers, posters, banners announcing activities
- Interviews with local officials that you organized
- New documents uploaded to the website
- Public service announcements submitted to the local radio or television stations
- Community forums or meetings organized
- Speeches by government leaders to community groups
- Visitors to your website
- Forms downloaded from your website

In public affairs planning, you can identify how many different process measures you seek to accomplish in the forthcoming communication effort. For instance, you can create a goal of sending out 20 news releases to the local media over the next year about recycling. Or, you can set a goal of creating an archive of speeches of community leaders that is available on the website. Some public affairs professionals may identify a certain number of community events, interviews, or even getting certain forms uploaded to the Internet as process measures. Almost any public relations tactic that you use can be incorporated into a communication plan and counted as a process measure.

Process measures are a great way of planning and then evaluating public affairs efforts. The benefit of identifying in advance what you will accomplish is that you actually control whether or not you meet your goal. In other words, if you sit down at the beginning of every quarter and say, "We will send at least one news release each week to the community newspaper and distribute 100 flyers to local businesses about recycling," then you actually have set up a process indicator objective that can be easily measured at the end of the quarter.

Few managers or budget mavens will care, however, if you met all of your process indictors if you failed to achieve your overall objectives. In the end, most organizations care about whether or not the outcome indictors have been met. *Outcome indicators* measure the impact of the process indicators and tap into changes in awareness, attitude, or behavior of the target audience. For instance, outcome indicators might include increases in the following measures: the overall level of recycling; awareness of the procedures for curbside recycling; positive attitudes about the value of recycling; and greater amounts of paper, aluminum, or glass being recycled.

How do you know if there has been an increase or decrease in the topics associated with the outcome indicators? The formula is simple: (1) the baseline tells you where you started; (2) the public relations plan identifies the process and outcome indicators of what you needed to do to change things; and (3) summative research provides evidence stating the difference between the place that you started and the place that you ended up. Summative research tells you if you met your goals.

Example: The final outcome objective is to increase the amount of cardboard, newspaper, glass, mixed paper, plastic, steel, and aluminum brought into the recycling centers in town over the one-year period. To accomplish this, you needed to have a systematic public relations information campaign telling people *how* to recycle. You also have to tell them *why* they should recycle. You incorporated a variety of *process measures* in your campaign over the course of the year:

■ Send out 20 news releases to the local media about the recycling effort
■ Convince 5 different neighborhoods to become involved in a contest to see which group could recycle the most materials
■ Update the amount of materials recycled on the website
■ Visit 10 to 15 elementary school classrooms to discuss recycling

- Recruit 20 small and medium-sized businesses to make a public commitment to recycling
- Design a pamphlet for recycling
- Print 1,000 copies of the pamphlet
- Distribute 800 copies of the pamphlet in the community

It is realistic to believe that you can accomplish all of these process measures, but the real success will be if recycling increases by the end of the year. The outcome indicators are clear: the baseline was 1,000 tons of cardboard, 700 tons of newspaper, 200 tons of glass, 100 tons of mixed paper, 150 tons of plastic, 30 tons of steel, and 20 tons of aluminum. A 50 percent increase means that at the end of the campaign (one year) you hope to have 1,500 tons of cardboard, 1,000 tons of newspaper, 300 tons of glass, 150 tons of mixed paper, 225 tons of plastic, 45 tons of steel, and 30 tons of aluminum recycled. How will you get these numbers to evaluate your efforts? The recycling unit of your local government office can provide you with these data.

The recycling example provides a concrete and measureable scenario to develop a monitoring and evaluation program. Some communication outreach activities, however, do not lend themselves to the same type of M&E. Yet, they can still be measured and their impact proven. Below are some examples of other types of M&E activities that have been used by the military, government implementers, NGOs, and others to track public affairs effectiveness. One of the easiest ways to create some measure of impact is to use content analysis to track the dissemination of messages through your media relations efforts.

Monitoring Media Content

Much of our communication in public relations is through the media. Although media relations is only one of many important functions of public relations, it is traditionally the one often associated with the practice. Media relations has a central role within the practice of public relations because the media are the "gatekeepers controlling the information that flows to other publics in a social system."[7] The media relations role is a traditional role for practitioners because it functions to "maintain media contacts, place news releases, and figure out what the media will find newsworthy about their organizations."[8] Government, businesses, not-for-profit organizations, and activist organizations rely on media relations to communicate important messages to multiple publics. While most discussion of media relations is focused on pragmatic relationships with the media, some scholars and practitioners have questioned what public relations would be like without the media relations function. Grunig has suggested that "the better public relations becomes, the less public relations practitioners will need the media."[9] Likewise, Hallahan

(1994) suggested that new technology may actually cut the media out of the public relations loop. But Hallahan has argued that this diminished relationship between organizations and the media will result in a negative outcome because "a loss of public reliance upon and confidence in the mass media could be devastating for public relations, journalism, and for society-at-large."[10] In other words, both the media and the organization help each other. Through what Gandy (1982) called the information subsidy, journalists get ideas and facts for news stories and public relations gains a venue through which to communicate information to publics. Without such information subsidies, small-town and medium-sized news organizations would not have the resources to report on the news. More than half of what appears on local television and in local newspapers comes from the information subsidy.

Practitioners of public relations generally agree that the most fundamental resource we provide to our organization is the quality of the relationships we create and manage with the media. It would be impossible to underestimate the value of open, frequent, honest, and mutually beneficial dialogue between an organization and the media that reports on it. In doing so, it is vital to maintain the highest levels of ethical and even-handed communication because not only is it the moral thing to do, but in the long run, it assures the organization of fair and accurate treatment of its news and information.

There are many M&E methodologies to study the effectiveness of our information subsidies. In qualitative methods, researchers have interviewed journalists and editors, conducted focus groups, and become members of news organizations (ethnographies). Using quantitative methods, researchers have surveyed media organizations and audiences. Another valuable tool in media monitoring is content analysis.

Content Analysis

Berelson defined content analysis as "a research technique for the objective, systematic and quantitative description of the manifest content of communication."[11] It allows the researcher to "make inferences by objectively and systematically identifying specified characteristics of messages."[12] The key to content analysis is to create a scientific way to identify and measure specific content features of news. Content analysis is a quantitative tool to count and measure what the media are saying about the organization. It is one way to measure the impact of your messages. This allows you to count the number of times the public affairs output has appeared in the media. It does not have to be statistics or science. What you are looking for just needs to be clearly articulated. More importantly, content analysis allows you to examine the tone, prominence, and placement of your strategic messages. For most government offices, you will want to measure the tone of newspaper, blog, and electronic media stories about key issues. This will let you know if your key messages are making it to your public through the media. Generally, we can code stories for three distinct dimensions of *tone*:

1. *Positive stories* use adjectives that are supportive of the project or person in question.
2. *Neutral stories* are basic facts about the project or person in question with no slant or attempt to sway the reader or viewer.
3. *Negative stories* place the organization or person in a negative light. These types of stories create doubt, raise questions, and cause distrust in readers and viewers. They may contain errors or use quotes or data out of context. These are the stories that need the public affairs officer to respond to correct the record.

Tone is the crucial first step in monitoring media coverage. Placement and prominence are also key factors in monitoring content. *Placement analysis* refers to the actual location of the story in the media outlet (lead story on the nightly news, above the fold in a newspaper). *Prominence analysis* combines the location of the story with circulation and readership numbers. It assumes that "bigger and earlier" is better (although this is not always the case). Tone, prominence, and placement analysis all provide details about whether or not your message is getting through.

How Effective Are Your Media Relations Efforts?

Sending information subsidies to the media about upcoming events is an easy way to publicize your activities. Sometimes, media coverage takes a different turn and your organization is under scrutiny. Dr. Suzanne Holroyd provided an illustration of how a public affairs officer working at Walter Reed Army Medical Center might have monitored the content of the first week of news coverage that broke in February 2006 identifying problems at the facility (see Table 12.1). The first column identifies the general tone of the stories (–3 to +3), the placement column identifies where it was placed in the paper or radio show (1–10 with 10 meaning the highest placement value), and the prominence score shows how important that outlet was to decision makers and opinion leaders (–3 to +3).

The chart shows that no story was positive and that some of the most negative ones were the most prominent. This allows the public administrator to figure out what to do next. The U.S. military created a full public relations effort to reach out to the public and people affected. Significant changes in medical care for those wounded in the wars occurred due to the scandal.

Table 12.1 Walter Reed Hospital Media Coverage (1 Week)

Date	Title Reporter, Placement	Outlet	Tone	Placement	Prominence
2/25	"Admin Issues Cited at Walter Reed" Steve Vogel, A9	Washington Post	0	8	3
2/24	"Review at Walter Reed Is Ordered" Steve Vogel, A1	Washington Post	0	10	3
2/24	"Army's Preemptive News Briefing" Howard Kurtz, Columnist, C1	Washington Post	−3	6	3
2/21	"Swift Action Promised at Walter Reed" Dana Priest, Anne Hull, A8	Washington Post	−3	8	3
2/20	"Army Fixing Patient's Housing" Dana Priest, Anne Hull, A1	Washington Post	−3	10	3
2/19	"U.S. Army Facility Reported in Poor Shape" Robert Siegel (with Dana Priest, Anne Hull)	National Public Radio	−3	6	3
2/18	"Soldiers Face Neglect, Frustration at Army's Top Medical Facility" Dana Priest, Anne Hull, A1	Washington Post	−3	10	3

Can Information Workshops for Media Really Inform the Public?

Content analysis can also be used to see if information that is shared with the media is actually being incorporated into media stories. It can tell you if your media relations efforts are working. For instance, a US-based legal organization helping to create the new court system in Kosovo created a series of informational workshops to explain the legal system to Albanian reporters. The organization used content analysis to evaluate the impact of the informational workshops. The workshops themselves were process indicators (the organization controlled them) and the media coverage of the legal system was considered an outcome indicator. The legal organization wanted more stories about the new legal system in Kosovo.

Workshop impact was measured by content analysis over the three time periods (before the workshops, during the workshops, and after the workshops). This allowed the legal organization to directly address the causal issue. Could media training about a certain topic increase and improve the media coverage of this topic? The answer for the Kosovo legal project was yes. First, the content analysis attempted to detect increases in the number of news stories reporting about the legal process and court cases by the journalists attending the workshops. Over the three time periods of the content analysis, the number of stories about the legal system increased. Second, the workshop also worked to promote improved quality of the articles on this topic over time. The findings suggest that quality of the stories stayed about the same over the three time periods. Third, the content analysis monitored if there was increased editorial support for articles about the new legal system in Kosovo by asking if the articles appeared with greater prominence in the newspapers. The findings of the content analysis reported that the legal stories generated from the journalists who attended the workshops did indeed gain editorial support through better placement, larger font in headlines, and so on.

Traditional media provide a valuable tool to see how public affairs efforts are working; however, today much of what people learn is through Internet-facilitated channels. The public affairs function can also track the effectiveness of the organization's website as a communication tool.

Tracking Website Analytics

Another way to measure the impact of your communication outreach is to track the visits to your organization's website. One way to prove that the communication function has value is to be able to report how many people are visiting the website, which documents they are accessing, and in some cases, how much of the organization's business and services can be conducted online. Nearly every local and county government has a website. The website is used to inform the public about events and policies. The site is a controlled communication channel to reach the community. It can be used for both one-way and two-way communication.

There are many free or low-cost easy-to-use software packages that will allow the public affairs function to track outreach efforts including how many visits the website gets, how many times people download materials, calendar visits, and information requests. Software or online packages including GoogleAnalytics, Shineystats.com, and Statcounter.com offer different levels of website monitoring. Organizations can get data delivered about traffic analysis, path analysis, and even real-time visitor tracking.

Website analytics provide another valuable M&E tool. The daily, weekly, monthly, or annual data (you decide how you want to organize the results of the analytics tool) can help you prove that the communication function of the organization is valuable and has clear impact on the community. There are also popular press books that can tell you how to revise your website based on the analytic data.[13] Indeed, using website analytics to improve a website, make information easier to find, and anticipate what your public wants is the real value of M&E.

Concluding Thoughts about M&E

The monitoring and evaluation process provides the strategic planning and evaluation tools that public administrators need to create effective communication with publics. Monitoring and evaluation should be a part of the strategic planning process where you identify what you want to achieve and identify the steps of how you will achieve it. M&E allows you to prove that your efforts have had a desired impact. In tough economic times, a strategic approach to M&E may mean the difference between keeping scarce resources or losing them to other organizational functions.

Endnotes

1. http://www.whitehouse.gov/omb/mgmt-gpra_gplaw2m/#h2.
2. Committee on Evaluation of USAID Democracy Assistance Programs and National Research Council, *Improving Democracy Assistance*, 172.
3. Clapp-Wincek and Blue, *Evaluation of Recent USAID Evaluation Experiences*, 2–3.
4. Wholey and Hatry, "The Case for Performance Monitoring," 604.
5. Behn, "Why Measure Performance?"
6. Grunig and Huang, From organizational effectiveness to relationship indicators: Antecedents of relationships, public relations strategies, and relational outcomes. In J. A. Ledingham and S. D. Bruning (Eds.), *Public relations as relationship management: A relational approach to the study and practice of public relations*, 27.
7. Grunig and Hunt, *Managing Public Relations*, 223.

8. Dozier, Grunig, and Grunig, *Manager's Guide to Excellence in Communication Management*, 112.
9. Grunig, "Theory and Practice of Interactive Media Relations," 23.
10. Hallahan, "Public Relations and Circumvention of the Press," 19.
11. Berelson, *Content Analysis in Communication Research*, 18.
12. Holsti, *Content Analysis for the Social Sciences and Humanities*, 14.
13. Sostre and LeClaire, *Web Analytics for Dummies*.

Bibliography

Behn, R. D., "Why Measure Performance? Different Purposes Require Different Measures," *Public Administration Review* 63 (2003): 586–606.

Berelson, B., *Content Analysis in Communication Research* (New York: Free Press, 1952).

Clapp-Wincek, C., and R. Blue, *Evaluation of Recent USAID Evaluation Experiences* (Washington, DC: United States Agency for International Development, 2001).

Committee on Evaluation of USAID Democracy Assistance Programs and National Research Council, *Improving Democracy Assistance: Building Knowledge through Evaluations and Research* (Washington, DC: National Academies Press, 2008).

Dozier, D. M., J. Grunig, and L. Grunig, *Manager's Guide to Excellence in Communication Management* (Hillsdale, NJ: Lawrence Erlbaum, 1995).

Drucker, P. F., *The Practice of Management* (New York: Harper & Row, 1954).

Gandy, O. *Beyond Agenda Setting: Information Subsidies and Public Policy.* (Norwood, NJ: Ablex, 1982).

Grunig, J. E., "Theory and Practice of Interactive Media Relations," *Public Relations Quarterly* 35, no. 3 (1990): 18–23.

Grunig, J. E., and Y. H. Huang, (2000). From organizational effectiveness to relationship indicators: Antecedents of relationships, public relations strategies, and relational outcomes. In J. A. Ledingham and S. D. Bruning (Eds.), *Public relations as relationship management: A relational approach to the study and practice of public relations* (pp. 23–53). Mahwah, NJ: Lawrence Erlbaum Associates.

Grunig, J. E., and T. Hunt, *Managing Public Relations* (New York: Holt, Rinehart & Winston, 1984).

Hallahan, K., "Public Relations and Circumvention of the Press," *Public Relations Quarterly* 4, no. 1 (1994): 18–32.

Holsti, O. R., *Content Analysis for the Social Sciences and Humanities* (Reading, MA: Addison-Wesley, 1969).

Hunt T., and J. E. Grunig, *Public Relations Techniques* (New York: Holt, Rinehart & Winston, 1994).

Sostre, P., and J. LeClaire, *Web Analytics for Dummies* (Hoboken, NJ: Wiley, 2007).

Wholey, J. S., and H. P. Hatry, "The Case for Performance Monitoring," *Public Administration Review* 52 (1992): 604–610.

Chapter 13

Conclusion

Grant Neeley and Kendra Stewart

Contents

Public Relations as Public Service

Although the news media and technological advances play significant roles in the lives of most Americans today, our field has virtually ignored the topic of public affairs in government. However, effective communications strategies not only advance the mission of an agency, but also provide an important and required public service. Public information is one of the key aspects of government accountability. Accountability to the citizenry is a defining characteristic of public organizations and sets those organizations apart from others in society. These organizations exist to serve the public in myriad ways and their survival depends on public support, albeit often indirect. Communication of what a governmental organization does and how it does it is a crucial component of accountability and government transparency. Ultimately the responsibility for communicating with the public lies with government administrators. The notion that "democracies die behind closed doors"[1] was clear to our Founding Fathers and has been regularly upheld by the U.S. Supreme Court.[2] The press has historically served as the conduit for communication between the government and the public, often creating tension between public organizations and the media.

However, the Supreme Court has frequently sided with the right of the public to have access to information over the right of the government to withhold that information. More recently, President Obama has emphasized the importance of government transparency and openness when he took up the issue of freedom of information as one of his first presidential acts. In issuing a memorandum to his agency directors he wrote the following:

> In our democracy, the Freedom of Information Act (FOIA), which encourages accountability through transparency, is the most prominent expression of a profound national commitment to ensuring an open Government. At the heart of that commitment is the idea that accountability is in the interest of the Government and the citizenry alike.[3]

Obama went on to order that when responding to information requests, all executive agencies should "act promptly and in a spirit of cooperation, recognizing that such agencies are servants to the public."[4] This memorandum sends a clear message to federal agencies that the communication of public information is a critical aspect in ensuring transparency in government and that they should adopt "a presumption in favor of disclosure" in addressing public requests. The Obama memorandum reflects a growing public sentiment that policies clamping down on public access to information, "dampen public debate, diminish government accountability and actually hamper efforts to protect the United States."[5]

Not only is agency communication an obligation, it is a necessity for survival. Agencies that are perceived in a positive manner by the public and public officials have access to more resources. Graber found that when agencies manage to ingratiate themselves with political leaders and influential publics, they are more likely to be well financed, regardless of past efficiency or effectiveness. "Agencies are therefore greatly concerned about the images they present to important leaders. Agency heads strive to show off activities likely to attract favorable publicity."[6] Therefore, agencies that are better at conveying their message and communicating their mission, goals, and success will be more positively viewed by the public and their elected officials. Today, this type of communication takes on many forms.

Direct Accountability

Cooperation with the press through answering media inquiries or holding press conferences is a method of indirect accountability to one's citizens. Direct accountability is also undertaken by government agencies and is increasingly undergoing rapid transformation due to technological changes in the information sector. Once relegated to production of annual or otherwise time-specific reports, new communications media have created entirely new channels of communication to reach and inform those citizens interested in an organization's functioning. These new mediums extend and expand the concept of government public relations beyond the retrospective function of merely reporting an agency's activities through an asynchronous format—the printed report. New communication technologies create and expand opportunities for agencies to reach a wide audience of citizens through electronic dissemination of their annual reports, as well as providing data and information that citizens might find useful. The potential for interaction with citizens has greatly expanded, and with this interaction, agencies are poised to potentially provide the public with information in greater quantities, more frequently, and in more detail.

Throughout the pages of this book we have attempted to provide you with a very practical and applicable approach to implementing government public relations. The academics and practitioners who have contributed chapters have all worked firsthand in some capacity of government public relations.

Accompanying CD-ROM

To supplement this text, you will find an accompanying CD-ROM that contains material that is linked to the information in this book. This material includes case studies, checklists, PowerPoint slides, and important reference sites. The CD-ROM table of contents lists all the materials included on the CD.

We appreciate your commitment to public service accountability through open communication with the public, and wish you the best with your organizations' public relations activities.

Endnotes

1. *Detroit Free Press v. Ashcroft, 303 F3d. 681 (6th Cir. 2002).*
2. *New York Times Co. v. United States, 403 U.S. 713 (1971); Kleindienst v. Mandel, 408 U.S. 753 (1972); Detroit Free Press v. Ashcroft, 303 F3d. 681 (6th Cir. 2002); Thomas v. Collins, 323 U.S. 516 (1945).*
3. White House Press Office, 2009.
4. White House Press Office, 2009.
5. Kenneth Jost, "Government Secrecy." *CQ Researcher*, 1023, Vol. 15, No. 42, December 2, 2005.
6. Doris A. Graber, *The Power of Communication: Managing Information in Public Organizations* (Washington, DC: CQ Press, 2003), 9.

Index